WORDSWORTH CLASSICS
OF WORLD LITERATURE

General Editor: Tom Griffith

CONFESSIONS OF
SAINT AUGUSTINE

Confessions of Saint Augustine

*based on the translation
by E. B. Pusey*

**WORDSWORTH CLASSICS
OF WORLD LITERATURE**

For my husband
ANTHONY JOHN RANSON
with love from your wife, the publisher
Eternally grateful for your
unconditional love

Readers who are interested in other titles from
Wordsworth Editions are invited to visit our
website at www.wordsworth-editions.com

For our latest list and a full mail order service contact
Bibliophile Books, Unit 5 Datapoint,
South Crescent, London E16 4TL
Tel: +44 (0) 20 74 74 24 74
Fax: +44 (0) 20 74 74 85 89
orders@bibliophilebooks.com
www.bibliophilebooks.com

This edition published 2016 by Wordsworth Editions Limited
8B East Street, Ware, Hertfordshire SG12 9HJ

ISBN 978 1 84022 592 1

This edition © Wordsworth Editions Limited 2016

Wordsworth® is a registered trademark of
Wordsworth Editions Limited

Wordsworth Editions is
the company founded in 1987 by
MICHAEL TRAYLER

Typeset in Great Britain by Roperford Editorial
Printed and bound by Clays Ltd, St Ives plc

CONTENTS

CONTENTS

INTRODUCTION

Augustine's life

Augustine was born in 354 [CE] in Thagaste (in modern Algeria). His mother, Monica (Latin, Monnica), was a devout Christian; his father Patricius was a pagan who converted to Christianity on his deathbed. The family name, Aurelius, suggests they were Berber freedmen of the gens Aurelia, granted Roman citizenship by the Edict of Caracalla in 212. His mother may likewise have been of Berber origin, but Augustine's first language is likely to have been Latin.

Augustine was sent to school at Madaurus, a small city about 30 km south of Thagaste. There he was a brilliant student in Latin, but never fully mastered Greek. More from lack of inclination than lack of talent, we suspect. At school he encountered pagan beliefs and practices, and records also his developing sense of sin, not least when he and some friends stole fruit they did not want from a nearby garden. They stole, he says, not because they were hungry, but 'because it was not permitted'.

At 17, Augustine went to Carthage to continue his education in rhetoric. There he came across Cicero's dialogue *Hortensius* (now lost), which left a lasting impression and sparked his interest in philosophy. During this period, Augustine left the Christian church to follow the Manichaean religion (see below). For a time he lived a hedonistic life, associating with young men who boasted of their sexual conquests. He describes himself 'confessing' to sins he had not committed, in order to win credibility and gain the approbation of his fellows ('that I might not seem contemptible in proportion as I was innocent'). He also began an affair with a young woman whom he calls his concubine. We would probably call her his mistress. This relationship lasted for over fifteen years, and she was the mother of his son Adeodatus ('Given by God'). He never tells us the name of this woman.

For a while he ran a school of rhetoric in Carthage, but after struggling to overcome the unruliness of students in that city, he moved to set up a school in Rome. Here too, he was disappointed with the attitude of the students; not least with their attitude to paying his fees (which were payable, as a general rule, in arrears). He applied, successfully, for a post as rhetoric professor at the imperial court in Milan.

In Rome, Augustine had already turned away from Manichaeism, and when he got to Milan, his mother, his own studies (in Neoplatonism), and his friend Simplicianus all urged him in the direction of Christianity. He was lukewarm at first, but after he came in contact with Ambrose, bishop of Milan, things changed. Augustine was impressed by Ambrose. He writes, 'That man of God received me as a father would, and welcomed my coming as a good bishop should.' He goes on, 'And I began to love him . . . not at the first as a teacher of the truth, for I had entirely despaired of finding that in Your Church – but as a friendly man.'

In 385, Augustine's mother arranged a marriage for him, and he therefore felt compelled to end his relationship with his lover. This was not a trivial decision. He was parting from the mother of his son, and was deeply hurt by the loss. He describes his heart as 'racked, and wounded, and bleeding'. What follows is less creditable. The proposed bride was only ten years old, so no marriage was possible for the next two years. Despite the fact that his rejected mistress had taken a vow of chastity, Augustine quickly took another concubine for the period until his fiancée came of age (though by the time she *was* of an age to marry, he had decided to remain celibate).

In summer 386, Augustine converted to Christianity, prompted by a voice he heard telling him to 'take up and read'. He opened the Bible and read the first thing he saw, Saint Paul's Epistle to the Romans, chapters 12 to 15 – where Paul outlines how the Gospel transforms believers. The precise point at which Augustine opened his Bible was Romans chapter 13, verses 13 and 14:

Not in rioting and drunkenness, not in chambering and wantonness, not in strife and envying, but put on the Lord Jesus Christ, and make no provision for the flesh to fulfill the lusts thereof.

Ambrose baptized Augustine, along with his son Adeodatus, in 387 in Milan. In the following year, Adeodatus and Augustine returned home to Africa, a journey marked by the death of Augustine's mother at Ostia, as they prepared to embark. When Adeodatus, too, died, not long after, Augustine sold all his property, giving the money to the poor, and keeping only the family house, which he converted into a monastic foundation for himself and a group of friends.

In 391 Augustine was ordained priest in Hippo (modern Algeria). He became a famous preacher, and was noted for opposing the Manichaean religion. In 395 he was made first coadjutor bishop, and then full bishop, of Hippo, a position he retained until his death in 430. He wrote the *Confessions* in 397-398, followed by *The City of God* (prompted by the sack of Rome by the Visigoths in 410).

Augustine as a person

In general, our picture of Augustine is that of a man who was charismatic, proud, competitive, above all, human. He was clearly an inspiring teacher; attractive to women and attracted by them. A man with a high regard for truth; not truth in the Christian sense in which things are true because passionately believed, but in the conventional secular sense of being true if supported by evidence. Not 'true because believed', but 'believed because true'.

He does not try to conceal his faults; yet when he describes them, we find it hard to condemn him too strongly. We have seen this in the theft of the pears, and in his attempt to impress his fellows with sins he had not committed. When he eventually decides to convert to Christianity, he does it as quietly as possible, finishing his teaching term, and not offering lessons for the term following. This, he says, is to forestall malicious gossip about his motives. Fair enough. Is there also a touch of pride in not wanting to have his affairs discussed publicly at all? Quite possibly. But would we act so very differently? Sometimes, again, he poses questions which we find genuinely hard to answer. He has mentioned love of praise as a fault, so when he asks: 'Can we do without praise?' he clearly thinks we should be able to. But his next question is a bit of a poser: should we stop doing the praiseworthy things which elicit that praise?

Nowhere is Augustine's humanity more evident than in his final exhortation to the reader.

> Be not conformed to the world. Keep yourselves from it: the soul lives by avoiding what it dies by seeking . . . that is to say, the haughtiness of pride, the delight of lust, and the poison of curiosity, are the motions of a dead soul; for the soul dies not so as to lose all motion; it dies by forsaking the fountain of life, and so is taken up by this transitory world, and is conformed unto it.

Pride and lust are two of the seven deadly sins, but curiosity is not. Why include it here? We are taken back to an earlier passage, where he berates himself for precisely that quality _ for curiosity, for things which we might not find so very culpable. He says, for example, that he would not go to watch hare coursing, but if he is walking in the countryside, and passes someone hare coursing, he cannot walk on. He must stop and look. Likewise if his attention is caught by a spider spinning its web, or a lizard catching flies. Not such very serious faults as all that, we might think, and it is hard not to feel that the main reason for their inclusion at this point is that curiosity was something he regarded as a major flaw in himself. Whether or not we judge him as harshly as he judged himself, certainly we admire and like his self-criticism.

His writing has a directness and authenticity which are hard to resist. When Saint Paul talks about sex, you cannot help wondering if he has any real idea (from direct personal experience) what he is talking about. With Augustine the matter is not in doubt. He cannot conceal his liking for women (not that he tries), and does not deny that he finds them attractive. And, perhaps unusually for someone who comes to condemn sexual relations, he talks about women with respect: above all his mother; but also his concubine; and the girl he proposes to marry. And there is a happy ending (of sorts) when he eventually finds a position he can be comfortable with: it is not wrong to love the beauty of bodies, provided what we love is God *in* that beauty. Not much of Saint Paul there.

For everyone, and especially perhaps for the unbeliever, Augustine has an appeal shared by few others among the great names of the early church. His doubts and uncertainties, his hesitations, his weaknesses, his backslidings, are the doubts and uncertainties of countless people before and after him. The weaknesses he describes (pride, love of praise, lust) are shared by many people. He has doubts, but his doubts are very modern. Why do we confess to God, if He knows everything? If God in the beginning made heaven and earth, where did he make it? What did He make it out of? What was He doing before He made heaven and earth? Was there a 'before' at all? Did time exist before the creation? These are questions a theist would ask, and will ask. But apart from the question about confession, the same (or equivalent) questions can be and are asked by people who are not theists, who perhaps have had a theory of the origin of the universe explained to them, and found it raises as many questions as it answers.

Augustine as a writer, and Pusey's translation

Augustine, as you might expect from a teacher of rhetoric, has a fine ear for the telling phrase: 'the soul lives by avoiding what it dies by seeking.' Or the people who 'love their own opinion not because it is truth, but because it is theirs.' The Latin he writes is straightforward, not archaic, so with a consciously archaic translation, such as Pusey's, it has seemed to us legitimate to modernize it a little. There are three main elements to this modernization:

1. We have replaced 'thee' and 'thou' with 'you'.
2. We have tried to avoid archaic verb forms ('hath', 'hast', 'wast', 'wert', etc).
3. We have reduced the number of initial capital letters. We have preserved the (almost universal) convention of using capitals for (the Christian) God, and for You, Your, Him, His (when these refer to the Christian God). But where Augustine refers to God as creator, or to God's mercy, then we have used lower case for 'creator' and 'mercy'.

In addition, in a very few cases (e.g. 'cleave to' in the sense of 'hold fast to') we have replaced a word which may be totally unfamiliar to the modern reader with a more familiar synonym.

A brief note on Manichaeism

Most people believe in good and evil, even if they do not believe in a God. For those who do believe in a God, and who want to believe in an all-powerful, good God, evil is a problem. If God is all-powerful, all-knowing, and cares about human beings, why is the world the way it is? Why so much suffering? God may possess any two of these attributes, we may feel, but not all three. The Christian answer to this is that suffering is the result of free will and human sin. A more radical solution is to abandon the belief that there is only one God.

Manichaeism (named after its third-century founder Mani) explains the evil in the world by saying there is not one god, but two: a good god and an evil god. The world is a struggle between good (the spiritual world of light) and evil (the material world of darkness). Light is gradually removed from the world of matter and returned to the world of light whence it came.

In Mani's teaching, God is powerful, but not omnipotent. He is opposed by the semi-eternal evil power (Satan). Humanity, the world and the soul result from the battle between God's proxy, Primal Man, and Satan. The human person is seen as a battleground for these powers. So evil is the result of a flawed creation for which the good God is not responsible.

For the Christian church, much of the fourth century [CE] was taken up with defining and establishing creeds and beliefs; a lengthy proceeding, since it involved defining what was heresy and what was not. Manichaeism was one among the variants on Christianity which found support for a time, and was briefly the main rival to Christianity in the competition to replace paganism.

Saint Augustine dates

354	Augustine born at Thagaste, in N. Africa
365	Sent to school at Madaurus
371	Goes to Carthage to continue education in rehetoric
373	Begins relationship with his concubine
373-74	Teaches grammar at Thagaste
375	Moves to Carthage; disappointed by his encounter with Faustus, the Manichaean bishop
383-84	Moves first to Rome, then to Milan
385	Ends his relationship with his concubine
386	Converts to Christianity
387	Is baptized by Ambrose, bishop of Milan
391	Is ordained priest in Hippo, back in N. Africa
395	Becomes bishop of Hippo, and remains bishop there until his death
397-98	Writes the *Confessions*
410	Sack of Rome by the Vizigoths. In response, Saint Augustine writes the *City of God* (*Civitas Dei*)
430	Death of Saint Augustine

[All dates CE]

Confessions

Book 1

1. *He admires God's Majesty, and is inflamed with a deep desire of praising Him*

Great are You, O Lord, and greatly to be praised; great is Your power, and Your wisdom infinite. And You would man praise; man, but a particle of Your creation; man, that bears about him his mortality, the witness of his sin, the witness that You resist the proud: yet would man praise You; he, but a particle of Your creation. You awake us to delight in Your praise; for You made us for Yourself, and our heart is restless, until it repose in You. Grant me, Lord, to know and understand which is first, to call on You or to praise You? And, again, to know You or to call on You? For who can call on You, not knowing You? For he that knows You not, may call on You as other than You are. Or is it rather, that we call on You that we may know You? But how shall they call on Him in whom they have not believed? Or how shall they believe without a preacher? And they that seek the Lord shall praise Him: for they that seek shall find Him, and they that find shall praise Him. I will seek You, Lord, by calling on You; and will call on You, believing in You; for to us have You been preached. My faith, Lord, shall call on You, which You have given me, wherewith You have inspired me, through the incarnation of Your Son, through the ministry of the preacher.

2. *Man has his being from God; and that God is in man, and man is in God*

And how shall I call upon my God, my God and Lord, since, when I call for Him, I shall be calling Him to myself? And what room is there within me, whither my God can come into me? Whither can God come into me, God who made heaven and earth? Is there, indeed, O Lord my God, anything in me that can contain You? Do then heaven and earth, which You have made, and wherein You have made me, contain You? Or, because nothing which exists could exist without You, does therefore whatever exists contain You? Since, then, I too exist, why do I seek that You should enter into me, who were not, were You not in me? Why? Because I am not gone down in hell, and yet You are there also. For if I go down into hell, You are there. I could not be then, O my God, could not be at all, were You not in me; or, rather, unless I were in You, of whom are all things, by whom are all things, in whom are all things? Even so, Lord, even so. Whither do I call You, since I am in You? Or whence can You enter into me? For whither can I go beyond heaven and earth, that thence my God should come into me, who has said, I fill the heaven and the earth.

3. *God is wholly everywhere, and is not by parts contained by the Creation*

Do the heaven and earth then contain You, since You fill them? Or do You fill them and yet overflow, since they do not contain You? And whither, when the heaven and the earth are filled, pour You forth the remainder of Yourself? Or have You no need that anything contain You, who contain all things, since what You fill You fill by containing it? For the vessels which You fill uphold You not, since, though they were broken, You were not poured out. And when You are poured out on us, You are not cast down, but You uplift us; You are not dissipated, but You gather us. But You who fill all things, fill You them with Your whole self? Or, since all things cannot contain You wholly, do they contain part of You? And all at once the same part? Or each its own part, the greater more, the smaller less? And is, then, one part of You greater, another less? Or are You wholly everywhere, while nothing contains You wholly?

4. *An admirable description of God's attributes*

What are You then, my God? What, but the Lord God? For who is Lord but the Lord? Or who is God save our God? Most highest, most good, most potent, most omnipotent; most merciful, yet most just; most hidden, yet most present; most beautiful, yet most strong; stable, yet incomprehensible; unchangeable, yet all-changing; never new, never old; all-renewing, and bringing age upon the proud, and they know it not; ever working, ever at rest; still gathering, yet nothing lacking; supporting, filling, and overspreading; creating, nourishing, and maturing; seeking, yet having all things. You love, without passion; are jealous, without anxiety; repent, yet grieve not; are angry, yet serene; change Your works, Your purpose unchanged; receive again what You find, yet did never lose; never in need, yet rejoicing in gains; never covetous, yet exacting usury. You receive over and above, that You may owe; and who has anything that is not Yours? You pay debts, owing nothing; remit debts, losing nothing. And what had I now said, my God, my life, my holy joy? Or what says any man when he speaks of You? Yet woe to him that speaks not, since mute are even the most eloquent. Oh! that I might repose on You!

5. *He prays for forgiveness of sins, and the Love of God*

Oh! that You would enter into my heart, and inebriate it, that I may forget my ills, and embrace You, my sole good! What are You to me? In Your pity, teach me to utter it. Or what am I to You that You demand my love, and, if I give it not, are angry with me, and threaten me with grievous woes? Is it then a slight woe to love You not? Oh! for Your mercies' sake, tell me, O Lord my God, what You are unto me. Say unto my soul, I am your salvation. So speak, that I may hear. Behold, Lord, my heart is before You; open You the ears thereof, and say unto my soul, I am your salvation. After this voice let me haste, and take hold on You. Hide not Your face from me; let me die – lest I die – that I may see it.

Narrow is the mansion of my soul; enlarge You it, that You may enter in. It is ruinous; repair You it. It has that within which must offend Your eyes; I confess and know it. But who shall cleanse it? Or to whom should I cry, save You? Lord, cleanse me from my secret faults, and spare Your servant from the power of the enemy. I believe, and therefore do I speak. Lord, You know. Have I not confessed against myself my transgressions unto You, and You, my God, have forgiven the iniquity of my heart? I contend not in judgment with You, who are the truth; I fear to deceive myself, lest mine iniquity lie unto itself. Therefore I contend not in judgment with You; for if You, Lord, should mark iniquities, O Lord, who shall abide it?

6. *That he has received all blessings from God: and how he has been preserved by Him*

Yet suffer me to speak unto Your mercy, me, dust and ashes. Yet suffer me to speak, since I speak to Your mercy, and not to scornful man. You too, perhaps, despise me, yet will You return and have compassion upon me. For what would I say, O Lord my God, but that I know not whence I came into this dying life (shall I call it?) or living death. Then immediately did the comforts of Your compassion take me up, as I heard (for I remember it not) from the parents of my flesh, out of whose substance You did sometime fashion me. Thus there received me the comforts of woman's milk. For neither my mother nor my nurses stored their own breasts for me; but You did bestow the food of my infancy through them, according to Your ordinance, whereby You distribute Your riches through the hidden springs of all things. You also gave me to desire no more than You gave; and to my nurses willingly to give me what You gave them. For they, with a heaven-taught affection, willingly gave me what they abounded with from You. For this my good from them, was good for them. Nor, indeed, from them was it, but through them; for from You, O God, are all good things, and from my God is all my health. This I since learned, You, through these Your gifts, within me and without, proclaiming Yourself unto me. For then I knew but to suck; to repose in what pleased, and cry at what offended my flesh; nothing more.

Afterwards I began to smile; first in sleep, then waking: for so it was told me of myself, and I believed it; for we see the like in other infants, though of myself I remember it not. Thus, little by little, I became conscious where I was; and to have a wish to express my wishes to those who could content them, and I could not; for the wishes were within me, and they without; nor could they by any sense of theirs enter within my spirit. So I flung about at random limbs and voice, making the few signs I could, and such as I could, like, though in truth very little like, what I wished. And when I was not presently obeyed (my wishes being hurtful or unintelligible), then I was indignant with my elders for not submitting to me; with those owing me no service, for not serving me; and avenged myself on them by tears. Such have I learnt infants to be from observing them; and that I was myself such, they, all unconscious, have shown me better than my nurses who knew it.

And, lo! my infancy died long since, and I live. But You, Lord, who for ever live, and in whom nothing dies: for before the foundation of the worlds, and before all that can be called 'before', You are, and are God and Lord of all which You have created: in You abide, fixed for ever, the first causes of all things unabiding; and of all things changeable, the springs abide in You unchangeable: and in You live the eternal reasons of all things unreasoning and temporal. Say, Lord, to me, Your suppliant; say, all-pitying, to me, Your pitiable one; say, did my infancy succeed another age of mine that died before it? Was it that which I spent within my mother's womb? For of that I have heard somewhat, and have myself seen women with child. And what before that life again, O God my joy, was I any where or any body? For this have I none to tell me, neither father nor mother, nor experience of others, nor mine own memory. Do You demand that You be praised by me, concerning that which I know; and that I confess myself to You?

I do confess to You, Lord of heaven and earth, and praise You for my first rudiments of being, and my infancy, whereof I remember nothing; for You have appointed that man should from others guess much as to himself; and believe much on the strength of weak females. Even then I had being and life, and (at my infancy's close) I could seek for signs whereby to make known to others my sensations. Whence could such a being be, save from You, Lord? Shall any be his own artificer? Or can there elsewhere be derived any vein, which may stream essence and life into us, save from You, O Lord, in whom essence and life are one? For You Yourself are supremely essence and life. For You are most high, and are not changed, neither in You does today come to a close; yet in You does it come to a close, because all such things also are in You. For they had no way to pass away, unless You upheld them. And since Your years fail not, Your years are one today. How many of ours and our fathers' years have flowed away through Your today, and from it received the measure and the mould of such being as they had; and still others shall flow away, and so receive the mould of their degree of being. But You are still the same, and all things of tomorrow, and all beyond, and all of yesterday, and all behind it, You have done today. What is it to me, though any comprehend

not this? Let him also rejoice and say, What thing is this? Let him
rejoice even thus, and be content rather by not discovering to
discover You, than by discovering not to discover You.

7. *That even his infancy was subject to sin*

Hear, O God. Alas, for man's sin! So says man, and You pity him;
for You made him, but sin in him You made not. Who reminds me
of the sins of my infancy? For in Your sight none is pure from sin,
not even the infant whose life is but a day upon the earth. Who
reminds me? Does not each little infant, in whom I see what of
myself I remember not? What then was my sin? Was it that I hung
upon the breast and cried? For should I now so do for food suitable
to my age, justly should I be laughed at and reproved. What I then
did was worthy reproof; but since I could not understand reproof,
custom and reason forbade me to be reproved. For those habits,
when grown, we root out and cast away. Now no man, though he
prunes, wittingly casts away what is good. Or was it then good,
even for a while, to cry for what, if given, would hurt? Bitterly to
resent, that persons free, and its own elders, yea, the very authors
of its birth, served it not? That many besides, wiser than it, obeyed
not the nod of its good pleasure? To do its best to strike and hurt,
because commands were not obeyed, which had been obeyed to
its hurt? The weakness then of infant limbs, not its will, is its
innocence. Myself have seen and known even a baby envious; it
could not speak, yet it turned pale and looked bitterly on its
foster-brother. Who knows not this? Mothers and nurses tell you
that they allay these things by I know not what remedies. Is that
too innocence, when the fountain of milk is flowing in rich
abundance, not to endure one to share it, though in extremest
need, and whose very life as yet depends thereon? We bear gently
with all this, not as being no or slight evils, but because they will
disappear as years increase; for, though tolerated now, the very
same tempers are utterly intolerable when found in riper years.

   You, then, O Lord my God, who gave life to this my infancy,
furnishing thus with senses (as we see) the frame You gave,
compacting its limbs, ornamenting its proportions, and, for its
general good and safety, implanting in it all vital functions, You
command me to praise You in these things, to confess unto You,
and sing unto Your name, You most Highest. For You are God,

almighty and good, even had You done nothing but only this, which none could do but You: whose unity is the mould of all things; who out of Your own fairness make all things fair; and order all things by Your law. This age then, Lord, whereof I have no remembrance, which I take on others' word, and guess from other infants that I have passed, true though the guess be, I am yet loth to count in this life of mine which I live in this world. For no less than that which I spent in my mother's womb, is it hid from me in the shadows of forgetfulness. But if I was shaped in iniquity, and in sin did my mother conceive me, where, I beseech You, O my God, where, Lord, or when, was I Your servant guiltless? But, lo! that period I pass by; and what have I now to do with that, of which I can recall no vestige?

8. *A description of his childhood*

Passing hence from infancy, I came to boyhood, or rather it came to me, displacing infancy. Nor did that depart, (for whither went it?) and yet it was no more. For I was no longer a speechless infant, but a speaking boy. This I remember; and have since observed how I learned to speak. It was not that my elders taught me words (as, soon after, other learning) in any set method; but I, longing by cries and broken accents and various motions of my limbs to express my thoughts, that so I might have my will, and yet unable to express all I willed, or to whom I willed, did myself, by the understanding which You, my God, gave me, practice the sounds in my memory. When they named anything, and as they spoke turned towards it, I saw and remembered that they called what they would point out by the name they uttered. And that they meant this thing and no other was plain from the motion of their body, the natural language, as it were, of all nations, expressed by the countenance, glances of the eye, gestures of the limbs, and tones of the voice, indicating the affections of the mind, as it pursues, possesses, rejects, or shuns. And thus by constantly hearing words, as they occurred in various sentences, I collected gradually for what they stood; and having broken in my mouth to these signs, I thereby gave utterance to my will. Thus I exchanged with those about me these current signs of our wills, and so launched deeper into the stormy intercourse of human life, yet depending on parental authority and the beck of elders.

9. *The hatred children bear to learning,*
and their love to playing

O God my God, what miseries and mockeries did I now experience, when obedience to my teachers was proposed to me, as proper in a boy, in order that in this world I might prosper, and excel in tongue-science, which should serve to the 'praise of men', and to deceitful riches. Next I was put to school to get learning, in which I (poor wretch) knew not what use there was; and yet, if idle in learning, I was beaten. For this was judged right by our forefathers; and many, passing the same course before us, framed for us weary paths, through which we were obliged to pass; multiplying toil and grief upon the sons of Adam.

But, Lord, we found that men called upon You, and we learnt from them to think of You (according to our powers) as of some great one, who, though hidden from our senses, could hear and help us. For so I began, as a boy, to pray to You, my aid and refuge; and broke the fetters of my tongue to call on You, praying You, though small, yet with no small earnestness, that I might not be beaten at school. And when You heard me not (not thereby giving me over to folly), my elders, yea my very parents, who yet wished me no ill, mocked my stripes, my then great and grievous ill. Is there, Lord, any of soul so great, and holding fast to You with so intense affection (for a sort of stupidity will in a way do it); but is there anyone who, from cleaving devoutly to You, is endued with so great a spirit, that he can think as lightly of the racks and hooks and other torments (against which, throughout all lands, men call on You with extreme dread), mocking at those by whom they are feared most bitterly, as our parents mocked the torments which we suffered in boyhood from our masters? For we feared not our torments less; nor prayed we less to You to escape them. And yet we sinned, in writing or reading or studying less than was exacted of us. For we wanted not, O Lord, memory or capacity, whereof Your will gave enough for our age; but our sole delight was play; and for this we were punished by those who yet themselves were doing the like. But elder folks' idleness is called 'business'; that of boys, being really the same, is punished by those elders; and none commiserates either boys or men. For will any of sound discretion approve of my being beaten as a boy, because, by playing a ball, I made less progress in studies which I was to learn, only that, as a man, I might play more unbeseemingly? And what else did he who beat me? Who, if worsted in some trifling discussion with his fellow-tutor, was more embittered and jealous than I when beaten at ball by a play-fellow?

10. *How for his play he neglected his parents' commandments*

And yet, I sinned herein, O Lord God, the creator and disposer of all things in nature, of sin the disposer only, O Lord my God; I sinned in transgressing the commands of my parents and those of my masters. For what they, with whatever motive, would have me learn, I might afterwards have put to good use. For I disobeyed, not from a better choice, but from love of play, loving the pride of victory in my contests, and to have my ears tickled with lying fables, that they might itch the more; the same curiosity flashing from my eyes more and more, for the shows and games of my elders. Yet those who give these shows are in such esteem, that almost all wish the same for their children, and yet are very willing that they should be beaten, if those very games detain them from the studies, whereby they would have them attain to be the givers of them. Look with pity, Lord, on these things, and deliver us who call upon You now; deliver those too who call not on You yet, that they may call on You, and You may deliver them.

11. *How he fell sick, and how, recovering, his baptism was deferred*

As a boy, then, I had already heard of an eternal life, promised us through the humility of the Lord our God stooping to our pride; and even from the womb of my mother, who greatly hoped in You, I was sealed with the mark of His cross and salted with His salt. You saw, Lord, how while yet a boy, being seized on a time with sudden oppression of the stomach, and like near to death – You saw, my God (for You were my keeper), with what eagerness and what faith I sought, from the pious care of my mother and Your Church, the mother of us all, the baptism of Your Christ, my God and Lord. Whereupon the mother my flesh, being much troubled (since, with a heart pure in Your faith, she even more lovingly travailed in birth of my salvation), would in eager haste have provided for my consecration and

cleansing by the health-giving sacraments, confessing You, Lord
Jesus, for the remission of sins, unless I had suddenly recovered.
And so, as if I must needs be again polluted should I live, my
cleansing was deferred, because the defilements of sin would,
after that washing, bring greater and more perilous guilt. I then
already believed: and my mother, and the whole household,
except my father: yet did not he prevail over the power of my
mother's piety in me, that as he did not yet believe, so neither
should I. For it was her earnest care that You my God, rather
than he, should be my father; and in this You did aid her to
prevail over her husband, whom she, the better, obeyed, therein
also obeying You, who have so commanded.

I beseech You, my God, I would gladly know, if so You will,
for what purpose my baptism was then deferred? Was it for my
good that the rein was laid loose, as it were, upon me, for me to
sin? Or was it not laid loose? If not, why does it still echo in our
ears on all sides, 'Let him alone, let him do as he will, for he is not
yet baptized'? but as to bodily health, no one says, 'Let him be
worse wounded, for he is not yet healed.' How much better then,
had I been at once healed; and then, by my friends' and my own
diligence, my soul's recovered health had been kept safe in Your
keeping who gave it. Better truly. But how many and great waves
of temptation seemed to hang over me after my boyhood! These
my mother foresaw; and preferred to expose to them the clay
whence I might afterwards be moulded, rather than the actual
cast, when made.

12. *He is forced to his book: which*
God turned to good purpose

In boyhood itself, however (so much less feared on my behalf than
youth), I loved not study, and hated to be forced to it. Yet I was
forced; and this was well done towards me, but I did not well; for,
unless forced, I had not learnt. But no one does well against his
will, even though what he does, be well. Yet neither did they
well who forced me, but what was well came to me from You,
my God. For they were regardless how I should employ what they
forced me to learn, except to satiate the insatiate desires of a
wealthy beggary, and a shameful glory. But You, by whom the
very hairs of our head are numbered, did use for my good the

error of all who urged me to learn; and my own, who would not learn, You did use for my punishment – a fit penalty for so small a boy and so great a sinner. So by those who did not well, You did well for me; and by my own sin You did justly punish me. For You have commanded, and so it is, that every inordinate affection should be its own punishment.

13. *With what studies he was chiefly delighted*

But why did I so much hate the Greek, which I studied as a boy? I do not yet fully know. For the Latin I loved; not what my first masters, but what the so-called grammarians taught me. For those first lessons, reading, writing and arithmetic, I thought as great a burden and penalty as any Greek. And yet whence was this too, but from the sin and vanity of this life, because I was flesh, and a breath that passes away and comes not again? For those first lessons were better certainly, because more certain; by them I obtained, and still retain, the power of reading what I find written, and myself writing what I will; whereas in the others, I was forced to learn the wanderings of one Aeneas, forgetful of my own, and to weep for dead Dido, because she killed herself for love; the while, with dry eyes, I endured my miserable self dying among these things, far from You, O God my life.

For what more miserable than a miserable being who commiserates not himself; weeping the death of Dido for love to Aeneas, but weeping not his own death for want of love to You, O God? You light of my heart, You bread of my inmost soul, You power who give vigor to my mind, who quicken my thoughts, I loved You not. I committed fornication against You, and all around me thus fornicating there echoed 'Well done! well done!' for the friendship of this world is fornication against You; and 'Well done! well done!' echoes on till one is ashamed not to be thus a man. And for all this I wept not, I who wept for Dido slain, and 'seeking by the sword a stroke and wound extreme', myself seeking the while a worse extreme, the extremest and lowest of Your creatures, having forsaken You, earth passing into the earth. And if forbidden to read all this, I was grieved that I might not read what grieved me. Madness like this is thought a higher and a richer learning, than that by which I learned to read and write.

But now, my God, cry You aloud in my soul; and let Your truth tell me, 'Not so, not so. Far better was that first study.' For, lo, I would readily forget the wanderings of Aeneas and all the rest, rather than how to read and write. But over the entrance of the grammar school is a veil drawn! True; yet is this not so much an emblem of anything recondite, as a cloak of error. Let not those, whom I no longer fear, cry out against me, while I confess to You, my God, whatever my soul will, and acquiesce in the condemnation of my evil ways, that I may love Your good ways. Let not either buyers or sellers of grammar-learning cry out against me. For if I question them whether it be true that Aeneas came on a time to Carthage, as the poet tells, the less learned will reply that they know not, the more learned that he never did. But should I ask with what letters the name 'Aeneas' is written, everyone who has learnt this will answer me aright, as to the signs which men have conventionally settled. If, again, I should ask which might be forgotten with least detriment to the concerns of life, reading and writing or these poetic fictions, who does not foresee what all must answer who have not wholly forgotten themselves? I sinned, then, when as a boy I preferred those empty to those more profitable studies, or rather loved the one and hated the other. 'One and one, two'; 'two and two, four'; this was to me a hateful singsong: 'the wooden horse lined with armed men', and 'the burning of Troy', and 'Creusa's shade and sad similitude', were the choice spectacle of my vanity.

14. *Of the Greek and Latin tongues*

Why then did I hate the Greek classics, which have the like tales? For Homer also curiously wove the like fictions, and is most sweetly vain, yet was he bitter to my boyish taste. And so I suppose would Virgil be to Grecian children, when forced to learn him as I was Homer. Difficulty, in truth, the difficulty of a foreign tongue, dashed, as it were, with gall all the sweetness of Grecian fable. For not one word of it did I understand, and to make me understand I was urged vehemently with cruel threats and punishments. Time was also (as an infant) I knew no Latin; but this I learned without fear or suffering, by mere observation, amid the caresses of my nursery and jests of friends, smiling and sportively encouraging me. This I learned without any pressure of punishment to urge me on, for my heart urged me to give birth to its conceptions, which I could only do by learning words not of those who taught, but of those who talked with me; in whose ears also I gave birth to the thoughts, whatever I conceived. No doubt, then, that a free curiosity has more force in our learning these things, than a frightful enforcement. But this enforcement restrains the flow of that freedom, through Your laws, O my God, Your laws, from the master's cane to the martyr's trials, being able to temper for us a wholesome bitterness, recalling us to Yourself from that deadly pleasure which lures us from You.

15. *His prayer to God*

Hear, Lord, my prayer; let not my soul faint under Your discipline, nor let me faint in confessing unto You all Your mercies, whereby You have drawn me out of all my most evil ways, that You might become a delight to me above all the allurements which I once pursued; that I may most entirely love You, and clasp Your hand with all my affections, and You may yet rescue me from every temptation, even unto the end. For lo, O Lord, my king and my God, for Your service be whatever useful thing my childhood learned; for Your service, that I speak, write, read, reckon. For You did grant me Your discipline, while I was learning vanities; and my sin of delighting in those vanities You have forgiven. In them, indeed, I learnt many a useful word, but these may as well be learned in things not vain; and that is the safe path for the steps of youth.

16. *Against lascivious fables*

But woe is you, you torrent of human custom! Who shall stand against you? How long shall you not be dried up? How long roll the sons of Eve into that huge and hideous ocean, which even they scarcely overpass who climb the cross? Did not I read in you of Jove the thunderer and the adulterer? Both, doubtless, he could not be; but so the feigned thunder might countenance and pander to real adultery. And now which of our gowned masters lends a sober ear to one who from their own school cries out, 'These were Homer's fictions, transferring things human to the gods; would he had brought down things divine to us!' Yet more truly had he said, 'These are indeed his fictions; but attributing a divine nature to wicked men, that crimes might be no longer crimes, and whoso commits them might seem to imitate not abandoned men, but the celestial gods.'

And yet, you hellish torrent, into you are cast the sons of men with rich rewards, for compassing such learning; and a great solemnity is made of it, when this is going on in the forum, within sight of laws appointing a salary beside the scholar's payments; and you break upon your rocks and roar, 'Hence words are learnt; hence eloquence; most necessary to gain your ends, or maintain opinions.' As if we should have never known such words as 'golden shower', 'lap', 'beguile', 'temples of the heavens', or others in that passage, unless Terence had brought a lewd youth upon the stage, setting up Jupiter as his example of seduction.

> Viewing a picture, where the tale was drawn,
> Of Jove's descending in a golden shower
> To Danaë's lap a woman to beguile.

And then mark how he excites himself to lust as by celestial authority:

> And what god? Great Jove,
> Who shakes heaven's highest temples with his thunder,
> And I, poor mortal man, not do the same!
> I did it, and with all my heart I did it.

Not one whit more easily are the words learnt for all this vileness; but by their means the vileness is committed with less shame. Not that I blame the words, being, as it were, choice and precious vessels; but that wine of error which is drunk to us in them by intoxicated teachers; and if we, too, drink not, we are beaten, and have no sober judge to whom we may appeal. Yet, O my God (in whose presence I now without hurt may remember this), all this I learnt willingly with great delight, and for this, wretched, was pronounced a hopeful boy.

17. *The way of exercizing youth in repeating and varying of verses*

Bear with me, my God, while I say somewhat of my wit, Your gift, and on what dotages I wasted it. For a task was set me, troublesome enough to my soul, upon terms of praise or shame, and fear of stripes, to speak the words of Juno, as she raged and mourned that she could not

> this Trojan prince from Latium turn.

which words I had heard that Juno never uttered; but we were forced to go astray in the footsteps of these poetic fictions, and to say in prose roughly what the poet expressed in verse. And his speaking was most applauded, in whom the passions of rage and grief were most preëminent, and clothed in the most fitting language, maintaining the dignity of the character.

What is it to me, O my true life, my God, that my declamation was applauded above so many of my own age and class? Is not all this smoke and wind? And was there nothing else whereon to exercise my wit and tongue? Your praises, Lord, Your praises might have stayed the yet tender shoot of my heart by the prop of Your scriptures; so had it not trailed away amid these empty trifles, a defiled prey for the fowls of the air. For in more ways than one do men sacrifice to the rebellious angels.

18. *That men care more to observe the rules of grammar than the laws of God*

But what marvel that I was thus carried away to vanities, and went out from Your presence, O my God, when men were set before me as models, who if, in relating some action of theirs, in itself not ill, they committed some barbarism or solecism, being censured, were abashed; but when in rich and adorned and well-ordered discourse they related their own disordered life, being praised, they gloried? These things You see, Lord, and hold Your peace; long-suffering, and plenteous in mercy and truth. Will You hold Your peace for ever? Even now You draw out of this horrible gulf the soul that seeks You, that thirsts for Your pleasures, whose heart says unto You, I have sought Your face; Your face, Lord, will I seek. For darkness of affections is distance from You. For it is not by our feet, or change of place, that men leave You, or return unto You. Or did that Your Son look out for horses or chariots, or ships, fly with visible wings, or journey by the motion of his limbs, that he might in a far country waste in riotous living all You gave at his departure? A loving father, when You gave, and more loving unto him who returns empty. So then in lustful, that is, in darkness of affection, is the true distance from Your face.

Behold, O Lord God, yea, behold patiently as You are wont how carefully the sons of men observe the covenanted rules of letters and syllables received from those who spoke before them, neglecting the eternal covenant of everlasting salvation received from You. Insomuch, that a teacher or learner of the hereditary laws of pronunciation will more offend men by speaking without the aspirate, of a 'uman being, in despite of the laws of grammar, than if he, a human being, hate a human being in despite of Your laws. As if any enemy could be more hurtful than that very hatred with which he himself is incensed against him; or could wound more deeply him whom he persecutes, than he wounds his own soul by his enmity. Assuredly no science of letters can be so innate as the record of conscience, 'that he is doing to another what from another he would be loth to suffer.' How deep are Your ways, O God, You only great, that sit silent on high and by an unwearied law dispense punishable blindness to lawless desires. In quest of the fame of eloquence, a man standing before a human judge, surrounded by a human throng, declaiming against his enemy with fiercest hatred, will take heed most watch-fully lest, by an error of the tongue, he murder the word 'human being'; but takes no heed lest, through the fury of his spirit, he murder the real human being.

19. *How he was more careful to avoid barbarisms of speech, than corruption of manners*

This was the world at whose gate unhappy I lay in my boyhood; this the stage where I had feared more to commit a barbarism, than having committed one, to envy those who had not. These things I speak and confess to You, my God; for which I had praise from them, whom I then thought it all virtue to please. For I saw not the abyss of vileness, wherein I was cast away from Your eyes. Before them what more foul than I was already, displeasing even such as myself? With innumerable lies deceiving my tutor, my masters, my parents, from love of play, eagerness to see vain shows and restlessness to imitate them!

Thefts also I committed, from my parents' cellar and table, enslaved by greediness, or that I might have to give to boys, who sold me their play, which all the while they liked no less than I. In this play, too, I often sought unfair conquests, myself conquered meanwhile by vain desire of preëminence. And what could I so ill endure, or, when I detected it, did I upbraid so fiercely, as that I was doing to others? And for which if, detected, I was upbraided, I chose rather to quarrel than to yield.

And is this the innocence of boyhood? Not so, Lord, not so; I cry Your mercy, my God. For these very sins, as riper years succeed, these very sins are transferred from tutors and masters, from nuts and balls and sparrows, to magistrates and kings, to gold and manors and slaves, just as severer punishments displace the cane. It was the low stature then of childhood which You our King did commend as an emblem of lowliness, when You said, Of such is the kingdom of heaven.

20. *He thanks God for his benefits*

Yet, Lord, to You, the creator and governor of the universe, most excellent and most good, thanks were due to You our God, even had You destined for me boyhood only. For even then I was, I lived, and felt; and had an implanted providence over my well-being – a trace of that mysterious unity whence I was derived; I guarded by the inward sense the entireness of my senses, and in these minute pursuits, and in my thoughts on things minute, I learnt to delight in truth, I hated to be deceived, had a vigorous memory, was gifted with speech, was soothed by friendship, avoided pain, baseness, ignorance. In so small a creature, what was not wonderful, not admirable? But all are gifts of my God: it was not I who gave them me; and good these are, and these together are myself. Good, then, is He that made me, and He is my good; and before Him will I exult for every good which as a boy I had. For it was my sin, that not in Him, but in His creatures – myself and others – I sought for pleasures, sublimities, truths, and so fell headlong into sorrows, confusions, errors. Thanks be to You, my joy and my glory and my confidence, my God, thanks be to You for Your gifts; but do You preserve them to me. For so will You preserve me, and those things shall be enlarged and perfected which You have given me, and I myself shall be with You, since even to be You have given me.

Book 2

1. *He enters upon the years and sins of his youth*

I will now call to mind my past foulness, and the carnal corruptions of my soul; not because I love them, but that I may love You, O my God. For love of Your love I do it; reviewing my most wicked ways in the very bitterness of my remembrance, that You may grow sweet unto me (You sweetness never failing, You blissful and assured sweetness); and gathering me again out of that my dissipation, wherein I was torn piecemeal, while turned from You, the one good, I lost myself among a multiplicity of things. For I even burnt in my youth heretofore, to be satiated in things below; and I dared to grow wild again, with these various and shadowy loves: my beauty consumed away, and I stank in Your eyes; pleasing myself, and desirous to please in the eyes of men.

2. *He accuses his youth spent in the heat of lustfulness*

And what was it that I delighted in, but to love, and be loved? But I kept not the measure of love, of mind to mind, friendship's bright boundary: but out of the muddy concupiscence of the flesh, and the bubblings of youth, mists fumed up which clouded and overcast my heart, that I could not discern the clear brightness of love from the fog of lustfulness. Both did confusedly boil in me, and hurried my unstayed youth over the precipice of unholy desires, and sunk me in a whirlpool of impurities. Your wrath had gathered over me, and I knew it not. I was grown deaf by the clanking of the chain of my mortality, the punishment of the pride of my soul, and I strayed further from You, and You let me alone, and I was tossed about, and wasted, and dissipated, and I boiled over in my fornications, and You held Your peace, O how late, my joy! You then held Your peace, and I wandered further and further from You, into more and more fruitless seed-plots of sorrows, with a proud dejectedness, and a restless weariness.

Oh! that someone had then attempered my disorder, and turned to account the fleeting beauties of these, the extreme points of Your creation! had put a bound to their pleasureableness, that so the tides of my youth might have cast themselves upon the marriage shore, if they could not be calmed, and kept within the object of a family, as Your law prescribes, O Lord: who this way form the offspring of this our death, being able with a gentle hand to blunt the thorns which were excluded from Your paradise? For Your omnipotency is not far from us, even when we be far from You. Else ought I more watchfully to have heeded the voice from the clouds: Nevertheless such shall have trouble in the flesh, but I spare you; and, It is good for a man not to touch a woman. And, He that is unmarried thinks of the things of the Lord, how he may please the Lord; but he that is married cares for the things of this world, how he may please his wife. To these words I should have listened more attentively, and being severed for the kingdom of heaven's sake, had more happily awaited Your embraces.

But I, poor wretch, foamed like a troubled sea, following the rushing of my own tide; I forsook You, and exceeded all Your limits; yet I escaped not Your scourges. For what mortal can? For You were ever with me mercifully rigorous, and sprinkling with most bitter alloy all my unlawful pleasures, that I might seek pleasures without alloy. But where to find such, I could not discover, save in You, O Lord, who teach by sorrow, and wound us, to heal; and kill us, lest we die from You. Where was I, and how far was I exiled from the delights of Your house, in that sixteenth year of the age of my flesh, when the madness of lust (to which human shamelessness gives free licence, though unlicensed by Your laws) took the rule over me, and I resigned myself wholly to it? My friends meanwhile took no care by marriage to save my fall; their only care was that I should learn to speak excellently, and be a persuasive orator.

3. *Of his travels for his studies' sake, and his parents' purpose in it*

In that year were my studies interrupted, when after my return from Madaura (a neighbour city, whither I had journeyed to learn grammar and rhetoric) the expenses for a further journey to Carthage were provided for me; and that rather by the resolution than the means of my father, who was but a poor freeman of Thagaste. To whom tell I this? Not to You, my God; but in Your presence to mine own kind, even to that small portion of mankind as may light upon these writings of mine. And to what purpose? That whosoever reads this, may think out of what depths we are to cry unto You. For what is nearer to Your ears than a confessing heart, and a life of faith? Who did not extol my father, for that beyond the ability of his means, he would furnish his son with all necessaries for a far journey for his studies' sake? For many far abler citizens did no such thing for their children. But yet this same father had no concern how I grew towards You, or how chaste I were; so that I were but copious in speech, however barren I were to Your culture, O God, who are the only true and good Lord of Your field, my heart.

But while in that my sixteenth year I lived with my parents, leaving all school for a while (a season of idleness being interposed through the narrowness of my parents' fortunes), the briers of unclean desires grew rank over my head, and there was no hand to root them out. When that my father saw me at the baths, now growing towards manhood, and endued with a restless youthfulness, he, as already hence anticipating his descendants, gladly told it to my mother; rejoicing in that tumult of the senses wherein the world forgets You its Creator, and becomes enamoured of Your creature, instead of Yourself, through the fumes of that invisible wine of its self-will, turning aside and bowing down to the very basest things. But in my mother's breast You had already begun Your temple, and the foundation of Your holy habitation, whereas my father was as yet but a catechumen, and that but recently. She then was startled with a holy fear and trembling; and though I was not as yet baptized, feared for me those crooked ways in which they walk who turn their back to You, and not their face.

Woe is me! and dare I say that You held Your peace, O my God, while I wandered further from You? Did You then indeed hold Your peace to me? And whose but Yours were these words which by my mother, Your faithful one, You sang in my ears? Nothing whereof sunk into my heart, so as to do it. Her wish was, and I remember in private with great anxiety her warning, 'not to commit fornication; but especially never to defile another man's wife'. These seemed to me womanish advices, which I should blush to obey. But they were Yours, and I knew it not: and I thought You were silent and that it was she who spoke; by whom You were not silent unto me; and in her were despised by me, her son, the son of Your handmaid, Your servant. But I knew it not; and ran headlong with such blindness, that amongst my equals I was ashamed of a less shamelessness, when I heard them boast of their immorality, yea, and the more boasting, the more they were degraded: and I took pleasure, not only in the pleasure of the deed, but in the praise. What is worthy of dispraise but vice? But I made myself worse than I was, that I might not be dispraised; and when in anything I had not sinned as the abandoned ones, I would say that I had done what I had not done, that I might not seem contemptible in proportion as I was innocent; or of less account, the more chaste. Behold with what companions I walked the streets of Babylon, and wallowed in the mire thereof, as if in a bed of spices and precious ointments. And that I might hold the faster to its very centre, the invisible enemy trod me down, and seduced me, for that I was easy to be seduced. Neither did the mother of my flesh (who had now fled out of the centre of Babylon, yet went more slowly in the skirts thereof as she advised me to chastity), so heed what she had heard of me from her husband, as to restrain within the bounds of conjugal affection (if it could not be pared away to the quick) what she felt to be pestilent at present, and for the future dangerous. She heeded not this, for she feared lest a wife should prove a clog and hindrance to my hopes. Not those hopes of the world to come, which my mother reposed in You; but the hope of learning, which both my parents were too desirous I should attain; my father, because he had next to no thought of You, and of me but vain conceits; my mother, because she accounted that those usual courses of learning would not only be no hindrance, but even some furtherance towards attaining You. For thus I conjecture, recalling, as well as I may, the disposition of my parents. The reins, meantime, were slackened to me, beyond all temper of due severity, to spend my time in sport, yea, even unto dissoluteness in whatsoever I affected. And in all was a mist, intercepting from me, O my God, the brightness of Your truth; and mine iniquity burst out as from very fatness.

4. *How he robbed a pear-tree*

Theft is punished by Your law, O Lord, and the law written in the hearts of men, which iniquity itself effaces not. For what thief will abide a thief? Even a rich thief will not abide one stealing through want. Yet I lusted to thieve, and did it, compelled by no hunger, nor poverty, but through a cloyedness of well-doing, and a pamperedness of iniquity. For I stole that, of which I had enough, and much better. Nor cared I to enjoy what I stole, but joyed in the theft and sin itself. A pear tree there was near our vineyard, laden with fruit, tempting neither for color nor taste. To shake and rob this, some lewd young fellows of us went, late one night (having according to our pestilent custom prolonged our sports in the streets till then), and took huge loads, not for our eating, but to fling to the very hogs, having only tasted them. And this, but to do what we liked only, because it was misliked. Behold my heart, O God, behold my heart, which You had pity upon in the bottom of the bottomless pit. Now, behold, let my heart tell You what it sought there, that I should be gratuitously evil, having no temptation to ill, but the ill itself. It was foul, and I loved it; I loved to perish, I loved mine own fault, not that for which I was faulty, but my fault itself. Foul soul, falling from Your firmament to utter destruction; not seeking anything through the shame, but the shame itself!

5. *No man sins, but provoked by some cause*

For there is a charm in beautiful bodies, in gold and silver, and all things; and in bodily touch, sympathy has much influence, and each other sense has his proper object answerably tempered. Worldly honor has also its grace, and the power of overcoming, and of mastery; whence springs also the thirst of revenge. But yet, to obtain all these, we may not depart from You, O Lord, nor decline from Your law. The life also which here we live has its own enchantment, through a certain proportion of its own, and a correspondence with all things beautiful here below. Human friendship also is endeared with a sweet tie, by reason of the unity formed of many souls. Upon occasion of all these, and the like, is sin committed, while through an immoderate inclination towards these goods of the lowest order, the better and higher are forsaken – You, our Lord God, Your truth, and Your law. For these lower things have their delights, but not like my God, who made all things; for in Him does the righteous delight, and He is the joy of the upright in heart.

When, then, we ask why a crime was done, we believe it not, unless it appear that there might have been some desire of obtaining some of those which we called lower goods, or a fear of losing them. For they are beautiful and comely; although compared with those higher and beatific goods, they be abject and low. A man has murdered another; why? He loved his wife or his estate; or would rob for his own livelihood; or feared to lose some such things by him; or, wronged, was on fire to be revenged. Would any commit murder upon no cause, delighted simply in murdering? Who would believe it? For as for that furious and savage man, of whom it is said that he was gratuitously evil and cruel, yet is the cause assigned; 'lest' (says he) 'through idleness hand or heart should grow inactive.' And to what end? That, through that practice of guilt, he might, having taken the city, attain to honors, empire, riches, and be freed from fear of the laws, and his embarrassments from domestic needs, and consciousness of villainies. So then, not even Catiline himself loved his own villainies, but something else, for whose sake he did them.

6. All those things which under the show of good invite us to sin, are in God alone to be found true and perfect

What then did wretched I so love in you, you theft of mine, you deed of darkness, in that sixteenth year of my age? Lovely you were not, because you were theft. But are you anything, that thus I speak to You? Fair were the pears we stole, because they were Your creation, You fairest of all, creator of all, You good God; God, the sovereign good and my true good. Fair were those pears, but not them did my wretched soul desire; for I had store of better, and those I gathered, only that I might steal. For, when gathered, I flung them away, my only feast therein being my own sin, which I was pleased to enjoy. For if anything of those pears came within my mouth, what sweetened it was the sin. And now, O Lord my God, I enquire what in that theft delighted me; and behold it has no loveliness; I mean not such loveliness as in justice and wisdom; nor such as is in the mind and memory, and senses, and animal life of man; nor yet as the stars are glorious and beautiful in their orbs; or the earth, or sea, full of embryo-life, replacing by its birth that which decays; nay, nor even that false and shadowy beauty which belongs to deceiving vices.

For so does pride imitate exaltedness; whereas You alone are God exalted over all. Ambition, what seeks it, but honors and glory? Whereas You alone are to be honored above all, and glorious for evermore. The cruelty of the great would fain be feared; but who is to be feared but God alone, out of whose power what can be wrested or withdrawn? When, or where, or whither, or by whom? The tendernesses of the wanton would fain be counted love: yet is nothing more tender than Your charity; nor is anything loved more healthfully than that Your truth, bright and beautiful above all. Curiosity makes semblance of a desire of knowledge; whereas You supremely know all. Yea, ignorance and foolishness itself is cloaked under the name of simplicity and uninjuriousness; because nothing is found more simple than You: and what less injurious, since they are his own works which injure the sinner? Yea, sloth would fain be at rest; but what stable rest is there other than the Lord? Luxury affects to be called plenty and abundance; but You are the fullness and never-failing plenteousness of incorruptible pleasures. Prodigality presents a shadow of liberality: but You are the most overflowing giver of all good. Covetousness would possess many things; and You possess all things. Envy disputes for excellency: what more excellent than You? Anger seeks revenge: who revenges more justly than You? Fear startles at things unwonted and sudden, which endangers things beloved, and takes forethought for their safety; but to You what is unwonted or sudden, or who separates from You what You love? Or where but with You is unshaken safety? Grief pines away for things lost, the delight of its desires; because it would have nothing taken from it, as nothing can be taken from You.

Thus does the soul commit fornication, when she turns from You, seeking without You, what she finds not pure and untainted, till she returns to You. Thus all pervertedly imitate You, who remove far from You, and lift themselves up against You. But even by thus imitating You, they imply You to be the creator of all nature; whence there is no place whither altogether to retire from You. What then did I love in that theft? And wherein did I even corruptly and pervertedly imitate my Lord? Did I wish even by stealth to do contrary to Your law, because by power I could not, so that being a prisoner, I might mimic a maimed liberty by doing with impunity things unpermitted me, a darkened likeness of Your omnipotency? Behold, Your servant, fleeing from his Lord, and obtaining a shadow. O rottenness, O monstrousness of life, and depth of death! Could I like what I might not, only because I might not?

7. *He returns thanks to God for remitting these sins, and for keeping him from many others*

What shall I render unto the Lord, that, whilst my memory recalls these things, my soul is not affrighted at them? I will love You, O Lord, and thank You, and confess unto Your name; because You have forgiven me these so great and heinous deeds of mine. To Your grace I ascribe it, and to Your mercy, that You have melted away my sins as it were ice. To Your grace I ascribe also whatsoever I have not done of evil; for what might I not have done, who even loved a sin for its own sake? Yea, all I confess to have been forgiven me; both what evils I committed by my own wilfulness, and what by Your guidance I committed not. What man is he, who, weighing his own infirmity, dares to ascribe his purity and innocency to his own strength; that so he should love You the less, as if he had less needed Your mercy, whereby You remit sins to those that turn to You? For whosoever, called by You, followed Your voice, and avoided those things which he reads me recalling and confessing of myself, let him not scorn me, who being sick, was cured by that physician, through whose aid it was that he was not, or rather was less, sick: and for this let him love You as much, yea and more; since by whom he sees me to have been recovered from such deep consumption of sin, by Him he sees himself to have been from the like consumption of sin preserved.

8. *What he loved in that his theft*

What fruit had I then (wretched man!) in those things, of the remembrance whereof I am now ashamed? Especially, in that theft which I loved for the theft's sake; and it too was nothing, and therefore the more miserable I, who loved it. Yet alone I had not done it: such was I then, I remember, alone I had never done it. I loved then in it also the company of the accomplices, with whom I did it. I did not then love nothing else but the theft, yea rather I did love nothing else; for that circumstance of the company was also nothing. What truly is? Who can teach me, save He that enlightens my heart, and discovers its dark corners? What is it which has come into my mind to enquire, and discuss, and consider? For had I then loved the pears I stole, and wished to enjoy them, I might have done it alone, had the bare commission of the theft sufficed to attain my pleasure; nor needed I have inflamed the itching of my desires by the excitement of accomplices. But since my pleasure was not in those pears, it was in the offence itself, which the company of fellow-sinners occasioned.

9. *Bad company is infectious*

What then was this feeling? For of a truth it was too foul: and woe was me, who had it. But yet what was it? Who can understand his errors? It was the sport, which as it were tickled our hearts, that we beguiled those who little thought what we were doing, and much disliked it. Why then was my delight of such sort that I did it not alone? Because none does ordinarily laugh alone? Ordinarily no one; yet laughter sometimes masters men alone and singly when no one whatever is with them, if anything very ludicrous presents itself to their senses or mind. Yet I had not done this alone; alone I had never done it.

Behold my God, before You, the vivid remembrance of my soul; alone, I had never committed that theft wherein what I stole pleased me not, but that I stole; it would not have pleased me to do iton my own, nor would I have I done it. O friendship too unfriendly! you incomprehensible inveigler of the soul, you greediness to do mischief out of mirth and wantonness, you thirst for others' loss, with none for my own gain or revenge: but when it is said, 'Let's go, let's do it', we are ashamed not to be shameless.

10. *Whatsoever is good, is in God*

Who can disentangle that twisted and intricate knottiness? Foul is it: I hate to think on it, to look on it. But You I long for, O righteousness and innocency, beautiful and comely to all pure eyes, and of a satisfaction unsating. With You is rest entire, and life imperturbable. Whoso enters into You, enters into the joy of his Lord and shall not fear; he shall do excellently in the all-excellent. I sank away from You, and I wandered, O my God, too much astray from You my stay, in these days of my youth, and I became to myself a barren land.

Book 3

1. *He is caught with love, which he hunted after*

To Carthage I came, where there sang all around me in my ears a cauldron of unholy loves. I loved not yet, yet I loved to love, and out of a deep-seated want, I hated myself for wanting not. I sought what I might love, in love with loving, and safety I hated, and a way without snares. For within me was a famine of that inward food, Yourself, my God; yet, through that famine I was not hungered; but was without all longing for incorruptible sustenance, not because filled therewith, but the more empty, the more I loathed it. For this cause my soul was sickly and full of sores, it miserably cast itself forth, desiring to be scraped by the touch of objects of sense. Yet if these had not a soul, they would not be objects of love. To love then, and to be beloved, was sweet to me; but more, when I obtained to enjoy the person I loved, I defiled, therefore, the spring of friendship with the filth of concupiscence, and I clouded its brightness with the hell of lustfulness; and thus foul and unseemly, I would fain, through exceeding vanity, be fine and courtly. I fell headlong then into the love wherein I longed to be ensnared. My God, my mercy, with how much gall did You out of Your great goodness sprinkle for me that sweetness? For I was both beloved, and secretly arrived at the bond of enjoying; and was with joy fettered with sorrow-bringing bonds, that I might be scourged with the iron-burning rods of jealousy, and suspicions, and fears, and angers, and quarrels.

2. *Of stage plays*

Stage-plays also carried me away, full of images of my miseries, and of fuel to my fire. Why is it, that man desires to be made sad, beholding doleful and tragical things, which yet himself would no means suffer? Yet he desires as a spectator to feel sorrow at them, this very sorrow is his pleasure. What is this but a miserable madness? For a man is the more affected with these actions, the less free he is from such affections. Howsoever, when he suffers in his own person, it is generally styled misery: when he compassionates others, then it is mercy. But what sort of compassion is this for feigned and scenical passions? For the auditor is not called on to relieve, but only to grieve: and he applauds the actor of these fictions the more, the more he grieves. And if the calamities of those persons (whether of old times, or mere fiction) be so acted, that the spectator is not moved to tears, he goes away disgusted and criticizing; but if he be moved to passion, he stays intent, and weeps for joy. Griefs, then, are loved, and sorrows. Certainly all men desire joy. Or whereas no man likes to be miserable, is he yet pleased to be merciful? Which because it cannot be without passion, for this reason alone are passions loved? This also springs from that vein of friendship.

But whither goes that vein? Whither flows it? Wherefore runs it into that torrent of pitch bubbling forth those monstrous tides of foul lustfulness, into which it is wilfully changed and transformed, being of its own will precipitated and corrupted from its heavenly clearness? Shall compassion then be put away? By no means. Let griefs then sometimes be loved. But beware of uncleanness, O my soul, under the guardianship of my God, the God of our fathers, who is to be praised and exalted above all for ever, beware of uncleanness. For I have not now ceased to pity; but then in the theatres I rejoiced with lovers when they wickedly enjoyed one another, although this was imaginary, and only in the play. And when they lost one another, as if very compassionate, I sorrowed with them, yet had my delight in both. But now I much more pity him that rejoices in his wickedness, than him who is thought to suffer hardship, by missing some pernicious pleasure, and the loss of some miserable felicity. This certainly is the truer mercy, but in it grief delights not. For though he that grieves for the miserable, be commended for his office of charity; yet had he, who is genuinely compassionate, rather there were nothing for him to grieve for. For if good will be ill willed (which can never be), then may he who truly and sincerely commiserates, wish there might be some miserable, that he might commiserate. Some sorrow may then be allowed, none loved. For thus do You, O Lord God, who love souls far more purely than we, and have more incorruptibly pity on them, yet are wounded with no sorrowfulness. And who is sufficient for these things?

But I, miserable, then loved to grieve, and sought out what to grieve at, when in another's and that feigned and personated misery, that acting best pleased me, and attracted me the most vehemently, which drew tears from me. What marvel that an unhappy sheep, straying from Your flock, and impatient of Your keeping, I became infected with a foul disease? And hence the love of griefs; not such as should sink deep into me; for I loved not to suffer, what I loved to look on; but such as upon hearing their fictions should lightly scratch the surface; upon which, as on envenomed nails, followed inflamed swelling, impostumes, and a putrefied sore. My life being such, was it life, O my God?

3. *His conversation with young lawyers*

And Your faithful mercy hovered over me from afar. Upon how grievous iniquities consumed I myself, pursuing a sacrilegious curiosity, that having forsaken You, it might bring me to the treacherous abyss, and the beguiling service of devils, to whom I sacrificed my evil actions, and in all these things You did scourge me! I dared even, while Your solemnities were celebrated within the walls of Your Church, to desire, and to compass a business deserving death for its fruits, for which You scourged me with grievous punishments, though nothing to my fault, O You my exceeding mercy, my God, my refuge from those terrible destroyers, among whom I wandered with a stiff neck, withdrawing further from You, loving mine own ways, and not Yours, loving a fugitive liberty.

Those studies also, which were accounted commendable, had a view to excelling in the courts of litigation; the more praised, the craftier. Such is men's blindness, glorying even in their blindness. And now I was chief in the rhetoric school, whereat I joyed proudly, and I swelled with arrogancy, though (Lord, You know) far quieter and altogether removed from the subvertings of those 'subverters' (for this ill-omened and devilish name was the very badge of gallantry) among whom I lived, with a shameless shame that I was not even as they. With them I lived, and was sometimes delighted with their friendship, whose doings I ever did abhor — i.e. their 'subvertings', wherewith they wantonly persecuted the modesty of strangers, which they disturbed by a gratuitous jeering, feeding thereon their malicious birth. Nothing can be more like the very actions of devils than these. What then could they be more truly called than 'subverters'? Themselves subverted and altogether perverted first, the deceiving spirits secretly deriding and seducing them, wherein themselves delight to jeer at and deceive others.

4. *How Tully's* Hortensius *provoked him to study philosophy*

Among such as these, in that unsettled age of mine, I learned books of eloquence, wherein I desired to be eminent, out of a damnable and vainglorious end, a joy in human vanity. In the ordinary course of study, I fell upon a certain book of Cicero, whose speech almost all admire, not so his heart. This book of his contains an exhortation to philosophy, and is called *Hortensius*. But this book altered my affections, and turned my prayers to Yourself, O Lord; and made me have other purposes and desires. Every vain hope at once became worthless to me; and I longed with an incredibly burning desire for an immortality of wisdom, and began now to arise, that I might return to You. For not to sharpen my tongue (which thing I seemed to be purchasing with my mother's allowances, in that my nineteenth year, my father being dead two years before), not to sharpen my tongue did I employ that book; nor did it infuse into me its style, but its matter.

How did I burn then, my God, how did I burn to re-mount from earthly things to You, nor knew I what You would do with me? For with You is wisdom. But the love of wisdom is in Greek called 'philosophy', with which that book inflamed me. Some there be that seduce through philosophy, under a great, and smooth, and honorable name coloring and disguising their own errors: and almost all who in that and former ages were such, are in that book censured and set forth: there also is made plain that wholesome advice of Your Spirit, by Your good and devout servant: Beware lest any man spoil you through philosophy and vain deceit, after the tradition of men, after the rudiments of the world, and not after Christ. For in Him dwells all the fullness of the godhead bodily. And since at that time (You, O light of my heart, know) apostolic scripture was not known to me, I was delighted with that exhortation, so far only, that I was thereby strongly roused, and kindled, and inflamed to love and seek and obtain and hold and embrace not this or that sect, but wisdom itself whatever it were; and this alone checked me thus unkindled, that the name of Christ was not in it. For this name, according to Your mercy, O Lord, this name of my Saviour Your Son, had my tender heart, even with my mother's milk, devoutly drunk in and deeply treasured; and whatsoever was without that name, though never so learned, polished, or true, took not entire hold of me.

5. He undervalues the holy scriptures because of the simplicity of their style

I resolved then to bend my mind to the holy scriptures, that I might see what they were. But behold, I see a thing not understood by the proud, nor laid open to children, lowly in access, in its recesses lofty, and veiled with mysteries; and I was not such as could enter into it, or stoop my neck to follow its steps. For not as I now speak, did I feel when I turned to those scriptures; but they seemed to me unworthy to be compared to the stateliness of Tully: for my swelling pride shrunk from their lowliness, nor could my sharp wit pierce the interior thereof. Yet were they such as would grow up in a little one. But I disdained to be a little one; and, swollen with pride, took myself to be a great one.

6. How he was ensnared by the Manichees

Therefore I fell among men proudly doting, exceeding carnal and prating, in whose mouths were the snares of the Devil, limed with the mixture of the syllables of Your name, and of our Lord Jesus Christ, and of the Holy Ghost, the Paraclete, our Comforter. These names departed not out of their mouth but so far forth as the sound only and the noise of the tongue, for the heart was void of truth. Yet they cried out 'truth, truth', and spoke much thereof to me, yet it was not in them: but they spoke falsehood, not of You only (who truly are truth), but even of those elements of this world, Your creatures. And I indeed ought to have passed by even philosophers who spoke truth concerning them, for love of You, my Father, supremely good, beauty of all things beautiful. O truth, truth, how inwardly did even then the marrow of my soul pant after You, when they often and diversely, and in many and huge books, echoed of You to me, though it was but an echo? And these were the dishes wherein to me, hungering after You, they, instead of You, served up the sun and moon, beautiful works of Yours, but yet Your works, not Yourself, no nor Your first works. For Your spiritual works are before these corporeal works, celestial though they be, and shining. But I hungered and thirsted not even after those first works of Yours, but after You Yourself, the truth, in whom is no variableness, neither shadow of turning: yet they still set before me in those dishes, glittering fantasies, than which it were better to love this very sun (which is real to our sight at least), than those fantasies which by our eyes deceive our mind. Yet because I thought them to be You, I fed thereon; not eagerly, for You did not in them taste to me as You are; for You were not these emptinesses, nor was I nourished by them, but exhausted rather. Food in sleep shows very like our food awake; yet are not those asleep nourished by it, for they are asleep. But those were not even any way like to You, as You have now spoken to me; for those were corporeal fantasies, false bodies, than which these true bodies, celestial or terrestrial, which with our fleshly sight we behold, are far more certain: these things the beasts and birds discern as well as we, and they are more certain than when we fancy them. And again, we do with more certainty fancy them, than by them conjecture other vaster and infinite bodies which have no being. Such empty husks was I then fed on; and was not fed. But You, my soul's Love, in looking for whom I fail, that I may become strong, are neither those bodies which we see, though in heaven; nor those which we see not there; for You have created them, nor do You account them among the chiefest of Your works. How far then are You from those fantasies of mine, fantasies of bodies which altogether are not, than which the images of those bodies which are, are far more certain, and more certain still the bodies themselves, which yet You are not; no, nor yet the soul, which is the life of the bodies. So then, better and more certain is the life of the bodies than the bodies. But You are the life of souls, the life of lives, having life in Yourself; and You change not, life of my soul.

Where then were You then to me, and how far from me? Far verily was I straying from You, barred from the very husks of the swine, whom with husks I fed. For how much better are the fables of poets and grammarians than these snares! For verses, and poems, and 'Medea flying', are more profitable truly than these men's five elements, variously disguised, answering to five dens of darkness, which have no being, yet slay the believer. For verses and poems I can turn to true food, and 'Medea flying', though I did sing, I maintained not; though I heard it sung, I believed not: but those things I did believe. Woe, woe, by what steps was I brought down to the depths of hell, toiling and turmoiling through want of truth, since I sought after You, my God (to You I confess it, who had mercy on me, not as yet confessing), not according to the understanding of the mind, wherein You willed that I should excel the beasts, but according to the sense of the flesh. But You were more inward to me than my most inward part; and higher than my highest. I lighted upon that bold woman, simple and knowing nothing, shadowed out in Solomon, sitting at the door, and saying, Eat ye bread of secrecies willingly, and drink ye stolen waters which are sweet: she seduced me, because she found my soul dwelling abroad in the eye of my flesh, and ruminating on such food as through it I had devoured.

7. *The absurd doctrine of the Manichees*

For other than this, that which really is I knew not; and was, as it were through sharpness of wit, persuaded to assent to foolish deceivers, when they asked me, Whence is evil? Is God bounded by a bodily shape, and has hairs and nails? Are they to be esteemed righteous who had many wives at once, and did kill men, and sacrifice living creatures? At which I, in my ignorance, was much troubled, and departing from the truth, seemed to myself to be making towards it; because as yet I knew not that evil was nothing but a privation of good, until at last a thing ceases altogether to be; which how should I see, the sight of whose eyes reached only to bodies, and of my mind to a phantasm? And I knew not God to be a spirit, not one who has parts extended in length and breadth, or whose being was bulk; for every bulk is less in a part than in the whole: and if it be infinite, it must be less in such part as is defined by a certain space, than in its infinitude; and so is not wholly everywhere, as spirit, as God. And what that should be in us, by which we were like to God, and might be rightly said to be after the image of God, I was altogether ignorant.

Nor knew I that true inward righteousness which judges not according to custom, but out of the most rightful law of God Almighty, whereby the ways of places and times were disposed according to those times and places; itself meantime being the same always and everywhere, not one thing in one place, and another in another; according to which Abraham, and Isaac, and Jacob, and Moses, and David, were righteous, and all those commended by the mouth of God; but were judged unrighteous by silly men, judging out of man's judgment, and measuring by their own petty habits, the moral habits of the whole human race. As if in an armory, one ignorant of what were adapted to each part should cover his head with greaves, or seek to be shod with a helmet, and complain that they fitted not: or as if on a day when business is publicly stopped in the afternoon, one were angered at not being allowed to keep open shop, because he had been in the forenoon; or when in one house he observe some servant take a thing in his hand, which the butler is not suffered to meddle with; or something permitted out of doors, which is forbidden in the dining-room; and should be angry, that in one house, and one family, the same thing is not allowed everywhere, and to all. Even such are they who are fretted to hear something to have been lawful for righteous men formerly, which now is not; or that God, for certain temporal respects, commanded them one thing, and these another, obeying both the same righteousness: whereas they see, in one man, and one day, and one house, different things to be fit for different members, and a thing formerly lawful, after a certain time not so; in one corner permitted or commanded, but in another rightly forbidden and punished. Is justice therefore various or mutable? No, but the times, over which it presides, flow not evenly, because they are times. But men whose days are few upon the earth, for that by their senses they cannot harmonize the causes of things in former

ages and other nations, which they had not experience of, with
these which they have experience of, whereas in one and the
same body, day, or family, they easily see what is fitting for each
member, and season, part, and person; to the one they take
exceptions, to the other they submit.

These things I then knew not, nor observed; they struck my
sight on all sides, and I saw them not. I indited verses, in which I
might not place every foot everywhere, but differently in different metres; nor even in any one metre the self-same foot in all
places. Yet the art itself, by which I indited, had not different
principles for these different cases, but comprised all in one. Still
I saw not how that righteousness, which good and holy men
obeyed, did far more excellently and sublimely contain in one all
those things which God commanded, and in no part varied;
although in varying times it prescribed not every thing at once,
but apportioned and ordered what was fit for each. And I in
my blindness, censured the holy Fathers, not only wherein they
made use of things present as God commanded and inspired
them, but also wherein they were foretelling things to come, as
God was revealing in them.

8. *Heinous offences, and how punished*

Can it at any time or place be unjust to love God with all his
heart, with all his soul, and with all his mind; and his neighbour
as himself? Therefore are those foul offences which be against
nature, to be everywhere and at all times detested and punished;
such as were those of the men of Sodom: which should all nations
commit, they should all stand guilty of the same crime, by the law
of God, which has not so made men that they should so abuse one
another. For even that intercourse which should be between God
and us is violated, when that same nature, of which He is author,
is polluted by perversity of lust. But those actions which are
offences against the customs of men, are to be avoided according
to the customs severally prevailing; so that a thing agreed upon,
and confirmed, by custom or law of any city or nation, may not be
violated at the lawless pleasure of any, whether native or foreigner.
For any part which harmonises not with its whole, is offensive.
But when God commands a thing to be done, against the customs
or compact of any people, though it were never by them done

heretofore, it is to be done; and if intermitted, it is to be restored; and if never ordained, is now to be ordained. For if it be lawful for a king, in the state which he reigns over, to command that which no one before him, nor he himself heretofore, had commanded, and to obey him cannot be against the common weal of the state (nay, it were against it if he were not obeyed, for to obey princes is a general compact of human society); how much more unhesitatingly ought we to obey God, in all which He commands, the Ruler of all His creatures! For as among the powers in man's society, the greater authority is obeyed in preference to the lesser, so must God above all.

So in acts of violence, where there is a wish to hurt, whether by reproach or injury; and these either for revenge, as one enemy against another; or for some profit belonging to another, as the robber to the traveller; or to avoid some evil, as towards one who is feared; or through envy, as one less fortunate to one more so; or one well thriven in anything, to him whose being on a par with himself he fears, or grieves at; or for the mere pleasure at another's pain, as spectators of gladiators, or deriders and mockers of others. These be the heads of iniquity which spring from the lust of the flesh, of the eye, or of rule, either singly, or two combined, or all together; and so do men live ill against the three, and seven, that psaltery of ten strings, Your Ten Commandments, O God, most high, and most sweet. But what foul offences can there be against You, who can not be defiled? Or what acts of violence against You, who can not be harmed? But You avenge what men commit against themselves, seeing also when they sin against You, they do wickedly against their own souls, and iniquity gives itself the lie, by corrupting and perverting their nature, which You have created and ordained, or by an immoderate use of things allowed, or in burning in things unallowed, to that use which is against nature; or are found guilty, raging with heart and tongue against You, kicking against the pricks; or when, bursting the pale of human society, they boldly joy in self-willed combinations or divisions, according as they have any object to gain or subject of offence. And these things are done when You are forsaken, O fountain of life, who are the only and true creator and governor of the universe, and by a self-willed pride, any one false thing is selected therefrom and loved. So then by a humble devoutness we return to You; and You cleanse us from our evil habits, and are merciful to their sins who confess, and hear the groaning of the prisoner, and loose us from the chains which we made for ourselves, if we lift not up against You the horns of an unreal liberty, suffering the loss of all, through covetousness of more, by loving more our own private good than You, the Good of all.

9. *The difference that is between sins, and between the judgment of God and men*

Amidst these offences of foulness and violence, and so many iniquities, are sins of men, who are on the whole making proficiency; which by those that judge rightly, are, after the rule of perfection, discommended, yet the persons commended, upon hope of future fruit, as in the green blade of growing corn. And there are some, resembling offences of foulness or violence, which yet are no sins; because they offend neither You, our Lord God, nor human society; when, namely, things fitting for a given period are obtained for the service of life, and we know not whether out of a lust of having; or when things are, for the sake of correction, by constituted authority punished, and we know not whether out of a lust of hurting. Many an action then which in men's sight is disapproved, is by Your testimony approved; and many, by men praised, are (You being witness) condemned: because the show of the action, and the mind of the doer, and the unknown exigency of the period, severally vary. But when You on a sudden command an unwonted and unthought of thing, yea, although You have sometime forbidden it, and still for the time hide the reason of Your command, and it be against the ordinance of some society of men, who doubts but it is to be done, seeing that society of men is just which serves You? But blessed are they who know Your commands! For all things were done by Your servants; either to show forth something needful for the present, or to foreshow things to come.

10. *He speaks again of the fig-tree, and derides the Manichees' foolish conceits about it*

These things I being ignorant of, scoffed at those Your holy servants and prophets. And what gained I by scoffing at them, but to be scoffed at by You, being insensibly and step by step drawn on to those follies, as to believe that a fig-tree wept when it was plucked, and the tree, its mother, shed milky tears? Which fig notwithstanding (plucked by some other's, not his own, guilt) had some Manichaean saint eaten, and mingled with his bowels, he should breathe out of it angels, yea, there shall burst forth particles of divinity, at every moan or groan in his prayer, which particles of the most high and true God had remained bound in that fig, unless they had been set at liberty by the teeth or belly of some 'elect' saint! And I, miserable, believed that more mercy was to be shown to the fruits of the earth than men, for whom they were created. For if anyone an-hungered, not a Manichaean, should ask for any, that morsel would seem as it were condemned to capital punishment, which should be given him.

11. *His mother's dream*

And You sent Your hand from above, and drew my soul out of that profound darkness; my mother, Your faithful one, weeping to You for me, more than mothers weep the bodily deaths of their children. For she, by that faith and spirit which she had from You, discerned the death wherein I lay, and You heard her, O Lord; You heard her, and despised not her tears, when streaming down, they watered the ground under her eyes in every place where she prayed; yea You heard her. For whence was that dream whereby You comforted her; so that she allowed me to live with her, and to eat at the same table in the house, which she had begun to shrink from, abhorring and detesting the blasphemies of my error? For she saw herself standing on a certain wooden rule, and a shining youth coming towards her, cheerful and smiling upon her, herself grieving, and overwhelmed with grief. But he having (in order to instruct, as is their wont not to be instructed) enquired of her the causes of her grief and daily tears, and she answering that she was bewailing my perdition, he bade her rest contented, and told her to look and observe, 'That where she was, there was I also.' And when she looked, she saw me standing by her in the same rule. Whence was this, but that Your ears were towards her heart? O You good omnipotent, who so care for every one of us, as if You cared for him only; and so for all, as if they were but one!

Whence was this also, that when she had told me this vision, and I would fain bend it to mean, that she rather should not despair of being one day what I was; she presently, without any hesitation, replies: No; for it was not told me that, 'where he, there you also;' but 'where you, there he also.' I confess to You, O Lord, that to the best of my remembrance (and I have oft spoken of this), Your answer, through my waking mother, that she was not perplexed by the plausibility of my false interpretation, and so quickly saw what was to be seen, and which I certainly had not perceived before she spoke – even then moved me more than the dream itself, by which a joy to the holy woman, to be fulfilled so long after, was, for the consolation of her present anguish, so long before foresignified. For almost nine years passed, in which I wallowed in the mire of that deep pit, and the darkness of falsehood, often assaying to rise, but dashed down the more grievously. All which time that chaste, godly, and sober widow (such as You love), now more cheered with hope, yet no whit relaxing in her weeping and mourning, ceased not at all hours of her devotions to bewail my case unto You. And her prayers entered into Your presence; and yet You suffered me to be yet involved and reinvolved in that darkness.

12. *The answer his mother received from a bishop, concerning his conversion*

You gave her meantime another answer, which I call to mind; for much I pass by, hasting to those things which more press me to confess unto You, and much I do not remember. You gave her then another answer, by a priest of Yours, a certain bishop brought up in Your Church, and well studied in Your books. Whom when this woman had entreated to vouchsafe to converse with me, refute my errors, unteach me ill things, and teach me good things (for this he was wont to do, when he found persons fitted to receive it), he refused, wisely, as I afterwards perceived. For he answered, that I was yet unteachable, being puffed up with the novelty of that heresy, and had already perplexed divers unskilful persons with captious questions, as she had told him: 'but let him alone a while' (says he), 'only pray God for him, he will of himself by reading find what that error is, and how great its impiety.' At the same time he told her, how himself, when a little

CONFESSIONS BOOK 3

one, had by his seduced mother been consigned over to the Manichees, and had not only read, but frequently copied out almost all, their books, and had (without any argument or proof from anyone) seen how much that sect was to be avoided; and had avoided it. Which when he had said, and she would not be satisfied, but urged him more, with entreaties and many tears, that he would see me and discourse with me; he, a little displeased at her importunity, says, 'Go your ways and God bless you, for it is not possible that the son of these tears should perish.' Which answer she took (as she often mentioned in her conversations with me) as if it had sounded from heaven.

Book 4

1. *How long, and what ways, he seduced others*

For this space of nine years (from my nineteenth year to my eight-and-twentieth) we lived seduced and seducing, deceived and deceiving, in divers lusts; openly, by sciences which they call liberal; secretly, with a false-named religion; here proud, there superstitious, everywhere vain. Here, hunting after the emptiness of popular praise, down even to theatrical applauses, and poetic prizes, and strifes for grassy garlands, and the follies of shows, and the intemperance of desires. There, desiring to be cleansed from these defilements, by carrying food to those who were called 'elect' and 'holy', out of which, in the workhouse of their stomachs, they should forge for us angels and gods, by whom we might be cleansed. These things did I follow, and practice with my friends, deceived by me and with me. Let the arrogant mock me, and such as have not been, to their soul's health, stricken and cast down by You, O my God; but I would still confess to You mine own shame in Your praise. Suffer me, I beseech You, and give me grace to go over in my present remembrance the wanderings of my forepassed time, and to offer unto You the sacrifice of thanksgiving. For what am I to myself without You, but a guide to mine own downfall? Or what am I even at the best, but an infant sucking the milk You give, and feeding upon You, the food that perishes not? But what sort of man is any man, seeing he is but a man? Let now the strong and the mighty laugh at us, but let us poor and needy confess unto You.

2. *He teaches rhetoric, and despises a wizard*
who promised him the victory

In those years I taught rhetoric, and, overcome by cupidity, made sale of a loquacity to overcome by. Yet I preferred (Lord, You know) honest scholars (as they are accounted), and these I, without artifice, taught artifices not to be practiced against the life of the guiltless, though sometimes for the life of the guilty. And You, O God, from afar perceived me stumbling in that slippery course, and amid much smoke sending out some sparks of faithfulness, which I showed in that my guidance of such as loved vanity and pursued what was false, myself their companion. In those years I had one – not in that which is called lawful marriage, but whom I had found out in a wayward passion, void of understanding; yet but one, remaining faithful even to her; in whom I in my own case experienced what difference there is betwixt the self-restraint of the marriage-covenant, for the sake of issue, and the bargain of a lustful love, where children are born against their parents' will, although, once born, they constrain love.

I remember also, that when I had settled to enter the lists for a theatrical prize, some wizard asked me what I would give him to win; but I, detesting and abhorring such foul mysteries, answered, Though the garland were of imperishable gold, I would not suffer a fly to be killed to gain me it. For he was to kill some living creatures in his sacrifices, and by those honors to invite the devils to favor me. But this ill also I rejected, not out of a pure love for You, O God of my heart; for I knew not how to love You, since I knew not how to conceive anything beyond a material brightness. And does not a soul, sighing after such fictions, commit fornication against You, trust in things unreal, and feed the wind? But still. for sure, I would not have sacrifices offered to devils for me, to whom I was sacrificing myself by that superstition. For what else is it to feed the wind, but to feed them, that is by going astray to become their pleasure and derision?

3. *Giving himself to astrology, he is reclaimed by an ancient physician*

Those impostors then, whom they style mathematicians, I consulted without scruple; because they seemed to use no sacrifice, nor to pray to any spirit for their divinations: which art, however, Christian and true piety consistently rejects and condemns. For, it is a good thing to confess unto You, and to say, Have mercy upon me, heal my soul, for I have sinned against You; and not to abuse Your mercy for a licence to sin, but to remember the Lord's words, Behold, you are made whole, sin no more, lest a worse thing come unto you. All which wholesome advice they labour to destroy, saying, 'The cause of your sin is inevitably determined in heaven'; and 'This did Venus, or Saturn, or Mars': that man, I suppose, flesh and blood, and proud corruption, might be blameless; while the creator and ordainer of heaven and the stars is to bear the blame. And who is he but our God, the very sweetness and well-spring of righteousness? Who render to every man according to his works: and a broken and contrite heart will You not despise.

There was in those days a wise man, very skilful in physic, and renowned therein, who as proconsul had with his own hand put the competition garland upon my distempered head, but not as a physician: for this disease You only cure, who resist the proud, and give grace to the humble. But did You fail me even by that old man, or forbear to heal my soul? For having become more acquainted with him, and hanging assiduously and fixedly on his speech (for though in simple terms, it was vivid, lively, and earnest), when he had gathered by my discourse that I was given to the books of astrologers, he kindly and fatherly advised me to cast them away, and not fruitlessly bestow a care and diligence, necessary for useful things, upon these vanities; saying, that he had in his earliest years studied that art, so as to make it the profession whereby he should live, and that, understanding Hippocrates, he could soon have understood such a study as this; and yet he had given it over, and taken to physic, for no other reason but that he found it utterly false; and he, a serious man, would not get his living by deluding people. 'But you,' says he, 'have rhetoric to maintain yourself by, so that you follow this of free choice, not of necessity: the more then ought you to give me credit herein, who laboured to acquire it so perfectly as to get my living by it alone.' Of whom when I had demanded, how then could many true things be foretold by it, he answered me (as he could) 'that the force of chance, diffused throughout the whole order of things, brought this about. For if when a man by haphazard opens the pages of some poet, who sang and thought of something wholly different, a verse oftentimes fell out, wondrously agreeable to the present business, it were not to be wondered at, if out of the soul of man, unconscious what takes place in it, by some higher instinct an answer should be given, by hap, not by art, corresponding to the business and actions of the demander.'

And thus much, either from or through him, You conveyed to me, and traced in my memory, which I might hereafter examine for myself. But at that time neither he, nor my dearest Nebridius, a youth singularly good and of a holy fear, who derided the whole body of divination, could persuade me to cast it aside, the authority of the authors swaying me yet more, and as yet I had found no certain proof (such as I sought) whereby it might without all doubt appear, that what had been truly foretold by those consulted was the result of haphazard, not of the art of the star-gazers.

4. He relates the sickness and baptism of his friend, whom himself had affected with heresy; he grievously laments his death

In those years when I first began to teach rhetoric in my native town, I had made one my friend, but too dear to me, from a community of pursuits, of mine own age, and, as myself, in the first opening flower of youth. He had grown up as a child with me, and we had been both school-fellows and play-fellows. But he was not yet my friend as afterwards, nor even then, as true friendship is; for true it cannot be, unless in such as You cement together, cleaving unto You, by that love which is shed abroad in our hearts by the Holy Ghost, which is given unto us. Yet was it but too sweet, ripened by the warmth of kindred studies: for, from the true faith (which he as a youth had not soundly and thoroughly imbibed), I had warped him also to those superstitious and pernicious fables, for which my mother bewailed me. With me he now erred in mind, nor could my soul be without him. But behold You were close on the steps of Your fugitives, at once God of vengeance, and fountain of mercies, turning us to Yourself by wonderful means; You took that man out of this life, when he had scarce filled up one whole year of my friendship, sweet to me above all sweetness of that my life.

Who can recount all Your praises, which he has felt in his one self? What did You then, my God, and how unsearchable is the abyss of Your judgments? For long, sore sick of a fever, he lay senseless in a death-sweat; and his recovery being despaired of, he was baptized, unknowing; myself meanwhile little regarding, and presuming that his soul would retain rather what it had received of me, not what was wrought on his unconscious body. But it proved far otherwise: for he was refreshed, and restored. Forthwith, as soon as I could speak with him (and I could, so soon as he was able, for I never left him, and we hung but too much upon each other), I essayed to jest with him, as though he would jest with me at that baptism which he had received, when utterly absent in mind and feeling, but had now understood that he had received. But he so shrunk from me, as from an enemy; and with a wonderful and sudden freedom bade me, as I would continue his friend, forbear such language to him. I, all astonished and amazed, suppressed all my emotions till he should grow well, and his health were strong enough for me to deal with him as I would. But he was taken away from my frenzy, that with You he might be preserved for my comfort; a few days after, in my absence, he was attacked again by the fever, and so departed.

At this grief my heart was utterly darkened; and whatever I beheld was death. My native country was a torment to me, and my father's house a strange unhappiness; and whatever I had shared with him, wanting him, became a distracting torture. Mine eyes sought him everywhere, but he was not granted them; and I hated all places, for that they had not him; nor could they now tell me, 'he is coming', as when he was alive and absent. I became a great riddle to myself, and I asked my soul, why she was so sad, and why she disquieted me sorely: but she knew not what to answer me. And if I said, Trust in God, she very rightly obeyed me not; because that most dear friend, whom she had lost, was, being man, both truer and better than that phantasm she was bid to trust in. Only tears were sweet to me, for they succeeded my friend, in the dearest of my affections.

5. *Of tears in our prayers for, and bewailing of, the thing beloved*

And now, Lord, these things are passed by, and time has assuaged my wound. May I learn from You, who are truth, and approach the ear of my heart unto Your mouth, that You may tell me why weeping is sweet to the miserable? Have You, although present everywhere, cast away our misery far from You? And You abide in Yourself, but we are tossed about in divers trials. And yet unless we mourned in Your ears, we should have no hope left. Whence then is sweet fruit gathered from the bitterness of life, from groaning, tears, sighs, and complaints? Does this sweeten it, that we hope You hear? This is true of prayer, for therein is a longing to approach unto You. But is it also in grief for a thing lost, and the sorrow wherewith I was then overwhelmed? For I neither hoped he should return to life nor did I desire this with my tears; but I wept only and grieved. For I was miserable, and had lost my joy. Or is weeping indeed a bitter thing, and for very loathing of the things which we before enjoyed, does it then, when we shrink from them, please us?

6. *He tells with what great affection he loved his friend*

But what speak I of these things? For now is no time to question, but to confess unto You. Wretched I was; and wretched is every soul bound by the friendship of perishable things; he is torn asunder when he loses them, and then he feels the wretchedness which he had before yet he lost them. So was it then with me; I wept most bitterly, and found my repose in bitterness. Thus was I wretched, and that wretched life I held dearer than my friend. For though I would willingly have changed it, yet was I more unwilling to part with it than with him; yea, I know not whether I would have parted with it even for him, as is related (if not feigned) of Pylades and Orestes, that they would gladly have died for each other or together, not to live together being to them worse than death. But in me there had arisen some unexplained feeling, too contrary to this, for at once I loathed exceedingly to live and feared to die. I suppose, the more I loved him, the more did I hate, and fear (as a most cruel enemy) death, which had bereaved me of him: and I imagined it would speedily make an end of all men, since it had power over him. Thus was it with me, I remember. Behold my heart, O my God, behold and see into me; for well I remember it, O my hope, who cleanse me from the impurity of such affections, directing mine eyes towards You, and plucking my feet out of the snare. For I wondered that others, subject to death, did live, since he whom I loved, as if he should never die, was dead; and I wondered yet more that myself, who was to him a second self, could live, he being dead. Well said one of his friend, 'You half of my soul'; for I felt that my soul and his soul were 'one soul in two bodies': and therefore was my life a horror to me, because I would not live halved. And therefore perchance I feared to die, lest he whom I had much loved should die wholly.

7. *The impatientness of grief constrains us to shift our dwellings*

O madness, which knows not how to love men, like men! O foolish man that I then was, enduring impatiently the lot of man! I fretted then, sighed, wept, was distracted; had neither rest nor counsel. For I bore about a shattered and bleeding soul, impatient of being borne by me, yet where to repose it, I found not. Not in calm groves, not in games and music, nor in fragrant spots, nor in curious banquetings, nor in the pleasures of the bed and the couch; nor (finally) in books or poesy, did it find repose. All things looked ghastly, yea, the very light; whatsoever was not what he was, was revolting and hateful, except groaning and tears. For in those alone found I a little refreshment. But when my soul was withdrawn from them a huge load of misery weighed me down. To You, O Lord, it ought to have been raised, for You to lighten; I knew it; but neither could nor would; the more, since when I thought of You, You were not to me any solid or substantial thing. For You were not Yourself, but a mere phantom, and my error was my God. If I offered to discharge my load thereon, that it might rest, it glided through the void, and came rushing down again on me; and I had remained to myself a hapless spot, where I could neither be, nor be from thence. For whither should my heart flee from my heart? Whither should I flee from myself? Whither not follow myself? And yet I fled out of my country; for so should mine eyes less look for him, where they were not wont to see him. And thus from Thagaste, I came to Carthage.

8. *Time cures sorrow*

Times lose no time; nor do they roll idly by; through our senses they work strange operations on the mind. Behold, they went and came day by day, and by coming and going, introduced into my mind other imaginations and other remembrances; and little by little patched me up again with my old kind of delights, unto which that my sorrow gave way. And yet there succeeded, not indeed other griefs, yet the causes of other griefs. For whence had that former grief so easily reached my very inmost soul, but that I had poured out my soul upon the dust, in loving one that must die, as if he would never die? For what restored and refreshed me chiefly was the solaces of other friends, with whom I did love, what instead of You I loved; and this was a great fable, and protracted lie, by whose adulterous stimulus, our soul, which lay itching in our ears, was being defiled. But that fable would not die to me, so oft as any of my friends died. There were other things which in them did more take my mind; to talk and jest together, to do kind offices by turns; to read together honeyed books; to play the fool or be earnest together; to dissent at times without discontent, as a man might with his own self; and even with the seldomness of these dissentings, to season our more frequent consentings; sometimes to teach, and sometimes learn; long for the absent with impatience; and welcome the coming with joy. These and the like expressions, proceeding out of the hearts of those that loved and were loved again, by the countenance, the tongue, the eyes, and a thousand pleasing gestures, were so much fuel to melt our souls together, and out of many make but one.

9. *The comparing of human friendship with divine*

This is it that is loved in friends; and so loved, that a man's conscience condemns itself, if he love not him that loves him again, or love not again him that loves him, looking for nothing from his person but indications of his love. Hence that mourning, if one die, and darkenings of sorrows, that steeping of the heart in tears, all sweetness turned to bitterness; and upon the loss of life of the dying, the death of the living. Blessed whoso loves You, and his friend in You, and his enemy for You. For he alone loses none dear to him, to whom all are dear in Him who cannot be lost. And who is this but our God, the God that made heaven and earth, and fills them, because by filling them He created them? No one loses You, but he who lets You go. And he who lets You go; whither goes or whither flees he, but from You well-pleased, to You displeased? For where does he not find Your law in his own punishment? And Your law is truth, and truth You.

10. *All beauty is from God, who is to be prayed for all*

Turn us, O God of Hosts, show us Your countenance, and we shall be whole. For whithersoever the soul of man turns itself, unless toward You, it is riveted upon sorrows, yea though it is riveted on things beautiful. And yet they, out of You, and out of the soul, were not, unless they were from You. They rise, and set; and by rising, they begin as it were to be; they grow, that they may be perfected; and perfected, they wax old and wither; and all grow not old, but all wither. So then when they rise and tend to be, the more quickly they grow that they may be, so much the more they haste not to be. This is the law of them. Thus much have You allotted them, because they are portions of things, which exist not all at once, but by passing away and succeeding, they together complete that universe, whereof they are portions. And even thus is our speech completed by signs giving forth a sound: but this again is not perfected unless one word pass away when it has sounded its part, that another may succeed. Out of all these things let my soul praise You, O God, creator of all; yet let not my soul be riveted unto these things with the glue of love, through the senses of the body. For they go whither they were to go, that they might not be; and they rend her with pestilent longings, because she longs to be, yet loves to repose in what she loves. But in these things is no place of repose; they abide not, they flee; and who can follow them with the senses of the flesh? Yea, who can grasp them, when they are hard by? For the sense of the flesh is slow, because it is the sense of the flesh; and thereby is it bounded. It suffices for that it was made for; but it suffices not to stay things running their course from their appointed starting-place to the end appointed. For in Your word, by which they are created, they hear their decree, 'hence and hitherto'.

11. *All things are created mutable in themselves, and immutable in God*

Be not foolish, O my soul, nor become deaf in the ear of your heart with the tumult of your folly. Hearken you too.

The word itself calls you to return: and there is the place of rest imperturbable, where love is not forsaken, if itself forsakes not. Behold, these things pass away, that others may replace them, and so this lower universe be completed by all his parts. But do I depart any whither? says the word of God. There fix your dwelling, trust there whatsoever you have from there, O my soul, at least now you are tired out with vanities. Entrust to truth, whatsoever you have from the truth, and you shall lose nothing; and your decay shall bloom again, and all your diseases be healed, and your mortal parts be reformed and renewed, and bound around you: nor shall they lay you whither themselves descend; but they shall stand fast with you, and abide for ever before God, who abides and stands fast for ever.

Why then be perverted and follow your flesh? Be it converted and follow you. Whatever by her you have sense of, is in part; and the whole, whereof these are parts, you know not; and yet they delight you. But had the sense of your flesh a capacity for comprehending the whole, had it not itself also, for your punishment, been justly restricted to a part of the whole, you would wish, that whatsoever exists at this present, should pass away, that so the whole might better please you. For what we speak also, by the same sense of the flesh you hear; yet would you not have the syllables stay, but fly away, that others may come, and you hear the whole. And so ever, when any one thing is made up of many, all of which do not exist together, all collectively would please more than they do severally, could all be perceived collectively. But far better than these is He who made all; and He is our God, nor does He pass away, for neither does anything succeed Him.

12. *Love of the creatures is not forbidden, provided that, in those which please us, God be loved*

If bodies please you, praise God on occasion of them, and turn back your love upon their maker; lest in these things which please you, you displease. If souls please you, be they loved in God: for they too are mutable, but in Him are they firmly stablished; else would they pass, and pass away. In Him then, be they beloved; and carry unto Him along with you what souls you can, and say to them, Him let us love, Him let us love: He made these, nor is He far off. For He did not make them, and so depart, but they are of Him, and in Him. See there He is, where truth is loved. He is within the very heart, yet has the heart strayed from Him. Go back into your heart, you transgressors, and hold fast to Him that made you. Stand with Him, and you shall stand fast. Rest in

Him, and you shall be at rest. Whither go you in rough ways?
Whither go you? The good that you love is from Him; but it is
good and pleasant through reference to Him, and justly shall it be
embittered, because unjustly is anything loved which is from Him,
if He be forsaken for it. To what end then would you still and still
walk these difficult and toilsome ways? There is no rest, where
you seek it. Seek what you seek; but it is not there where you
seek. You seek a blessed life in the land of death; it is not there.
For how should there be a blessed life where life itself is not?

But our true Life came down hither, and bore our death, and
slew him, out of the abundance of His own life: and He thun-
dered, calling aloud to us to return hence to Him into that secret
place, whence He came forth to us, first into the virgin's womb,
wherein He espoused the human creation, our mortal flesh, that
it might not be for ever mortal, and thence like a bridegroom
coming out of his chamber, rejoicing as a giant to run his course.
For He lingered not, but ran, calling aloud by words, deeds, death,
life, descent, ascension; crying aloud to us to return unto Him.
And He departed from our eyes, that we might return into our
heart, and there find Him. For He departed, and so, He is here.
He would not be long with us, yet left us not; for He departed
thither, whence He never parted, because the world was made by
Him. And in this world He was, and into this world He came to
save sinners, unto whom my soul confesses, and He heals it, for it
has sinned against Him. O you sons of men, how long so slow of
heart? Even now, after the descent of Life to you, will you not
ascend and live? But whither do you ascend, when you are on
high, and set your mouth against the heavens? Descend, that you
may ascend, and ascend to God. For you have fallen, by ascending
against Him. Tell them this, that they may weep in the valley of
tears, and so carry them up with you unto God; because out of His
spirit you speak thus unto them, if you speak, burning with the
fire of charity.

13. *Love, whence it comes*

These things I then knew not, and I loved these lower beauties,
and I was sinking to the very depths, and to my friends I said, 'Do
we love anything but the beautiful? What then is the beautiful?
And what is beauty? What is it that attracts and wins us to the

things we love? For unless there were in them a grace and beauty, they could by no means draw us unto them.' And I marked and perceived that in bodies themselves, there was a beauty, from their forming a sort of whole, and again, another from apt and mutual correspondence, as of a part of the body with its whole, or a shoe with a foot, and the like. And this consideration sprang up in my mind, out of my inmost heart, and I wrote *On the Fair and Fit*, I think, two or three books. You know, O Lord, for it is gone from me; for I have them not, but they are strayed from me, I know not how.

14. *Of his book,* Fair and Fit

But what moved me, O Lord my God, to dedicate these books unto Hierius, an orator of Rome, whom I knew not by face, but loved for the fame of his learning which was eminent in him, and some words of his I had heard, which pleased me? But more did he please me, for that he pleased others, who highly extolled him, amazed that out of a Syrian, first instructed in Greek eloquence, should afterwards be formed a wonderful Latin orator, and one most learned in things pertaining unto philosophy. One is commended and, unseen, he is loved: does this love enter the heart of the hearer from the mouth of the commender? Not so. But by one who loves is another kindled. For hence he is loved who is commended, when the commender is believed to extol him with an unfeigned heart; that is, when one that loves him, praises him.

For so did I then love men, upon the judgment of men, not Yours, O my God, in whom no man is deceived. But yet why not for qualities like those of a famous charioteer, or fighter with beasts in the theatre, known far and wide by a vulgar popularity, but far otherwise, and earnestly, and so as I would be myself commended? For I would not be commended or loved as actors are (though I myself did commend and love them), but had rather be unknown than so known; and even hated, than so loved. Where now are the impulses to such various and divers kinds of loves laid up in one soul? What is it I love in another, and which again, did I not hate it, I should not spurn and cast from myself, seeing we are both of us men? It is not like the way a good horse is loved by him, who would not want to *be* that horse, even if he could; the same may not be said of an actor,

who shares our nature. Do I then love in a man, what I hate to
be, who am a man? Man himself is a great deep, whose very hairs
You number, O Lord, and they fall not to the ground without
You. And yet are the hairs of his head easier to be numbered than
his feelings, and the beatings of his heart.

But that orator was of that sort whom I loved, as wishing to be
myself such; and I erred through a swelling pride, and was tossed
about with every wind, but yet was steered by You, though very
secretly. And whence do I know, and whence do I confidently
confess unto You, that I had loved him more for the love of his
commenders, than for the very things for which he was commended? Because, had he been unpraised, and these self-same
men had dispraised him, and with dispraise and contempt told
the very same things of him, I had never been so kindled and
excited to love him. And yet the things had not been other, nor
he himself other; but only the feelings of the relators. See where
the impotent soul flies along, that is not yet stayed up by the
solidity of truth! Just as the gales of tongues blow from the breast
of the opinionated, so is the soul carried this way and that, driven
forward and backward, and the light is overclouded to it, and the
truth unseen. And lo, it is before us. And it was to me a great
matter, that my discourse and labours should be known to that
man: which should he approve, I were the more kindled; but if he
disapproved, my empty heart, void of Your solidity, had been
wounded. And yet the *Fair and Fit*, whereon I wrote to him, I
dwelt on with pleasure, and surveyed it, and admired it, though
none joined therein.

15. *How his understanding being overshadowed with
corporeal images, he could not discern the spiritual*

But I saw not yet, whereon this weighty matter turned in Your
wisdom, O You omnipotent, who alone do wonders; and my
mind ranged through corporeal forms; and 'fair' I defined and
distinguished what is so in itself, and 'fit', whose beauty is in
correspondence to some other thing: and this I supported by
corporeal examples. And I turned to the nature of the mind, but
the false notion which I had of spiritual things, did not let me see
the truth. Yet the force of truth did of itself flash into mine eyes,
and I turned away my panting soul from incorporeal substance

to lineaments, and colors, and bulky magnitudes. And not being able to see these in the mind, I thought I could not see my mind. And whereas in virtue I loved peace, and in viciousness I abhorred discord, in the first I observed a unity, but in the other, a sort of division. And in that unity I conceived the rational soul, and the nature of truth and of the chief good to consist; but in this division I miserably imagined there to be some unknown substance of irrational life, and the nature of the chief evil, which should not only be a substance, but real life also, and yet not derived from You, O my God, of whom are all things. And yet that first I called a *monad*, as it had been a soul without sex; but the latter a *dyad* – anger, in deeds of violence, and in immorality, lust; not knowing whereof I spoke. For I had not known or learned that neither was evil a substance, nor our soul that chief and unchangeable good.

For as deeds of violence arise, if that emotion of the soul be corrupted, whence vehement action springs, stirring itself insolently and unrulily; and lusts, when that affection of the soul is ungoverned, whereby carnal pleasures are drunk in, so do errors and false opinions defile the conversation, if the reasonable soul itself be corrupted; as it was then in me, who knew not that it must be enlightened by another light, that it may be partaker of truth, seeing itself is not that nature of truth. For You shall light my candle, O Lord my God, You shall enlighten my darkness: and of Your fullness have we all received, for You are the true light that lights every man that comes into the world; for in You there is no variation, neither shadow of change.

But I pressed towards You, and was thrust from You, that I might taste of death: for you resist the proud. But what prouder, than for me with a strange madness to maintain myself to be that by nature which You are? For whereas I was subject to change (so much being manifest to me, my very desire to become wise being the wish, of worse to become better), yet chose I rather to imagine You subject to change, and myself not to be that which You are. Therefore I was repelled by You, and You resisted my vain stiffneckedness, and I imagined corporeal forms, and, myself flesh, I accused flesh; and, a wind that passes away, I returned not to You, but I passed on and on to things which have no being, neither in You, nor in me, nor in the body. Neither were they created for me by Your truth, but by my vanity devised out of things corporeal. And I was wont to ask Your faithful little ones, my fellow-citizens (from whom, unknown to myself, I stood exiled), I was wont, prating and foolishly, to ask them, 'Why then does the soul err which God created?' But I would not be asked, 'Why then does God err?' And I maintained that Your unchangeable substance did err upon constraint, rather than confess that my changeable substance had gone astray voluntarily, and now, in punishment, lay in error.

I was then some six or seven and twenty years old when I wrote those volumes; revolving within me corporeal fictions, buzzing in the ears of my heart, which I turned, O sweet truth, to your inward melody, meditating on the 'fair and fit', and longing to stand and hearken to You, and to rejoice greatly at the bridegroom's voice; but I could not, for by the voices of mine own errors, I was hurried abroad, and through the weight of my own pride, I was sinking into the lowest pit. For You did not make me to hear joy and gladness, nor did the bones exult which were not yet humbled.

16. *The admirable aptness to learning, and the great understanding Saint Augustine had*

And what did it profit me, that scarce twenty years old, when a book of Aristotle, which they call the Ten Categories, fell into my hands (on whose very name I hung, as on something great and divine, so often as my rhetoric master of Carthage, and others accounted learned, mouthed it with cheeks bursting with pride), I read and understood it unaided? And on my conferring with others, who said that they scarcely understood it with very able tutors not only orally explaining it, but drawing many things in sand, they could tell me no more of it than I had learned, reading it by myself. And the book appeared to me to speak very clearly of substances, such as 'man', and of their qualities, as the figure of a man, of what sort it is; and stature, how many feet high; and his relationship, whose brother he is; or where placed; or when born; or whether he stands or sits; or be shod or armed; or does or suffers anything; and all the innumerable things which might be ranged under these nine categories, of which I have given some specimens, or under that chief category of Substance.

CONFESSIONS BOOK 4   59

What did all this further me, seeing it even hindered me when, imagining whatever was, was comprehended under those ten categories, I essayed in such wise to understand You also, O my God, in Your wonderful simplicity and changelessness, as if You also had been subjected to Your own greatness or beauty; so that (as in bodies) they should exist in You, as their subject: whereas You Yourself are Your greatness and beauty; but a body is not great or fair in that it is a body, seeing that, though it were less great or fair, it should notwithstanding be a body. But it was falsehood, what I thought about You, not truth, fictions of my misery, not the realities of Your blessedness. For You had commanded, and it was done in me, that the earth should bring forth briars and thorns to me, and that in the sweat of my brows I should eat my bread.

And what did it profit me, that all the books I could procure of the so-called liberal arts, I, the vile slave of vile affections, read by myself, and understood? And I delighted in them, but knew not whence came all that therein was true or certain. For I had my back to the light, and my face to the things enlightened; whence my face, with which I discerned the things enlightened, itself was not enlightened. Whatever was written, either on rhetoric, or logic, geometry, music, and arithmetic, by myself without much difficulty or any instructor, I understood, You know, O Lord my God; because both quickness of understanding, and acuteness in discerning, is Your gift: yet did I not thence sacrifice to You. So then it served not to my use, but rather to my perdition, since I went about to get so good a portion of my substance into my own keeping; and I kept not my strength for You, but wandered from You into a far country, to spend it upon harlotries. What profited me good abilities, not employed to good uses? For I felt not that those arts were attained with great difficulty, even by the studious and talented, until I attempted to explain them to such; when he most excelled in them who followed me not altogether slowly.

But what did this further me, imagining that You, O Lord God, the truth, were a vast and bright body, and I a fragment of that body? Perverseness too great! But such was I. Nor do I blush, O my God, to confess to You Your mercies towards me, and to call upon You, I who blushed not then to profess to men my blasphemies, and to bark against You. What profited me then my nimble wit in those sciences and all those most knotty volumes, unravelled by me, without aid from human instruction; seeing I erred so foully, and with such sacrilegious shamefulness, in the doctrine of piety? Or what hindrance was a far slower wit to Your little ones, since they departed not far from You, that in the nest of Your Church they might securely be fledged, and nourish the wings of charity, by the food of a sound faith. O Lord our God, under the shadow of Your wings let us hope; protect us, and carry us. You will carry us both when little, and even to hoar hairs will You carry us; for our firmness, when it is You, then is it firmness; but when our own, it is infirmity. Our good ever lives with You; from which when we turn away, we are turned aside. Let us now, O Lord, return, that we may not be overturned, because with You our good lives without any decay, which good are You; nor need we fear, lest there be no place whither to return, because we fell from it: fsinceit is not our absence which causes our mansion, which is Your eternity, to fall.

Book 5

1. *He stirs his own soul to praise God*

Accept the sacrifice of my confessions from the ministry of my tongue, which You have formed and stirred up to confess unto Your name. Heal You all my bones, and let them say, O Lord, who is like unto You. For he who confesses to You does not teach You what takes place within him; seeing a closed heart closes not out Your eye, nor can man's hard-heartedness thrust back Your hand: for You dissolve it at Your will in pity or in vengeance, and nothing can hide itself from Your heat. But let my soul praise You, that it may love You; and let it confess Your own mercies to You, that it may praise You. Your whole creation ceases not, nor is silent in Your praises; neither the spirit of man with voice directed unto You, nor creation animate or inanimate, by the voice of those who meditate thereon: that so our souls may from their weariness arise towards You, leaning on those things which You have created, and passing on to Yourself, who made them wonderfully; and there is refreshment and true strength.

2. *God's presence can no man avoid, seeing he is everywhere*

Let the restless, the wicked, depart and flee from You; yet You see them, and can penetrate the shades. And behold, everything with them is fair, though they are foul. And how have they injured You? Or how have they disgraced Your government, which, from the heaven to this lowest earth, is just and perfect? For whither fled they, when they fled from Your presence? Or where do not You find them? But they fled, that they might not see You seeing them, and, blinded, might stumble against You (because You forsake nothing You have made) – that the unjust might stumble upon You, and justly be hurt; withdrawing themselves from Your gentleness, and stumbling at Your uprightness, and falling into Your harshness. Ignorant, in truth, that You are everywhere, whom no place encompasses, and that You alone are near, even to those that remove far from You. Let them then be turned, and seek You; because You have not forsaken Your creation as they have forsaken their creator. Let them be turned and seek You; and behold, You are there in their heart, in the heart of those that confess to You, and cast themselves upon You, and weep in Your bosom, after all their taxing journeys. Then do You gently wipe away their tears, and they weep the more, and joy in weeping; even for that You, Lord – not man of flesh and blood, but – You, Lord, who made them, re-make and comfort them. But where was I, when I was seeking You? And You were before me, but I had gone away from You; nor did I find myself, how much less You!

3. *Of Faustus the Manichee: and of astrologies*

I would lay open before my God that nine-and-twentieth year of mine age. There had then come to Carthage a certain bishop of the Manichees, Faustus by name, a great snare of the Devil, and many were entangled by him through that lure of his smooth language: which though I did commend, yet could I separate from the truth of the things which I was earnest to learn: nor did I so much regard the service of oratory as the science which this Faustus, so praised among them, set before me to feed upon. Fame had before bespoken him most knowing in all valuable learning, and exquisitely skilled in the liberal sciences.

And since I had read and well remembered much of the philosophers, I compared some things of theirs with those long fables of the Manichees, and found the former the more probable; even although they could only prevail so far as to make judgment of this lower world, the Lord of it they could by no means find out. For You are great, O Lord, and have respect unto the humble, but the proud You behold afar off. Nor do You draw near, but to the contrite in heart, nor are found by the proud, no, not though by painstaking skill they could number the stars and the sand, and measure the starry heavens, and track the courses of the planets.

For with their understanding and wit, which You bestowed on them, they search out these things; and much have they found out; and foretold, many years before, eclipses of those luminaries, the sun and moon – what day and hour, and how many digits – nor did their calculation fail; and it came to pass as they foretold; and they wrote down the rules they had found out, and these are read at this day, and out of them do others foretell in what year and month of the year, and what day of the month, and what hour of the day, and what part of its light, moon or sun is to be eclipsed, and so it shall be, as it is foreshowed. At these things men, that know not this art, marvel and are astonished, and they that know it, exult, and are puffed up; and by an ungodly pride departing from You, and failing of Your light, they foresee a failure of the sun's light, which shall be, so long before, but see not their own, which is in the preent. For they search not religiously where their wit comes from, wherewith they search out this. And finding that You made them, they give not themselves up to You, to preserve what You made, nor sacrifice to You what they have made themselves; nor slay their own soaring imaginations, as fowls of the air, nor their own diving curiosities (wherewith, like the fishes of the sea, they wander over the unknown paths of the abyss), nor their own luxuriousness, as beasts of the field, that You, Lord, a consuming fire, may burn up those dead cares of theirs, and re-create them immortally.

But they knew not the way, Your word, by whom You made these things which they number, and themselves who number, and the sense whereby they perceive what they number, and the understanding, out of which they number; or that of Your wisdom there is no number. But the only begotten is Himself made unto us wisdom, and righteousness, and sanctification, and was numbered among us, and paid tribute unto Caesar. They knew not this way whereby to descend to Him from themselves, and by Him ascend unto Him. They knew not this way, and deemed themselves exalted amongst the stars and shining; and behold, they fell upon the earth, and their foolish heart was darkened. They discourse many things truly concerning the creature; but truth, artificer of the creature, they seek not piously, and therefore find Him not; or if they find Him, knowing Him to be God, they glorify Him not as God, neither are thankful, but become vain in their imaginations, and profess themselves to be wise, attributing to themselves what is Yours; and thereby with most perverse blindness, study to impute to You what is their own, forging lies of You who are the truth, and changing the glory of uncorruptible God into an image made like corruptible man, and to birds, and four-footed beasts, and creeping things, changing Your truth into a lie, and worshipping and serving the creature more than the creator.

Yet many truths concerning the creature I retained from these men, and saw the reason thereof from calculations, the succession of times, and the visible testimonies of the stars; and compared them with the saying of Manichaeus, which in his frenzy he had written most largely on these subjects; but discovered not any account of the solstices, or equinoxes, or the eclipses of the greater lights, nor whatever of this sort I had learned in the books of secular philosophy. But I was commanded to believe; and yet it corresponded not with what had been established by calculations and my own sight, but was quite contrary.

4. *Only the knowledge of God makes happy*

Does then, O Lord God of truth, whoever knows these things, therefore please You? Surely unhappy is he who knows all these, and knows not You: but happy whoso knows You, though he know not these. And whoso knows both You and them is not the happier for them, but for You only, if, knowing You, he glorifies You as God, and is thankful, and becomes not vain in his imaginations. For as he is better off who knows how to possess a tree, and return thanks to You for the use thereof, although he know not how many cubits high it is, or how wide it spreads, than he that can measure it, and count all its boughs, and neither owns it, nor knows or loves its creator: so a believer, whose all this world of wealth is, and who having nothing, yet possesses all things, by cleaving unto You, whom all things serve, though he know not even the circles of the Great Bear, yet is it folly to doubt but he is in a better state than one who can measure the heavens, and number the stars, and weigh the elements, yet neglects You who have made all things in number, weight, and measure.

5. *The rashness of Faustus, in teaching what he knew not*

But yet who bade some Manichaean or other to write on these things also, skill in which was no element of piety? For You have said to man, Behold piety and wisdom; of which he might be ignorant, though he had perfect knowledge of these things; but since, knowing not, he most impudently dared to teach these things, he plainly could have no knowledge of piety. For it is vanity to make profession of these worldly things even when known; but confession to You is piety. Wherefore this wanderer to this end spoke much of these things, that convicted by those who had truly learned them, it might be manifest what understanding he had in the other abstruser things. For he would not have himself meanly thought of, but went about to persuade men, that the Holy Ghost, the comforter and enricher of Your faithful ones, was with plenary authority personally within him. When then he was found out to have taught falsely of the heaven and stars, and of the motions of the sun and moon (although these things pertain not to the doctrine of religion), yet his sacrilegious presumption would become evident enough, seeing he delivered things which not only he knew not, but which were falsified, with so mad a vanity of pride, that he sought to ascribe them to himself, as to a divine person.

For when I hear any Christian brother ignorant of these things, and mistaken on them, I can patiently behold such a man holding his opinion; nor do I see that any ignorance as to the position or character of the corporeal creation can injure him, so long as he does not believe anything unworthy of You, O Lord, the creator of all. But it does injure him, if he imagine it to pertain to the form of the doctrine of piety, and will yet affirm that too stiffly whereof he is ignorant. And yet is even such an infirmity, in the infancy of faith, borne by our mother Charity, till the new-born may grow up unto a perfect man, so as not to be carried about with every wind of doctrine. But in him who in such wise presumed to be the teacher, source, guide, chief of all whom he could so persuade, that whoso followed him thought that he followed, not a mere man, but Your Holy Spirit; who would not judge that so great madness, when once convicted of having taught anything false, were to be detested and utterly rejected? But I had not as yet clearly ascertained whether the vicissitudes of longer and shorter days and nights, and of day and night itself, with the eclipses of the greater lights, and whatever else of the kind I had read of in other books, might be explained consistently with his sayings; so that, if they by any means might, it should still remain a question to me whether it were so or no; but I might, on account of his reputed sanctity, rest my credence upon his authority.

6. *Faustus was eloquent by nature, rather than by art*

And for almost all those nine years, wherein with unsettled mind I had been their disciple, I had longed but too intensely for the coming of this Faustus. For the rest of the sect, whom by chance I had lighted upon, when unable to solve my objections about these things, still held out to me the coming of this Faustus, by conference with whom these and greater difficulties, if I had them, were to be most readily and abundantly cleared. When then he came, I found him a man of pleasing discourse, and who could speak fluently and in better terms, yet still but the self-same things which they were wont to say. But what availed the utmost neatness of the cup-bearer to my thirst for a more precious draught? Mine ears were already cloyed with the like, nor did they seem to me therefore better, because better said; nor therefore true, because eloquent; nor the soul therefore wise, because the face was comely, and the language graceful. But they who held him out to me were no good judges of things; and therefore to them he appeared understanding and wise, because in words pleasing. I felt however that another sort of people were suspicious even of truth, and refused to assent to it, if delivered in a smooth and copious discourse. But You, O my God, had already taught me by wonderful and secret ways, and the reason I believe that You taught me, is because it is truth, nor is there besides You any teacher of truth, where or whencesoever it may shine upon us. Of Yourself therefore had I now learned, that neither ought anything to seem to be spoken truly, because eloquently; nor therefore falsely, because the utterance of the lips is inharmonious; nor, again, therefore true, because rudely delivered; nor therefore false, because the language is rich; but that wisdom and folly are as wholesome and unwholesome food; and adorned or unadorned phrases as courtly or country vessels; either kind of meats may be served up in either kind of dishes.

That greediness then, wherewith I had of so long time expected that man, was delighted verily with his action and feeling when disputing, and his choice and readiness of words to clothe his ideas. I was then delighted, and, with many others and more than they, did I praise and extol him. It troubled me, however, that in the assembly of his auditors, I was not allowed to put in and communicate those questions that troubled me, in familiar converse with him. Which when I might, and with my friends began to engage his ears at such times as it was not unbecoming for him to discuss with me, and had brought forward such things as moved me, I found him first utterly ignorant of liberal sciences, save grammar, and that but in an ordinary way. But because he had read some of Tully's *Orations*, a very few books of Seneca, some things of the poets, and such few volumes of his own sect as were written in Latin and neatly, and was daily practiced in speaking, he acquired a certain eloquence, which proved the more pleasing and seductive because under the guidance of a good wit, and with a kind of natural gracefulness. Is it not thus, as I recall it, O Lord my God, You judge of my conscience? Before You is my heart, and my remembrance, who did at that time direct me by the hidden mystery of Your providence, and did set those shameful errors of mine before my face, that I might see and hate them.

7. *He falls off from the Manichees*

For after it was clear that he was ignorant of those arts in which I thought he excelled, I began to despair of his opening and solving the difficulties which perplexed me (of which indeed however ignorant, he might have held the truths of piety, had he not been a Manichee). For their books are fraught with prolix fables, of the heaven, and stars, sun, and moon, and I now no longer thought him able satisfactorily to decide what I much desired, whether, on comparison of these things with the calculations I had elsewhere read, the account given in the books of Manichaeus were preferable, or at least as good. Which when I proposed to be considered and discussed, he, so far modestly, shrunk from the burthen. For he knew that he knew not these things, and was not ashamed to confess it. For he was not one of those talking persons, many of whom I had endured, who undertook to teach me these things, and said nothing. But this man had a heart, though not right towards You, yet neither altogether treacherous to himself. For he was not altogether ignorant of his own ignorance, nor would he rashly be entangled in a dispute, whence he could neither retreat nor extricate himself fairly. Even for this I liked him the better. For fairer is the modesty of a candid mind, than the knowledge of those things which I desired; and such I found him, in all the more difficult and subtile questions.

My zeal for the writings of Manichaeus being thus blunted, and despairing yet more of their other teachers, seeing that in divers things which perplexed me, he, so renowned among them, had so turned out, I began to engage with him in the study of that literature, on which he also was much set (and which as rhetoric-reader I was at that time teaching young students at Carthage), and to read with him, either what himself desired to hear, or such as I judged fit for his genius. But all my efforts whereby I had purposed to advance in that sect, upon knowledge of that man, came utterly to an end; not that I detached myself from them altogether, but as one finding nothing better, I had settled to be content meanwhile with what I had in whatever way fallen upon, unless by chance something more eligible should dawn upon me. Thus, that Faustus, to so many a snare of death, had now neither willing nor witting it, begun to loosen that wherein I was taken. For Your hands, O my God, in the secret purpose of Your providence, did not forsake my soul; and out of my mother's heart's blood, through her tears night and day poured out, was a sacrifice offered for me unto You; and You did deal with me by wondrous ways. You did it, O my God: for the steps of a man are ordered by the Lord, and He shall dispose his way. Or how shall we obtain salvation, but from Your hand, re-making what it made?

8. *He takes a voyage to Rome, against the will of his mother*

You did deal with me, that I should be persuaded to go to Rome, and to teach there rather, what I was teaching at Carthage. And how I was persuaded to this, I will not neglect to confess to You; because herein also the deepest recesses of Your wisdom, and Your most present mercy to us, must be considered and confessed. I did not wish to go to Rome, simply because higher gains and higher dignities were warranted me by my friends who persuaded me to this (though even these things had at that time an influence over my mind), but my chief and almost only reason was, that I heard that young men studied there more peacefully, and were kept quiet under a restraint of more regular discipline; so that they did not, at their pleasures, petulantly rush into the school of one whose pupils they were not, nor were even admitted without his permission. Whereas at Carthage there reigns among the scholars a most disgraceful and unruly licence. They burst in audaciously, and with gestures almost frantic, disturb all order which anyone has established for the good of his scholars. Divers outrages they commit, with a wonderful stolidity, punishable by law, did not custom uphold them; that custom evincing them to be the more miserable, in that they now do as lawful what by Your eternal law shall never be lawful; and they think they do it unpunished, whereas they are punished with the very blindness whereby they do it, and suffer incomparably worse than what they do. The manners then which, when a student, I would not make my own, I was forced as a teacher to endure in others: and so I was well pleased to go where all that knew it, assured me that the like was not done. But You, my refuge and my portion in the land of the living; that I might change my earthly dwelling for the salvation of my soul, at Carthage did goad me, that I might thereby be torn from it; and at Rome did proffer me allurements, whereby I might be drawn thither, by men in love with a dying life, on the one side doing frantic things, on the other promising vain things; and, to correct my steps, You did secretly use their and my own perverseness. For both they who disturbed my quiet were blinded with a disgraceful frenzy, and they who invited me elsewhere savored of earth. And I, who here detested real misery, was there seeking unreal happiness.

But why I went from one, and to the other, You knew, O God, yet showed it neither to me, nor to my mother, who grievously bewailed my journey, and followed me as far as the sea. But I deceived her, holding me by force, that either she might keep me back or go with me, and I pretended I had a friend whom I could not leave, till he had a fair wind to sail. And I lied to my mother, and such a mother, and escaped: for this also have You mercifully forgiven me, preserving me, thus full of execrable defilements, from the waters of the sea, for the water of Your grace; whereby when I was cleansed, the streams of my mother's eyes should be dried, with which for me she daily watered the ground under her face. And yet refusing to return without me, I scarcely persuaded her to stay that night in a place hard by our ship, where was an oratory in memory of the blessed Cyprian. That night I privily departed, but she was not behind in weeping and prayer. And what, O Lord, was she with so many tears asking of You, but that You would not suffer me to sail? But You, in the depth of Your counsels and hearing the main point of her desire, regarded not what she then asked, that You might make me what she ever asked. The wind blew and swelled our sails, and withdrew the shore from our sight; and she on the morrow was there, frantic with sorrow, and with complaints and groans filled Your ears, who did then disregard them; whilst through my desires, You were hurrying me to end all desire, and the earthly part of her affection to me was chastened by the allotted scourge of sorrows. For she loved my being with her, as mothers do, but much more than many; and she knew not how great joy You were about to work for her out of my absence. She knew not; therefore did she weep and wail, and by this agony there appeared in her the inheritance of Eve, with sorrow seeking what in sorrow she had brought forth. And yet, after accusing my treachery and hardheartedness, she betook herself again to intercede to You for me, went to her wonted place, and I to Rome.

9. Of a shrewd fever that he fell into

And lo, there was I received by the scourge of bodily sickness, and I was going down to hell, carrying all the sins which I had committed, both against You and myself and others, many and grievous, over and above that bond of original sin, whereby we all die in Adam. For You had not forgiven me any of these things in Christ, nor had He abolished by His cross the enmity which by my sins I had incurred with You. For how should He, by the crucifixion of a phantasm, which I believed Him to be? So true, then, was the death of my soul, as that of His flesh seemed to me false; and how true the death of His body, so false was the life of my soul, which did not believe it. And now the fever heightening, I was parting and departing for ever. For had I then parted hence, whither had I departed, but into fire and torments, such as my misdeeds deserved in the truth of Your ordinance? And this she knew not, yet in absence prayed for me. But You, everywhere present, heard her where she was, and, where I was, had compassion upon me, that I should recover the health of my body, though frenzied as yet in my sacrilegious heart. For I did not in all that danger desire Your baptism; and I was better as a boy, when I begged it of my mother's piety, as I have before recited and confessed. But I had grown up to my own shame, and I madly scoffed at the prescripts of Your medicine, who would not suffer me, being such, to die a double death. With which wound, had my mother's heart been pierced, it could never be healed. For I cannot express the affection she bore to me, and with how much more vehement anguish she was now in labour of me in the spirit, than at her childbearing in the flesh. I see not then how she should have been healed, had such a death of mine stricken through the bowels of her love. And where would have been those her so strong and unceasing prayers, unintermitting to You alone? But would You, God of mercies, despise the contrite and humbled heart of that chaste and sober widow, so frequent in alms-deeds, so full of duty and service to Your saints, no day intermitting the oblation at Your altar, twice a day, morning and evening, without any intermission, coming to Your church, not for idle tattlings and old wives' fables; but that she might hear You in Your discourses, and You her in her prayers. Could You despise and reject from Your aid the tears of such an one, wherewith she begged of You not gold or silver, nor any mutable or passing good, but the salvation of her son's soul? You, by whose gift she was such? Never, Lord. Yea, You were at hand, and were hearing and doing, in that order wherein You had determined before that it should be done. Far be it that You should deceive her in Your visions and answers, whereof some I have mentioned, others I have not mentioned, which she laid up in her faithful heart, and ever praying, urged upon You, as Your own handwriting. For You, because Your mercy endures for ever, to those to whom You forgive all of their debts, do vouchsafe to become also a debtor by Your promises.

10. *His errors before receiving the doctrine of the gospel*

You recovered me then of that sickness, and healed the son of Your handmaid in body, for the time, that he might live, for You to bestow upon him a better and more abiding health. And even then, at Rome, I joined myself to those deceiving and deceived 'holy ones'; not with their disciples only (of which number was he, in whose house I had fallen sick and recovered); but also with those whom they call 'the elect'. For I still thought 'that it was not we that sin, but that I know not what other nature sinned in us'; and it delighted my pride, to be free from blame; and when I had

done any evil, not to confess I had done any, that You might heal
my soul because it had sinned against You: but I loved to excuse
it, and to accuse I know not what other thing, which was with
me, but which I was not. But in truth it was wholly I, and mine
impiety had divided me against myself: and that sin was the more
incurable, whereby I did not judge myself a sinner; and execrable
iniquity it was, that I had rather have You, You, O God almighty,
to be overcome in me to my destruction, than myself be overcome by You, to my salvation.

Not as yet then had You set a watch before my mouth, and a
door of safe keeping around my lips, that my heart might not turn
aside to wicked speeches, to make excuses of sins, with men that
work iniquity; and therefore was I still united with their 'elect'.
But now despairing to make proficiency in that false doctrine,
I now held even those things with which I had resolved to rest
contented (should I find no better), more laxly and carelessly.

For there half arose a thought in me that those philosophers,
whom they call Academics, were wiser than the rest, for that
they held men ought to doubt everything, and laid down that no
truth can be comprehended by man: for so, not then understanding even their meaning, I also was clearly convinced that
they thought, as they are commonly reported. Yet did I freely and
openly discourage that host of mine from that over-confidence
which I perceived him to have in those fables, which the books of
Manichaeus are full of. Yet I lived in more familiar friendship with
them, than with others who were not of this heresy. Nor did I
maintain it with my ancient eagerness; still my intimacy with that
sect (Rome secretly harbouring many of them) made me slower to
seek any other way: especially since I despaired of finding the
truth, from which they had turned me aside, in Your church, O
Lord of heaven and earth, creator of all things visible and invisible:
and it seemed to me very unseemly to believe You to have the
shape of human flesh, and to be bounded by the bodily lineaments
of our members. And because, when I wished to think on my
God, I knew not what to think of, but a mass of bodies (for what
was not such did not seem to me to be anything), this was the
greatest, and almost only cause of my inevitable error.

For hence I believed evil also to be some such kind of substance, and to have its own foul and hideous bulk; whether gross,

which they called earth, or thin and subtile (like the body of the air), which they imagine to be some malignant mind, creeping through that earth. And because a piety, such as it was, constrained me to believe that the good God never created any evil nature, I conceived two masses, contrary to one another, both unbounded, but the evil narrower, the good more expansive. And from this pestilent beginning, the other sacrilegious conceits followed on me. For when my mind endeavored to recur to the Catholic faith, I was driven back, since that was not the Catholic faith which I thought to be so. And I seemed to myself more reverential, if I believed of You, my God (to whom Your mercies confess out of my mouth), as unbounded, at least on other sides, although on that one where the mass of evil was opposed to You, I was constrained to confess You bounded; than if on all sides I should imagine You to be bounded by the form of a human body. And it seemed to me better to believe You to have created no evil (which to me ignorant seemed not just a substance, but a bodily substance, because I could not conceive of mind unless as a subtile body, and that diffused in definite spaces), than to believe the nature of evil, such as I conceived it, could come from You. Yea, and our Saviour Himself, Your only begotten, I believed to have been reached forth (as it were) for our salvation, out of the mass of Your most lucid substance, so as to believe nothing of Him, but what I could imagine in my vanity. His nature, then, being such, I thought could not be born of the Virgin Mary, without being mingled with the flesh: and how that which I had so figured to myself could be mingled, and not defiled, I saw not. I feared therefore to believe Him born in the flesh, lest I should be forced to believe Him defiled by the flesh. Now will Your spiritual ones mildly and lovingly smile upon me, if they shall read these my confessions. Yet such was I.

11. How he compared the Manichees' tenets with the Catholics'

Furthermore, what the Manichees had criticized in Your scriptures, I thought could not be defended; yet at times verily I had a wish to confer upon these several points with someone very well skilled in those books, and to make trial what he thought

thereon; for the words of one Helpidius, as he spoke and dis-
puted face to face against the said Manichees, had begun to stir
me even at Carthage: in that he had produced things out of the
scriptures, not easily withstood, the Manichees' answer whereto
seemed to me weak. And this answer they liked not to give
publicly, but only to us in private. It was, that the scriptures of
the New Testament had been corrupted by I know not whom,
who wished to engraft the law of the Jews upon the Christian
faith: yet themselves produced not any uncorrupted copies.
But I, conceiving of things corporeal only, was mainly held
down, vehemently oppressed and in a manner suffocated by
those 'masses'; panting under which after the breath of Your
truth, I could not breathe it pure and untainted.

12. *The cunning tricks put upon their*
masters by scholars at Rome

I began then diligently to practice that for which I came to
Rome, to teach rhetoric; and first, to gather some to my house, to
whom, and through whom, I had begun to be known; when
lo, I found other offences committed in Rome, to which I was
not exposed in Africa. True, those 'subvertings' by profligate
young men were not here practiced, as was told me: but on a
sudden, said they, to avoid paying their master's stipend, a number of youths plot together, and remove to another − breakers
of faith, who for love of money hold justice cheap. These
also my heart hated, though not with a perfect hatred: for perchance I hated them more because I was to suffer by them, than
because they did things utterly unlawful. Of a truth such are
base persons, and they go a-whoring from You, loving these
fleeting mockeries of things temporal, and filthy lucre, which
fouls the hand that grasps it; hugging the fleeting world, and
despising You, who abide, and recall, and forgive the adulteress
soul of man, when she returns to You. And now I hate such
depraved and crooked persons, though I love them if corrigible,
so as to prefer to money the learning which they acquire, and to
learning, You, O God, the truth and fullness of assured good, and
most pure peace. But then I rather for my own sake misliked
them evil, than liked and wished them good for Yours.

13. *He goes to Milan to teach rhetoric, and how Saint Ambrose there entertains him*

When therefore they of Milan had sent to Rome to the prefect of the city, to furnish them with a rhetoric reader for their city, and sent him at the public expense, I made application (through those very persons, intoxicated with Manichaean vanities, to be freed wherefrom I was to go, neither of us however knowing it) that Symmachus, then prefect of the city, would try me by setting me some subject, and so send me. To Milan I came, to Ambrose the bishop, known to the whole world as among the best of men, Your devout servant; whose eloquent discourse did then plentifully dispense unto Your people the flour of Your wheat, the gladness of Your oil, and the sober inebriation of Your wine. To him was I unknowing led by You, that by him I might knowingly be led to You. That man of God received me as a father, and showed me an episcopal kindness on my coming. Thenceforth I began to love him, at first indeed not as a teacher of the truth (which I utterly despaired of in Your church), but as a person kind towards myself. And I listened diligently to him preaching to the people, not with that intent I ought, but, as it were, trying his eloquence, whether it answered the fame thereof, or flowed fuller or lower than was reported; and I hung on his words attentively; but of the matter I was as a careless and scornful looker-on; and I was delighted with the sweetness of his discourse, more recondite, yet in manner less winning and harmonious, than that of Faustus. Of the matter, however, there was no comparison; for the one was wandering amid Manichaean delusions, the other teaching salvation most soundly. But salvation is far from sinners, such as I then stood before him; and yet was I drawing nearer by little and little, and unconsciously.

14. *Upon his hearing of Saint Ambrose, he by little and little falls off from his errors*

For though I took no pains to learn what he spoke, but only to hear how he spoke (for that empty care alone was left me, despairing of a way, open for man, to You), yet together with the words which I would choose, came also into my mind the things which I would refuse; for I could not separate them. And while I opened my heart to admit 'how eloquently he spoke', there also entered 'how truly he spoke'; but this by degrees. For first, these things also had now begun to appear to me capable of defence; and the Catholic faith, for which I had thought nothing could be said against the Manichees' objections, I now thought might be maintained without shamelessness; especially after I had heard one or two places of the Old Testament resolved, and ofttimes 'in a figure', which when I understood literally, I was slain spiritually. Very many places then of those books having been explained, I now blamed my despair, in believing that no answer could be given to such as hated and scoffed at the Law and the Prophets. Yet did I not therefore then see that the Catholic way was to be held, because it also could find learned maintainers, who could at large and with some show of reason answer objections; nor that what I held was to be condemned, simply because both sides could be maintained. For the Catholic cause seemed to me in such sort not vanquished, as still not as yet to be victorious.

Hereupon I earnestly bent my mind, to see if in any way I could by any certain proof convict the Manichees of falsehood. Could I once have conceived a spiritual substance, all their strongholds had been beaten down, and cast utterly out of my mind; but I could not. Notwithstanding, concerning the frame of this world, and the whole of nature, which the senses of the flesh can reach to, as I more and more considered and compared things, I judged the tenets of most of the philosophers to have been much more probable. So then after the manner of the Academics (as they are supposed) doubting of every thing, and wavering between all, I settled so far, that the Manichees were to be abandoned; judging that, even while doubting, I might not continue in that sect, to which I already preferred some of the philosophers; to which philosophers notwithstanding, for that they were without the saving name of Christ, I utterly refused to commit the cure of my sick soul. I determined therefore so long to be a catechumen in the Catholic church, to which I had been commended by my parents, till something certain should dawn upon me, whither I might steer my course.

Book 6

1. *How Saint Augustine was neither Manichee, nor good Catholic*

O You, my hope from my youth, where were You to me, and whither were You gone? Had not You created me, and separated me from the beasts of the field, and fowls of the air? You had made me wiser, yet did I walk in darkness, and in slippery places, and sought You abroad out of myself, and found not the God of my heart; and had come into the depths of the sea, and distrusted and despaired of ever finding truth. My mother had now come to me, resolute through piety, following me over sea and land, in all perils confiding in You. For in perils of the sea, she comforted the very mariners (by whom passengers unacquainted with the deep, use rather to be comforted when troubled), assuring them of a safe arrival, because You had by a vision assured her thereof. She found me in grievous peril, through despair of ever finding truth. But when I had discovered to her that I was now no longer a Manichee, though not yet a Catholic Christian, she was not overjoyed, as at something unexpected; although she was now assured concerning that part of my misery, for which she bewailed me as one dead, though to be reawakened by You, carrying me forth upon the bier of her thoughts, that You might say to the son of the widow, Young man, I say unto You, Arise; and he should revive, and begin to speak, and You should deliver him to his mother. Her heart then was shaken with no tumultuous exultation, when she heard that what she daily with tears desired of You was already in so great part realized; in that, though I had not yet attained the truth, I was rescued from falsehood; but, as being assured, that You, who had promised the whole, would one day give the rest, most calmly, and with a heart full of confidence, she replied to me, 'She believed in Christ, that before she departed this life, she should see me a Catholic believer.' Thus much to me.

But to You, Fountain of mercies, poured she forth more copious prayers and tears, that You would hasten Your help, and enlighten my darkness; and she hastened the more eagerly to the Church, and hung upon the lips of Ambrose, praying for the fountain of that water, which springs up unto life everlasting. But that man she loved as an angel of God, because she knew that by him I had been brought for the present to that doubtful state of faith I now was in, through which she anticipated most confidently that I should pass from sickness unto health, after the access, as it were, of a sharper fit, which physicians call 'the crisis'.

2. *His mother is turned from her country superstitions*

When then my mother had once, as she was wont in Afric, brought to the churches built in memory of the saints, certain cakes, and bread and wine, and was forbidden by the door-keeper; so soon as she knew that the bishop had forbidden this, she so piously and obediently embraced his wishes, that I myself wondered how readily she censured her own practice, rather than discuss his prohibition. For wine-bibbing did not lay siege to her spirit, nor did love of wine provoke her to hatred of the truth, as it does too many (both men and women), who revolt at a lesson of sobriety, as men well-drunk at a draught mingled with water. But she, when she had brought her basket with the accustomed festival-food, to be but tasted by herself, and then given away, never joined therewith more than one small cup of wine, diluted according to her own abstemious habits, which for courtesy she would taste. And if there were many churches of the departed saints that were to be honored in that manner, she still carried round that same one cup, to be used everywhere; and this, though not only made very watery, but unpleasantly heated with carrying about, she would distribute to those about her by small sips; for she sought there devotion, not pleasure.

So soon, then, as she found this custom to be forbidden by that famous preacher and most pious prelate, even to those that would use it soberly, lest so an occasion of excess might be given to the drunken; and because these, as it were, anniversary funeral solemnities did much resemble the superstition of the gentiles, she most willingly forbare it: and for a basket filled with fruits of the earth, she had learned to bring to the churches of the martyrs a breast filled with more purified petitions, and to give what she could to the poor; that so the communication of the Lord's body might be there rightly celebrated, where, after the example of His passion, the martyrs had been sacrificed and crowned. But yet it seems to me, O Lord my God, and thus thinks my heart of it in Your sight, that perhaps she would not so readily have yielded to the cutting off of this custom, had it been forbidden by another, whom she loved not as Ambrose, whom, for my salvation, she loved most entirely; and he her again, for her most religious conversation, whereby in good works, so fervent in spirit, she was constant at church; so that, when he saw me, he often burst forth into her praises; congratulating me that I had such a mother; not knowing what a son she had in me, who doubted of all these things, and imagined the way to life could not be found out.

3. The employments and studies of Saint Ambrose

Nor did I yet groan in my prayers, that You would help me; but my spirit was wholly intent on learning, and restless to dispute. And Ambrose himself, as the world counts happy, I esteemed a happy man, whom personages so great held in such honor; only his celibacy seemed to me a painful course. But what hope he bore within him, what struggles he had against the temptations which beset his very excellencies, or what comfort in adversities, and what sweet joys Your bread had for the hidden mouth of his spirit, when chewing the cud thereof, I neither could conjecture, nor had experienced. Nor did he know the tides of my feelings, or the abyss of my danger. For I could not ask of him what I would as I would, being shut out both from his ear and speech by multitudes of busy people, whose weaknesses he served. With whom when he was not taken up (which was but a little time), he was either refreshing his body with the sustenance absolutely necessary, or his mind with reading. But when he was reading, his eye glided over the pages, and his heart searched out the sense, but his voice and tongue were at rest. Ofttimes when we had come (for no man was forbidden to enter, nor was it his wont that any who came should be announced to him), we saw him thus reading to himself, and never otherwise; and having long sat silent (for who durst intrude on one so intent?) we were fain to depart, conjecturing that in the small interval which he obtained, free from the din of others' business, for the recruiting of his mind, he was loth to be taken off; and perchance he dreaded lest if the author he read should deliver anything obscurely, some attentive or perplexed hearer should desire him to expound it, or to discuss some of the harder questions; so that his time being thus spent, he could not turn over so many volumes as he desired; although the preserving of his voice (which a very little speaking would weaken) might be the truer reason for his reading to himself. But with what intent soever he did it, certainly in such a man it was good.

I however certainly had no opportunity of enquiring what I wished of that so holy oracle of Yours, his breast, unless the thing might be answered briefly. But those tides in me, to be poured out to him, required his full leisure, and never found it. I heard him indeed every Lord's day, rightly expounding the Word of truth among the people; and I was more and more convinced that all the knots of those crafty calumnies, which those our deceivers had knit against the divine books, could be unravelled. But when I understood withal, that 'man created by You, after Your own image', was not so understood by Your spiritual sons, whom of the Catholic Mother You have regenerated through grace, as though they believed and conceived of You as bounded by human shape (although what a spiritual substance should be I had not even a faint or shadowy notion); yet, with joy I blushed at having so many years barked not against the Catholic faith, but against the fictions of carnal imaginations. For so rash and impious had I been, that what I ought by enquiring to have learned, I had pronounced on, condemning. For You, most high, and most near; most secret, and most present; who have not limbs some larger, some smaller, but are wholly everywhere and no where in space, are not of such corporeal shape, yet have You made man after Your own image; and behold, from head to foot is he contained in space.

4. Of the letter and the spirit

Ignorant then how this Your image should subsist, I should have knocked and proposed the doubt, how it was to be believed, not insultingly opposed it, as if believed. Doubt, then, what to hold for certain, the more sharply gnawed my heart, the more ashamed

I was, that so long deluded and deceived by the promise of cert-
ainties, I had with childish error and vehemence, prated of so
many uncertainties. For that they were falsehoods became clear
to me later. However I was certain that they were uncertain, and
that I had formerly accounted them certain, when with a blind
contentiousness, I accused Your Catholic church, whom I now
discovered, not indeed as yet to teach truly, but at least not to
teach that for which I had grievously censured her. So I was
confounded, and converted: and I joyed, O my God, that the
one only church, the body of Your only Son (wherein the name
of Christ had been put upon me as an infant), had no taste for
infantine conceits; nor in her sound doctrine maintained any
tenet which should confine You, the creator of all, in space,
however great and large, yet bounded everywhere by the limits
of a human form.

I joyed also that the old scriptures of the Law and the Prophets
were laid before me, not now to be perused with that eye to
which before they seemed absurd, when I reviled Your holy ones
for so thinking, whereas indeed they thought not so: and with
joy I heard Ambrose in his sermons to the people, oftentimes
most diligently recommend this text for a rule, The letter kills,
but the Spirit gives life; whilst he drew aside the mystic veil,
laying open spiritually what, according to the letter, seemed to
teach something unsound; teaching herein nothing that offended
me, though he taught what I knew not as yet, whether it were
true. For I kept my heart from assenting to anything, fearing to
fall headlong; but by hanging in suspense I was the worse killed.
For I wished to be as assured of the things I saw not, as I was that
seven and three are ten. For I was not so mad as to think that
even this could not be comprehended; but I desired to have
other things as clear as this, whether things corporeal, which
were not present to my senses, or spiritual, whereof I knew not
how to conceive, except corporeally. And by believing might I
have been cured, that so the eyesight of my soul being cleared,
might in some way be directed to Your truth, which abides
always, and in no part fails. But as it happens that one who has
tried a bad physician, fears to trust himself with a good one, so
was it with the health of my soul, which could not be healed but
by believing, and lest it should believe falsehoods, refused to be

cured; resisting Your hands, who have prepared the medicines of faith, and have applied them to the diseases of the whole world, and given unto them so great authority.

5. *Of the authority and necessary use of the Holy Bible*

Being led, however, from this to prefer the Catholic doctrine, I felt that her proceeding was more unassuming and honest, in that she required to be believed things not demonstrated (whether it was that they could in themselves be demonstrated but not to certain persons, or could not at all be), whereas among the Manichees our credulity was mocked by a promise of certain knowledge, and then so many most fabulous and absurd things were imposed to be believed, because they could not be demonstrated. Then You, O Lord, little by little with most tender and most merciful hand, touching and composing my heart, did persuade me – considering what innumerable things I believed, which I saw not, nor was present while they were done, as so many things in secular history, so many reports of places and of cities, which I had not seen; so many of friends, so many of physicians, so many continually of other men, which unless we should believe, we should do nothing at all in this life; lastly, with how unshaken an assurance I believed of what parents I was born, which I could not know, had I not believed upon hearsay – considering all this, You did persuade me, that not they who believed Your books (which You have established in so great authority among almost all nations), but they who believed them not, were to be blamed; and that they were not to be heard, who should say to me, 'How know you those scriptures to have been imparted unto mankind by the spirit of the one true and most true God?' For this very thing was of all most to be believed, since no contentiousness of blasphemous questionings, of all that multitude which I had read in the self-contradicting philosophers, could wring this belief from me, 'That You are' whatsoever You were (what I knew not), and 'That the government of human things belongs to You.'

This I believed, sometimes more strongly, otherwhiles more weakly; yet I ever believed both that You were, and had a care of us; though I was ignorant, both what was to be thought of Your substance, and what way led or led back to You. Since then we were too weak by abstract reasonings to find out truth; and for this very cause needed the authority of holy writ, I had now begun to believe that You would never have given such excellency of authority to that writ in all lands, had You not willed thereby to be believed in, thereby sought. For now what things, sounding strangely in the scripture, were wont to offend me, having heard divers of them expounded satisfactorily, I referred to the depth of the mysteries, and its authority appeared to me the more venerable, and more worthy of religious credence, in that, while it lay open to all to read, it reserved the majesty of its mysteries within its profounder meaning, stooping to all in the great plainness of its words and lowliness of its style, yet calling forth the intensest application of such as are not light of heart; that so it might receive all in its open bosom, and through narrow passages waft over towards You some few, yet many more than if it stood not aloft on such a height of authority, nor drew multitudes within its bosom by its holy lowliness. These things I thought on, and You were with me; I sighed, and You heard me; I wavered, and You did guide me; I wandered through the broad way of the world, and You did not forsake me.

6. The misery of the ambitious, shown by the example of a beggar

I panted after honors, gains, marriage; and you derided me. In these desires I underwent most bitter crosses, You being the more gracious, the less You suffered anything to grow sweet to me, which was not You. Behold my heart, O Lord, who would I should remember all this, and confess to You. Let my soul hold fast unto You, now that You have freed it from that fast-holding birdlime of death. How wretched was it! and You did irritate the feeling of its wound, that forsaking all else, it might be converted unto You, who are above all, and without whom all things would be nothing; be converted, and be healed. How miserable was I then, and how did You deal with me, to make me feel my misery on that day, when I was preparing to recite a panegyric of the Emperor, wherein I was to utter many a lie, and lying, was to be applauded by those who knew I lied, and my heart was panting with these anxieties, and boiling with the feverishness of consuming thoughts. For, passing through one of the streets of Milan, I observed a poor beggar, then, I suppose, with a full belly, joking and joyous: and I sighed, and spoke to the friends around me, of the many sorrows of our frenzies; for that by all such efforts of ours, as those wherein I then toiled dragging along, under the goading of desire, the burthen of my own wretchedness, and, by dragging, augmenting it, we yet looked to arrive only at that very joyousness whither that beggar-man had arrived before us, who should never perchance attain it. For what he had obtained by means of a few begged pence, the same was I plotting for by many a toilsome turning and winding; the joy of a temporary felicity. For he verily had not the true joy; but yet I with those my ambitious designs was seeking one much less true. And certainly he was joyous, I anxious; he void of care, I full of fears. But should any ask me, had I rather be merry or fearful? I would answer merry. Again, if he asked had I rather be such as he was, or what I then was? I should choose to be myself, though worn with cares and fears; but out of wrong judgment; for, was it the truth? For I ought not to prefer myself to him, because more learned than he, seeing I had no joy therein, but sought to please men by it; and that not to instruct, but simply to please. Wherefore also You did break my bones with the staff of Your correction.

Away with those then from my soul who say to her, 'It makes a difference whence a man's joy is. That beggar-man joyed in drunkenness; You desired to joy in glory.' What glory, Lord? That which is not in You. For even as his was no true joy, so was that no true glory: and it overthrew my soul more. He that very night should digest his drunkenness; but I had slept and risen again with mine, and was to sleep again, and again to rise with it, how many days, You, God, know. But 'it does make a difference whence a man's joy is.' I know it, and the joy of a faithful hope lies incomparably beyond such vanity. Yea, and so was he then beyond me: for he verily was the happier; not only for that he was thoroughly drenched in mirth, I disembowelled with cares: but he, by fair wishes, had gotten wine; I, by lying, was seeking for empty, swelling praise. Much to this purpose said I then to my friends: and I often marked in them how it fared with me; and I found it went ill with me, and grieved, and doubled that very ill; and if any prosperity smiled on me, I was loth to catch at it, for almost before I could grasp it, it flew away.

7. *He dissuades Alypius from his excessive delight in the games at the Circus*

These things we, who were living as friends together, bemoaned together, but chiefly and most familiarly did I speak thereof with Alypius and Nebridius, of whom Alypius was born in the same town with me, of persons of chief rank there, but younger than I. For he had studied under me, both when I first lectured in our town, and afterwards at Carthage, and he loved me much, because I seemed to him kind, and learned; and I him, for his great towardliness to virtue, which was eminent enough in one of no great years. Yet the whirlpool of Carthaginian habits (amongst whom those idle spectacles are hotly followed) had drawn him into the madness of the Circus. But while he was miserably tossed therein, and I, professing rhetoric there, had a public school, as yet he used not my teaching, by reason of some unkindness risen betwixt his father and me. I had found then how deadly he doted upon the Circus, and was deeply grieved that he seemed likely, nay, or had already thrown away so great promise: yet had I no means of advising or with a sort of constraint reclaiming him, either by the kindness of a friend, or the authority of a master. For I supposed that he thought of me as did his father, but he was not such; laying aside then his father's mind in that matter, he began to greet me, come sometimes into my lecture room, hear a little, and be gone.

I however had forgotten to deal with him, that he should not, through a blind and headlong desire of vain pastimes, undo so good a wit. But You, O Lord, who guide the course of all You have created, had not forgotten him, who was one day to be among Your children, priest and dispenser of Your sacrament; and that his amendment might plainly be attributed to Yourself, You effected it through me, unknowingly. For as one day I sat in my accustomed place, with my scholars before me, he entered, greeted me, sat down, and applied his mind to what I then handled. I had by chance a passage in hand, which while I was explaining, a likeness from the races at the Circus occurred to me, as likely to make what I would convey pleasanter and plainer, seasoned with biting mockery of those whom that madness had enthralled; God, You know that I then thought not of curing Alypius of that infection. But he took it wholly to himself, and

thought that I said it simply for his sake. And what another would
have taken as occasion of offence with me, that right-minded
youth took as a ground of being offended at himself, and loving
me more fervently. For You had said it long ago, and put it into
Your book, Rebuke a wise man and he will love you. But I had
not rebuked him, but You, who employ all, knowing or not
knowing, in that order which Yourself know (and that order is
just), did of my heart and tongue make burning coals, by which to
set on fire the hopeful mind, thus languishing, and so cure it. Let
him be silent in Your praises, who considers not Your mercies,
which confess unto You out of my inmost soul. For he upon that
speech burst out of that pit so deep, wherein he was wilfully
plunged, and was blinded with its wretched pastimes; and he
shook his mind with a strong self-command; whereupon all the
filths of the Circus entertainments flew off from him, nor came he
again thither. Upon this, he prevailed with his unwilling father
that he might be my scholar. He gave way, and gave in. And
Alypius beginning to be my hearer again, was involved in the
same superstition with me, loving in the Manichees that show of
continency which he supposed true and unfeigned. Whereas it
was a senseless and seducing continency, ensnaring precious souls,
unable as yet to reach the depth of virtue, yet readily beguiled
with the surface of what was but a shadowy and counterfeit virtue.

8. *Alypius is taken with a delight of the sword-plays, which before he hated*

He, not forsaking that secular course which his parents had
charmed him to pursue, had gone before me to Rome, to study
law, and there he was carried away incredibly with an incredible
eagerness after the shows of gladiators. For being utterly averse to
and detesting spectacles, he was one day by chance met by divers
of his acquaintance and fellow-students coming from dinner, and
they with a familiar violence haled him, vehemently refusing
and resisting, into the amphitheatre, during these cruel and deadly
shows, he thus protesting: 'Though you hale my body to that
place, and there set me, can you force me also to turn my mind
or my eyes to those shows? I shall then be absent while present,
and so shall overcome both you and them.' They, hearing this,
led him on nevertheless, desirous perchance to try that very thing,

whether he could do as he said. When they were come thither, and had taken their places as they could, the whole place kindled with that savage pastime. But he, closing the passage of his eyes, forbade his mind to range abroad after such evil; and would he had stopped his ears also! For in the fight, when one fell, a mighty cry of the whole people striking him strongly, overcome by curiosity, and as if prepared to despise and be superior to it whatsoever it were, even when seen, he opened his eyes, and was stricken with a deeper wound in his soul than the other, whom he desired to behold, was in his body; and he fell more miserably than he upon whose fall that mighty noise was raised, which entered through his ears, and unlocked his eyes, to make way for the striking and beating down of a soul, bold rather than resolute, and the weaker, in that it had presumed on itself, which ought to have relied on You. For so soon as he saw that blood, he therewith drunk down savageness; nor turned away, but fixed his eye, drinking in frenzy, unawares, and was delighted with that guilty fight, and intoxicated with the bloody pastime. Nor was he now the man he came, but one of the throng he came unto, yea, a true associate of theirs that brought him thither. Why say more? He beheld, shouted, kindled, carried thence with him the madness which should goad him to return not only with them who first drew him thither, but also before them, yea and to draw in others. Yet thence did You with a most strong and most merciful hand pluck him, and taught him to have confidence not in himself, but in You. But this was after.

9. *Alypius apprehended on suspicion of thievery*

But this was already being laid up in his memory to be a medicine hereafter. So was that also, that when he was yet studying under me at Carthage, and was thinking over at mid-day in the market-place what he was to say by heart (as scholars use to practise), You suffered him to be apprehended by the officers of the market-place for a thief. For no other cause, I deem, did You, our God, suffer it, but that he who was hereafter to prove so great a man, should already begin to learn that in judging of causes, man was not readily to be condemned by man out of a rash credulity. For as he was walking up and down by himself before the judgment-seat, with his note-book and pen, lo, a young man, a lawyer, the real thief, privily bringing a hatchet, got in, unperceived by Alypius, as far as the leaden gratings which fence in the silversmiths' shops, and began to cut away the lead. But the noise of the hatchet being heard, the silversmiths beneath began to make a stir, and sent to apprehend whomever they should find. But he, hearing their voices, ran away, leaving his hatchet, fearing to be taken with it. Alypius now, who had not seen him enter, was aware of his going, and saw with what speed he made away. And being desirous to know the matter, entered the place; where finding the hatchet, he was standing, wondering and considering it, when behold, those that had been sent, find him alone with the hatchet in his hand, the noise whereof had startled and brought them thither. They seize him, hale him away, and gathering the dwellers in the market-place together, boast of having taken a notorious thief, and so he was being led away to be taken before the judge.

But only so far was Alypius to be instructed. For forthwith, O Lord, You succoured his innocency, whereof You alone were witness. For as he was being led either to prison or to punishment, a certain architect met them, who had the chief charge of the public buildings. Glad they were to meet him especially, by whom they were wont to be suspected of stealing the goods lost out of the marketplace, as though to show him at last by whom these thefts were committed. He, however, had divers times seen Alypius at a certain senator's house, to whom he often went to pay his respects; and recognizing him immediately, took him aside by the hand, and enquiring the occasion of so great a calamity, heard the whole matter, and bade all present, amid much uproar and threats, to go with him. So they came to the house of the young man who had done the deed. There, before the door, was a boy so young as to be likely, not apprehending any harm to his master, to disclose the whole. For he had attended his master to the market-place. Whom so soon as Alypius remembered, he told the architect: and he showing the hatchet to the boy, asked him 'Whose that was?' 'Ours,' quoth he presently: and being further questioned, he discovered everything. Thus the crime being transferred to that house, and the multitude ashamed, which had begun to insult over Alypius, he who was to be a dispenser of Your word, and an examiner of many causes in Your church, went away better experienced and instructed.

10. *Of the great integrity of Alypius, and of Nebridius' coming*

Him then I had found at Rome, and he held fast to me by a most strong tie, and went with me to Milan, both that he might not leave me, and might practice something of the law he had studied, more to please his parents than himself. There he had thrice sat as assessor, with an uncorruptness much wondered at by others, he wondering at others rather who could prefer gold to honesty. His character was tried besides, not only with the bait of covetousness, but with the goad of fear. At Rome he was assessor to the count of the Italian treasury. There was at that time a very powerful senator, to whose favors many stood indebted, and whom many much feared. He would needs, by his usual power, have a thing allowed him which by the laws was unallowed. Alypius resisted it: a bribe was promised; with all his heart he scorned it: threats were held out; he trampled upon them: all wondering at so unwonted a spirit, which neither desired the friendship, nor feared the enmity of one so great and so mightily renowned for innumerable means of doing good or evil. And the very judge, whose councillor Alypius was, although also unwilling it should be, yet did not openly refuse, but put the matter off upon Alypius, alleging that he would not allow him to do it: for in truth had the judge done it, Alypius would have decided otherwise. With this one thing in the way of learning was he well-nigh seduced, that he might have books copied for him at the prices the praetors pay, but consulting justice, he altered his deliberation for the better, esteeming equity whereby he was hindered more gainful than the power whereby he were allowed. These are slight things, but he that is faithful in little, is faithful also in much. Nor can that any how be void, which proceeded out of the mouth of Your truth: If ye have not been faithful in the unrighteous Mammon, who will commit to your trust true riches? And if ye have not been faithful in that which is another man's, who shall give you that which is your own? He being such, did at that time hold fast to me, and with me wavered in purpose, what course of life was to be taken.

Nebridius also, who having left his native country near Carthage, yes and Carthage itself, where he had much lived, leaving his excellent family-estate and house, and a mother behind, who was not to follow him, had come to Milan, for no other reason but that with me he might live in a most ardent search after truth and wisdom. Like me he sighed, like me he wavered, an ardent searcher after true life, and a most acute examiner of the most difficult questions. Thus were there the mouths of three indigent persons, sighing out their wants one to another, and waiting upon You that You might give them their meat in due season. And in all the bitterness which by Your mercy followed our worldly affairs, as we looked towards the end, why we should suffer all this, darkness met us; and we turned away groaning, and saying, How long shall these things be? This too we often said; and so saying forsook them not, for as yet there dawned nothing certain, which these forsaken, we might embrace.

11. *He deliberates what course of life he were best to take*

And I, viewing and reviewing things, most wondered at the length of time from that my nineteenth year, wherein I had begun to kindle with the desire of wisdom, settling when I had found her, to abandon all the empty hopes and lying frenzies of vain desires. And lo, I was now in my thirtieth year, sticking in the same mire, greedy of enjoying things present, which passed away and wasted my soul; while I said to myself, Tomorrow I shall find it; it will appear manifestly and I shall grasp it; lo, Faustus the Manichee will come, and clear everything! O you great men, you Academicians, it is true then, that no certainty can be attained for the ordering of life! Nay, let us search the more diligently, and despair not. Lo, things in the ecclesiastical books are not absurd to us now, which sometimes seemed absurd, and may be otherwise taken, and in a good sense. I will take my stand where, as a child, my parents placed me, until the clear truth be found out. But where shall it be sought or when? Ambrose has no leisure; we have no leisure to read; where shall we find even the books? Whence, or when procure them? From whom borrow them? Let set times be appointed, and certain hours be ordered for the health of our soul. Great hope has dawned; the Catholic faith teaches not what we thought, and vainly accused it of; her instructed members hold it profane to believe God to be bounded by the figure of a human body: and do we doubt to 'knock', that the rest 'may be opened'? The forenoons our scholars take up; what do we during the rest? Why not this? But when then pay we court to our great friends, whose favor we need? When compose what we may sell to scholars? When refresh ourselves, unbending our minds from this intenseness of care?

Perish every thing, dismiss we these empty vanities, and betake ourselves to the one search for truth! Life is vain, death uncertain; if it steals upon us on a sudden, in what state shall we depart hence? And where shall we learn what here we have neglected? And shall we not rather suffer the punishment of this negligence? What, if death itself cut off and end all care and feeling? Then must this be ascertained. But God forbid this! It is no vain and empty thing, that the excellent dignity of the authority of the Christian faith has overspread the whole world. Never would such and so great things be by God wrought for us, if with the death of the body the life of the soul came to an end. Wherefore delay then to abandon worldly hopes, and give ourselves wholly to seek after God and the blessed life? But wait! Even the things of the world are pleasant; they have some, and no small sweetness. We must not lightly abandon them, for it were a shame to return again to them. See, it is no great matter now to obtain some position, and then what should we more wish for? We have store of powerful friends; if nothing else offer, and we be in much haste, at least a presidentship may be given us: and a wife with some money, that she increase not our charges: and this shall be the bound of desire. Many great men, and most worthy of imitation, have given themselves to the study of wisdom in the state of marriage.

While I went over these things, and these winds shifted and drove my heart this way and that, time passed on, but I delayed to turn to the Lord; and from day to day deferred to live in You, and deferred not daily to die in myself. Loving a happy life, I feared it in its own abode, and sought it by fleeing from it. I thought I should be too miserable, unless folded in female arms; and of the medicine of Your mercy to cure that infirmity I thought not, not having tried it. As for continency, I supposed it to be in our own power (though in myself I did not find that power), being so foolish as not to know what is written, None can be continent unless You give it; and that You would give it, if with inward groanings I did knock at Your ears, and with a settled faith did cast my care on You.

12. *A contention between Alypius and Augustine, about marriage and single life*

Alypius indeed kept me from marrying; alleging that so could we by no means with undistracted leisure live together in the love of wisdom, as we had long desired. For himself was even then most pure in this point, so that it was wonderful; and that the more, since in the outset of his youth he had entered into that course, but had not stuck fast therein; rather had he felt remorse and revolting at it, living thenceforth until now most continently. But I opposed him with the examples of those who as married men had cherished wisdom, and served God acceptably, and retained their friends, and loved them faithfully. Of whose greatness of spirit I was far short; and bound with the disease of the flesh, and its deadly sweetness, dragged along my chain, dreading to be loosed, and as if my wound had been fretted, put back his good persuasions, as it were the hand of one that would unchain me.

Moreover, by me did the serpent speak unto Alypius himself, by my tongue weaving and laying in his path pleasurable snares, wherein his virtuous and free feet might be entangled. For when he wondered that I, whom he esteemed not slightly, should stick so fast in the birdlime of that pleasure, as to protest (as oft as we discussed it) that I could never lead a single life; and urged in my defence when I saw him wonder, that there was great difference between his momentary and scarce-remembered knowledge of that life, which so he might easily despise, and my continued acquaintance with it if the honorable name of marriage were added, he ought not to wonder why I could not contemn that course; he began also to desire to be married; not as overcome with desire of such pleasure, but out of curiosity. For he would fain know, he said, what that should be, without which my life, to him so pleasing, would to me seem not life but a punishment. For his mind, free from that chain, was amazed at my slavery; and through that amazement was going on to a desire of trying it, thence to the trial itself, and thence perhaps to sink into that bondage whereat he wondered, seeing he was willing to make a covenant with death; and he that loves danger, shall fall into it. For whatever honor there be in the office of well-ordering a married life, and a family, moved us but slightly. But me for the most part the habit of satisfying an insatiable appetite tormented, while it held me captive; him, an admiring wonder was leading captive. So were we, until You, O most high, not forsaking our dust, commiserating us miserable, did come to our help, by wondrous and secret ways.

13. *Augustine lays out for a wife*

Continual effort was made to have me married. I wooed, I was promised, chiefly through my mother's pains, that so once married, the health-giving baptism might cleanse me, towards which she rejoiced that I was being daily fitted, and observed that her prayers, and Your promises, were being fulfilled in my faith. At which time verily, both at my request and her own longing, with strong cries of heart she daily begged of You, that You would by a vision discover unto her something concerning my future marriage; You never would. She saw indeed certain vain and fantastic things, such as the energy of the human spirit, busied thereon, brought together; and these she told me of, not with that confidence she was wont, when You showed her anything, but slighting them. For she could, she said, through a certain feeling, which in words she could not express, distinguish between Your revelations, and the dreams of her own soul. Yet the matter was pressed on, and a maiden asked in marriage, two years under the fit age; and, as pleasing, was waited for.

14. *A new plot is laid and broken*

And many of us friends conferring about, and detesting the turbulent turmoils of human life, had debated and now almost resolved on living apart from business and the bustle of men; and this was to be thus obtained; we were to bring whatever we might severally procure, and make one household of all; so that through the truth of our friendship nothing should belong especially to any; but the whole thus derived from all, should as a whole belong to each, and all to all. We thought there might be some ten persons in this society; some of whom were very rich, especially Romanianus our townsman, from childhood a very familiar friend of mine, whom the grievous perplexities of his affairs had brought up to court; who was the most earnest for this project; and therein was his voice of great weight, because his ample estate far exceeded any of the rest. We had settled also that two annual officers, as it were, should provide all things necessary, the rest being undisturbed. But when we began to consider whether the wives, which some of us already had, others hoped to have, would allow this, all that plan, which was being so well moulded, fell to pieces in our hands, was utterly dashed and cast aside. Thence we betook us to sighs and groans, and to steps following the broad and beaten ways of the world; for many thoughts were in our heart, but Your counsel stands for ever. Out of which counsel You did deride ours, and prepared Your own; purposing to give us meat in due season, and to fill our souls with blessing.

15. How his old concubine goes away from him, and he gets another

Meanwhile my sins were being multiplied, and my concubine being torn from my side as a hindrance to my marriage, my heart which held fast unto her was torn and wounded and bleeding. And she returned to Afric, vowing unto You never to know any other man, leaving with me my son by her. But unhappy I, who could not imitate a very woman, impatient of delay, inasmuch as not till after two years was I to obtain her I sought, not being so much a lover of marriage as a slave to lust, procured another, though no wife, that so by the servitude of an enduring custom, the disease of my soul might be kept up and carried on in its vigor, or even augmented, into the dominion of marriage. Nor was that my wound cured, which had been made by the cutting away of the former, but after inflammation and most acute pain, it mortified, and my pains became less acute, but more desperate.

16. Of the immortality of the soul

To You be praise, glory to You, Fountain of mercies. I was becoming more miserable, and You nearer. Your right hand was continually ready to pluck me out of the mire, and to wash me thoroughly, and I knew it not; nor did anything call me back from a yet deeper gulf of carnal pleasures, but the fear of death, and of Your judgment to come; which amid all my changes, never departed from my breast. And in my disputes with my friends Alypius and Nebridius of the nature of good and evil, I held that Epicurus would in my mind have won the palm, had I not believed that after death there remained a life for the soul, and places of requital according to men's deserts, which Epicurus would not believe. And I asked, Were we immortal, and to live in perpetual bodily pleasure, without fear of losing it, why should we not be happy? Or what else should we seek? not knowing that great misery was involved in this very thing, that, being thus sunk and blinded, I could not discern that light of excellence and beauty, to be embraced for its own sake, which the eye of flesh cannot see, and is seen by the inner man. Nor did I, unhappy, consider from what source it sprung, that even on these things, foul as they were, I with pleasure discoursed with my friends, nor could I, even according to the notions I then had of happiness, be happy without friends, amid what abundance soever of carnal pleasures. And yet these friends I loved for themselves only, and I felt that I was beloved of them again for myself only.

O crooked paths! Woe to the audacious soul, which hoped, by forsaking You, to gain some better thing! Turned it has, and turned again, upon back, sides, and belly, yet all was painful; and You alone rest. And behold, You are at hand, and deliver us from our wretched wanderings, and place us in Your way, and do comfort us, and say, Run; I will carry you; yea I will bring you through; there also will I carry you.

Book 7

Deceased now was that evil and abominable youth of mine, and I
was passing into early manhood; the more defiled by vain things as
I grew in years, who could not imagine any substance, but such
as is wont to be seen with these eyes. I thought not of You, O
God, under the figure of a human body; since I began to hear
anything of wisdom, I always avoided this; and rejoiced to have
found the same in the faith of our spiritual mother, Your Catholic
church. But what else to conceive of You I knew not. And I, a
man, and such a man, sought to conceive of You the sovereign,
only, true God; and I did in my inmost soul believe that You were
incorruptible, and uninjurable, and unchangeable; because though
not knowing whence or how, yet I saw plainly, and was sure, that
that which may be corrupted must be inferior to that which cannot;
what could not be injured I preferred unhesitatingly to what could
receive injury; the unchangeable to things subject to change. My
heart passionately cried out against all my phantoms, and with this
one blow I sought to beat away from the eye of my mind all that
unclean troop which buzzed around it. And lo, being scarce put off,
in the twinkling of an eye they gathered again thick about me, flew
against my face, and clouded it; so that though not under the form
of the human body, yet was I constrained to conceive of You (that
incorruptible, uninjurable, and unchangeable, which I preferred
before the corruptible, and injurable, and changeable) as being in
space, whether infused into the world, or diffused infinitely without
it. Because whatsoever I conceived, deprived of this space, seemed
to me nothing, yea altogether nothing, not even a void, as if a body
were taken out of its place, and the place should remain empty of
any body at all, of earth and water, air and heaven, yet would it
remain a void place, as it were a spacious nothing.

I then being thus gross-hearted, nor clear even to myself, what-soever was not extended over certain spaces, nor diffused, nor condensed, nor swelled out, or did not or could not receive some of these dimensions, I thought to be altogether nothing. For over such forms as my eyes are wont to range, did my heart then range: nor yet did I see that this same notion of the mind, whereby I formed those very images, was not of this sort, and yet it could not have formed them, had not itself been some great thing. So also did I endeavor to conceive of You, Life of my life, as vast, through infinite spaces on every side penetrating the whole mass of the universe, and beyond it, every way, through unmeasurable boundless spaces; so that the earth should have You, the heaven have You, all things have You, and they be bounded in You, and You bounded nowhere. For that as the body of this air which is above the earth, hinders not the light of the sun from passing through it, penetrating it, not by bursting or by cutting, but by filling it wholly: so I thought the body not of heaven, air, and sea only, but of the earth too, pervious to You, so that in all its parts, the greatest as the smallest, it should admit Your presence, by a secret inspiration, within and without, directing all things which You have created. So I guessed, only as unable to conceive anything else, for it was false. For thus should a greater part of the earth contain a greater portion of You, and a less, a lesser: and all things should in such sort be full of You, that the body of an elephant should contain more of You, than that of a sparrow, by how much larger it is, and takes up more room; and thus should You make the several portions of Yourself present unto the several portions of the world, in fragments, large to the large, petty to the petty. But such are not You. But as yet You had not enlightened my darkness.

2. *Nebridius confutes the Manichees*

It was enough for me, Lord, to oppose to those deceived deceivers, and dumb praters, since Your word sounded not out of them – that was enough which long ago, while we were yet at Carthage, Nebridius used to propound, at which all we that heard it were staggered: That said nation of darkness, which the Manichees are wont to set as an opposing mass over against You, what could it have done unto You, had You refused to fight with it? For, if they answered, 'It would have done You some hurt', then should You be subject to injury and corruption: but if it could do You no hurt, then was no reason brought for Your fighting with it; and fighting in such wise, as that a certain portion or member of You, or offspring of Your very substance, should be mingled with opposed powers, and natures not created by You, and be by them so far corrupted and changed to the worse, as to be turned from happiness into misery, and need assistance, whereby it might be extricated and purified; and that this offspring of Your substance was the soul, which being enthralled, defiled, corrupted, Your word, free, pure and whole, might relieve; that word itself being still corruptible because it was of one and the same substance. So then, should they affirm You, whatsoever You are, that is, Your substance whereby You are, to be incorruptible, then were all these sayings false and execrable; but if corruptible, the very statement showed it to be false and revolting. This argument then of Nebridius sufficed against those who deserved wholly to be vomited out of the overcharged stomach; for they had no escape, without horrible blasphemy of heart and tongue, thus thinking and speaking of You.

3. *Free will is the cause of sin*

But I also as yet, although I held and was firmly persuaded that You our Lord the true God, who made not only our souls, but our bodies, and not only our souls and bodies, but all beings, and all things, were undefilable and unalterable, and in no degree mutable; yet understood I not, clearly and without difficulty, the cause of evil. And yet whatever it were, I perceived it was in such wise to be sought out, as should not constrain me to believe the immutable God to be mutable, lest I should become that evil I was seeking out. I sought it out then, thus far free from anxiety, certain of the untruth of what these held, from whom I shrunk with my whole heart: for I saw, that through enquiring the origin of evil, they were filled with evil, in that they preferred to think that Your substance did suffer ill than their own did commit it.

And I strained to perceive what I now heard, that free-will was the cause of our doing ill, and Your just judgment of our suffering ill. But I was not able clearly to discern it. So then endeavoring to draw my soul's vision out of that deep pit, I was again plunged therein, and endeavoring often, I was plunged back as often. But this raised me a little into Your light, that I knew as well that I had a will, as that I lived: when then I did will or not will anything, I was most sure that no other than myself did will and not will: and I all but saw that there was the cause of my sin. But what I did against my will, I saw that I suffered rather than did, and I judged not to be my fault, but my punishment; whereby, however, holding You to be just, I speedily confessed myself to be not unjustly punished. But again I said, Who made me? Did not my God, who is not only good, but goodness itself? Whence then came I to will evil and not will good, so that I am thus justly punished? Who set this in me, and ingrafted into me this plant of bitterness, seeing I was wholly formed by my most sweet God? If the devil were the author, whence is that same devil? And if he also by his own perverse will, of a good angel became a devil, whence, again, came in him that evil will whereby he became a devil, seeing the whole nature of angels was made by that most good creator? By these thoughts I was again sunk down and choked; yet not brought down to that hell of error (where no man confesses unto You), to think rather that You do suffer ill, than that man does it.

4. *God cannot be compelled*

For I was in such wise striving to find out the rest, as one who had already found that the incorruptible must needs be better than the corruptible: and You therefore, whatsoever You were, I confessed to be incorruptible. For soul never was, nor shall be, able to conceive anything which may be better than You, who are the sovereign and the best good. But since most truly and certainly, the incorruptible is preferable to the corruptible (as I did now prefer it) then, were You not incorruptible, I could in thought have arrived at something better than my God. Where then I saw the incorruptible to be preferable to the corruptible, there ought I to seek for You, and there observe 'wherein evil itself was'; that is, whence corruption comes, by which Your substance can by no means be impaired. For corruption does in no way impair our God; by no will, by no necessity, by no unlooked-for chance: because He is God, and what He wills is good, and Himself is that good; but to be corrupted is not good. Nor are You against Your will constrained to anything, since Your will is not greater than

Your power. But greater should it be, were Yourself greater than Yourself. For the will and power of God is God Himself. And what can be unlooked-for by You, who know all things? Nor is there any nature in things, but You know it. And what should we more say, why that substance which God is should not be corruptible, seeing if it were so, it should not be God?

5. *He pursues his enquiries*

And I sought, whence is evil, and sought in an evil way; and saw not the evil in my very search. I set now before the sight of my spirit the whole creation, whatsoever we can see therein (as sea, earth, air, stars, trees, mortal creatures); yea, and whatever in it we do not see, as the firmament of heaven, all angels moreover, and all the spiritual inhabitants thereof. But these very beings, as though they were bodies, did my fancy dispose in place, and I made one great mass of Your creation, distinguished as to the kinds of bodies: some, real bodies; some, what myself had feigned for spirits. And this mass I made huge, not as it was (which I could not know), but as I thought convenient, yet every way finite. But You, O Lord, I imagined on every part environing and penetrating it, though every way infinite: as if there were a sea, everywhere and on every side, through unmeasured space, one only boundless sea, and it contained within it some sponge, huge but bounded; that sponge must needs, in all its parts, be filled from that unmeasurable sea: so conceived I Your creation, itself finite, full of You, the infinite; and I said, Behold God, and behold what God has created; and God is good, yea, most mightily and incomparably better than all these: but yet He, the good, created them good; and see how He environs and fulfils them. Where is evil then, and whence, and how crept it in hither? What is its root, and what its seed? Or has it no being? Why then do we fear and avoid what is not? Or if we fear it idly, then is that very fear evil, whereby the soul is thus idly goaded and racked. Yea, and so much a greater evil, as we have nothing to fear, and yet do fear. Therefore either that is evil which we fear, or else evil is the fact that we fear. Whence is it then, seeing God, the good, has created all these things good? He indeed, a greater and supreme good, has created these lesser goods; still both creator and created, all are good. Whence is evil? Or, was there some evil matter of which

He made, and formed, and ordered it, yet left something in it which He did not convert into good? Why so then? Was He powerless to turn and change the whole, so that no evil should remain in it, seeing He is all-powerful? Lastly, why would He make anything at all of it, and not rather by the same all-mightiness cause it not to be at all? Or, could it then be against His will? Or if it were from eternity, why suffered He it so to be for infinite spaces of times past, and was pleased so long after to make something out of it? Or if He were suddenly pleased now to effect somewhat, this rather should the all-powerful have effected, that this evil matter should not be, and He alone be, the whole, true, sovereign, and infinite good. Or if it was not good that He who was good should not also frame and create something that were good, then, that evil matter being taken away and brought to nothing, He might form good matter, whereof to create all things. For He should not be all-powerful, if He might not create something good without the aid of that matter which Himself had not created. These thoughts I revolved in my miserable heart, overcharged with most gnawing cares, lest I should die ere I had found the truth; yet was the faith of Your Christ, our Lord and Saviour, professed in the church Catholic, firmly fixed in my heart, in many points, indeed, as yet unformed, and fluctuating from the rule of doctrine; yet did not my mind utterly leave it, but rather daily took in more and more of it.

6. *Divinations made by the mathematicians are vain*

By this time also had I rejected the lying divinations and impious dotages of the astrologers. Let Your own mercies, out of my very inmost soul, confess unto You for this also, O my God. For You, You altogether (for who else calls us back from the death of all errors, save the life which cannot die, and the wisdom which needing no light enlightens the minds that need it, whereby the universe is directed, down to the whirling leaves of trees?) — You made provision for my obstinacy wherewith I struggled against Vindicianus, an acute old man, and Nebridius, a young man of admirable talents; the first vehemently affirming, and the latter often (though with some doubtfulness) saying, that there was no such art whereby to foresee things to come, but that men's conjectures were a sort of lottery, and that out of many things which they said should come to pass, some actually did, unawares to them who spoke it, who stumbled upon it, through their oft speaking. You provided then a friend for me, no negligent consulter of the astrologers, nor yet well skilled in those arts, but (as I said) a curious consulter with them, and yet knowing something, which he said he had heard of his father, which how far it went to overthrow the estimation of that art, he knew not. This man then, Firminus by name, having had a liberal education, and well taught in rhetoric, consulted me, as one very dear to him, what, according to his so-called constellations, I thought on certain affairs of his, wherein his worldly hopes had risen, and I, who had herein now begun to incline towards Nebridius' opinion, did not altogether refuse to conjecture, and tell him what came into my unresolved mind; but added, that I was now almost persuaded that these were but empty and ridiculous follies. Thereupon he told me that his father had been very curious in such books, and had a friend as earnest in them as himself, who with joint study and conference fanned the flame of their affections to these toys, so that they would observe the moments whereat the very dumb animals, which bred about their houses, gave birth, and then observed the relative position of the heavens, thereby to make fresh experiments in this so-called art. He said then that he had heard of his father, that what time his mother was about to give birth to him, Firminus, a woman-servant of that friend of his father's was also with child, which could not escape her master, who took care with most exact diligence to know the births of his very puppies. And so it was that (the one for his wife, and the other for his servant, with the most careful observation, reckoning days, hours, nay, the lesser divisions of the hours) both were delivered at the same instant; so that both were constrained to allow the same constellations, even to the minutest points, the one for his son, the other for his new-born slave. For so soon as the women began to be in labour, they each gave notice to the other what was fallen out in their houses, and had messengers ready to send to one another so soon as they had notice of the actual birth, of which they had easily provided, each in his own province, to give instant intelligence. Thus then the messengers of the respective parties met, he averred, at such an equal distance from either house that neither of them could make out any difference in the position of the stars, or any other minutest points; and yet Firminus, born in a high estate in his parents' house, ran his course through the gilded paths of life, was increased in riches, raised to honors; whereas that slave continued to serve his masters, without any relaxation of his yoke, as Firminus, who knew him, told me.

Upon hearing and believing these things, told by one of such credibility, all that my resistance gave way; and first I endeavored to reclaim Firminus himself from that curiosity, by telling him that upon inspecting his constellations, I ought if I were to predict truly, to have seen in them parents eminent among their neighbours, a noble family in its own city, high birth, good education, liberal learning. But if that servant had consulted me upon the same constellations, since they were his also, I ought again (to tell him too truly) to see in them a lineage the most abject, a slavish condition, and everything else utterly at variance with the former. Whence then, if I spoke the truth, I should, from the same constellations, speak diversely, or if I spoke the same, speak falsely: from that it followed most certainly that whatever, upon consideration of the constellations, was spoken truly, was spoken not out of art, but chance; and whatever spoken falsely, was not out of ignorance in the art, but the failure of the chance.

An opening thus made, ruminating with myself on the like things, so that no one of those dotards (who lived by such a trade, and whom I longed to attack, and with derision to confute) might urge against me that Firminus had informed me falsely, or his father him, I bent my thoughts on those that are born twins, who for the most part come out of the womb so near one to other, that the small interval (how much force soever in the nature of things folk may pretend it to have) cannot be noted by human observation, or be at all expressed in those figures which the astrologer is to inspect, that he may pronounce truly. Yet they cannot be true: for looking into the same figures, he must have predicted the same of Esau and Jacob, whereas the same happened not to them. Therefore he must speak falsely; or if truly, then, looking into the same figures, he must not give the same answer. Not by art, then, but by chance, would he speak truly. For You, O Lord, most righteous ruler of the universe, while consulters and consulted know it not, do by Your hidden inspiration effect that the consulter should hear what, according to the hidden deservings of souls, he ought to hear, out of the unsearchable depth of Your just judgment; to whom let no man say, What is this? Why that? Let him not so say, for he is man.

7. *He is miserably tortured in his enquiry after the root of evil*

Now then, O my helper, had You loosed me from those fetters: and I sought, whence is evil, and found no way. But You suffered me not by any fluctuations of thought to be carried away from the faith whereby I believed both You to be, and Your substance to be unchangeable, and that You have a care of, and would judge men, and that in Christ, Your Son, our Lord, and the holy scriptures, which the authority of Your Catholic church pressed upon me, You had set the way of man's salvation, to that life which is to be after this death. These things being safe and immovably settled in my mind, I sought anxiously, whence was evil? What were the pangs of my teeming heart, what groans, O my God! Yet even there were Your ears open, and I knew it not; and when in silence I vehemently sought, those silent contritions of my soul were strong cries unto Your mercy. You knew what I suffered, but no man. For, what was that which was thence through my tongue distilled into the ears of my most familiar friends? Did the whole tumult of my soul, for which neither time nor utterance sufficed, reach them? Yet went up the whole to Your hearing, all which I roared out from the groanings of my heart; and my desire was before You, and the light of mine eyes was not with me: for that was within, I without: nor was that confined to place, but I was intent on things contained in place, but there found I no resting-place, nor did they so receive me, that I could say, It is enough, It is well: nor did they yet suffer me to turn back, where it might be well enough with me. For to these things was I superior, but inferior to You; and You are my true joy when subjected to You, and You had subjected to me what You created below me. And this was the true temperament, and middle region of my safety, to remain in Your Image, and by serving You, rule the body. But when I rose proudly against You, and ran against the Lord with my neck, with the thick bosses of my buckler, even these inferior things were set above me, and pressed me down, and nowhere was there respite or space of breathing. They met my sight on all sides by heaps and troops, and in thought the images thereof presented themselves unsought, as I would return to You, as if they would say unto me, Whither do you go, unworthy and defiled? And these things had grown out of my wound; for You 'humbled the proud like one that is wounded', and through my own swelling was I separated from You; yea, my pride-swollen face closed up mine eyes.

8. *How the mercy of God at length relieved him*

But You, Lord, abide for ever, yet not for ever are You angry with us; because You pity our dust and ashes, and it was pleasing in Your sight to reform my deformities; and by inward goads did You rouse me, that I should be ill at ease, until You were manifested to my inward sight. Thus, by the secret hand of Your medicining was my swelling abated, and the troubled and bedimmed eyesight of my mind, by the smarting anointings of healthful sorrows, was from day to day healed.

9. *What he found in the books of the Platonists,*
agreeable to Christian doctrine

And You, willing first to show me how You resist the proud, but give grace unto the humble, and by how great an act of Your mercy You had traced out to men the way of humility, in that Your word was made flesh, and dwelt among men – You procured for me, by means of one puffed up with most unnatural pride, certain books of the Platonists, translated from Greek into Latin. And therein I read, not indeed in the very words, but to the very same purpose, enforced by many and divers reasons, that In the beginning was the word, and the word was with God, and the word was God: the same was in the beginning with God: all things were made by Him, and without Him was nothing made: that which was made by Him is life, and the life was the light of men, and the light shines in the darkness, and the darkness comprehended it not. And that the soul of man, though it bears witness to the light, yet itself is not that light; but the word of God, being God, is that true light that lights every man that comes into the world. And that He was in the world, and the world was made by Him, and the world knew Him not. But that He came unto His own, and His own received Him not; but as many as received Him, to them gave He power to become the sons of God, as many as believed in His name; this I read not there.

Again I read there, that God the word was born not of flesh nor of blood, nor of the will of man, nor of the will of the flesh, but of God. But that the word was made flesh, and dwelt among us, I read not there. For I traced in those books, though said in a variety of different ways, that the Son was in the form of the Father, and thought it not robbery to be equal with God, for that naturally He was the same substance. But that He emptied Himself, taking the form of a servant, being made in the likeness of men, and found in fashion as a man, humbled Himself, and became obedient unto death, and that the death of the cross: wherefore God exalted Him from the dead, and gave Him a name above every name, that at the name of Jesus every knee should bow, of things in heaven, and things in earth, and things under the earth; and that every tongue should confess that the Lord Jesus Christ is in the glory of God the Father; those books have not. For that before all times and above all times Your only-begotten Son remains unchangeable, co-eternal with You, and that of His fullness souls receive, that they may be blessed; and that by participation of wisdom abiding in them, they are renewed, so as to be wise, is there. But that in due time He died for the ungodly; and that You spared not Your only Son, but delivered Him for us all, is not there. For You hid these things from the wise, and revealed them to babes; that they that labour and are heavy laden might come unto Him, and He refresh them, because He is meek and lowly in heart; and the meek He directs in judgment, and the gentle He teaches His ways, beholding our lowliness and trouble, and forgiving all our sins. But such as are lifted up in the lofty walk of some would-be sublimer learning, hear not Him, saying, Learn of Me, for I am meek and lowly in heart, and you shall find rest to your souls. Although they knew God, yet they glorify Him not as God, nor are thankful, but wax vain in their thoughts; and their foolish heart is darkened; professing that they were wise, they became fools.

And therefore did I read there also, that they had changed the glory of Your incorruptible nature into idols and divers shapes, into the likeness of the image of corruptible man, and birds, and beasts, and creeping things; namely, into that Egyptian food for which Esau lost his birthright, for that Your first-born people worshipped the head of a four-footed beast instead of You; turning in heart back towards Egypt; and bowing Your image, their own soul, before the image of a calf that eats hay. These things found I here, but I fed not on them. For it pleased You, O Lord, to take away the reproach of diminution from Jacob, that the elder should serve the younger: and You called the gentiles into Your inheritance. And I had come to You from among the gentiles; and I set my mind upon the gold which You willed Your people to take from Egypt, seeing wheresoever it were, it was Yours. And to the Athenians You said by Your apostle, that in You we live, move, and have our being, as one of their own poets had said. And verily these books came from thence. But I set not my mind on the idols of Egypt, whom they served with Your gold, who changed the truth of God into a lie, and worshipped and served the creature more than the creator.

10. *Divine things are more clearly discovered unto him*

And being thence admonished to return to myself, I entered even into my inward self, You being my guide: and I was able, for You were become my helper. And I entered and beheld with the eye of my soul (such as it was), above the same eye of my soul, above my mind, the light unchangeable. Not this ordinary light, which all flesh may look upon, nor as it were a greater of the same kind, as though it would shine with a greater and greater brightness, and with its greatness take up all space. Not such was this light, but other, yea, far other from these. Nor was it above my soul, as oil is above water, nor yet as heaven above earth: but higher because it made me; and I below it, because I was made by it. He that knows the truth, knows what that light is; and he that knows it, knows eternity. Love knows it. O truth who are eternity! and love who are truth! and eternity who are love! You are my God, to You do I sigh night and day. You when I first knew, You lifted me up, that I might see there was what I might see, and that I was not yet such as to see. And You did beat back the weakness of my sight, streaming forth Your beams of light upon me most strongly, and I trembled with love and awe: and I perceived myself to be far off from You, in the region of unlikeness, as if I heard this Your voice from on high: I am the food of grown men. Grow, and you shall feed upon Me; nor shall you convert

Me, like the food of your flesh into you, but you shall be converted into Me. And I learned that You for iniquity chasten man, and You made my soul to consume away like a spider. And I said, Is truth therefore nothing, because it is not diffused through space finite or infinite? And You cried to me from afar: Yet verily, I am that I am. And I heard, as the heart hears, nor had I room to doubt, and I should sooner doubt that I live than that truth is not, which is clearly seen, being understood by those things which are made.

11. *How creatures are, and yet are not*

And I beheld the other things below You, and I perceived that they neither altogether are, nor altogether are not, for they are, since they are from You, but are not, because they are not what You are. For that truly is which remains unchangeably. It is good then for me to hold fast unto God; for if I remain not in Him, I cannot in myself; but He remaining in Himself, renews all things. And You are the Lord my God, since You stand not in need of my goodness.

12. *All that is, is good*

And it was manifested unto me, that those things be good which yet are corrupted; which neither were they sovereignly good, nor unless they were good could be corrupted: for if sovereignly good, they were incorruptible; if not good at all, there were nothing in them to be corrupted. For corruption injures, but unless it diminished goodness, it could not injure. Either then corruption injures not, which cannot be; or which is most certain, all which is corrupted is deprived of good. But if they be deprived of all good, they shall cease to be. For if they shall be, and can now no longer be corrupted, they shall be better than before, because they shall abide incorruptibly. And what more monstrous than to affirm things to become better by losing all their good? Therefore, if they shall be deprived of all good, they shall no longer be. So long therefore as they are, they are good: therefore whatsoever is, is good. That evil then which I sought, whence it is, is not any substance: for were it a substance, it should be good. For either it should be an incorruptible substance, and so a chief good: or a corruptible substance; which unless it were good, could not be corrupted. I perceived therefore, and it was manifested to me that You made all things good, nor is there any substance at all, which You made not; and for that You made not all things equal, therefore are all things; because each is good, and altogether very good, because our God has made all things very good.

13. *All created things praise God*

And to You is nothing whatsoever evil: yea, not only to You, but also to Your creation as a whole, because there is nothing without, which may break in, and corrupt that order which You have appointed it. But in the parts thereof some things, because unharmonizing with other some, are accounted evil: whereas those very things harmonize with others, and are good; and in themselves are good. And all these things which do not agree together, do yet agree with the inferior part, which we call earth, having its own cloudy and windy sky harmonizing with it. Far be it then that I should say, These things should not be: for should I see nothing but these, I should indeed long for the better; but still must even for these alone praise You; for that You are to be praised, do show from the earth, dragons, and all deeps, fire, hail, snow, ice, and stormy wind, which fulfil Your word; mountains, and all hills, fruitful trees, and all cedars; beasts, and all cattle, creeping things, and flying fowls; kings of the earth, and all people, princes, and all judges of the earth; young men and maidens, old men and young, praise Your name. But when, from heaven, these praise You, praise You, our God, in the heights all Your angels — all Your hosts, sun and moon, all the stars and light, the heaven of heavens, and the waters that be above the heavens, praise Your name; I did not now long for things better, because I conceived of all: and with a sounder judgment I apprehended that the things above were better than these below, but all together better than those above by themselves.

14. *To a sober mind, some of God's creatures are displeasing*

There is no soundness in them, whom anything of Your creation displeases: as neither in me, when much which You have made, displeased me. And because my soul did not dare be displeased at my God, it would fain not account that Yours, which displeased it. Hence it had gone into the opinion of two substances, and had no rest, but talked idly. And returning thence, it had made to itself a God, through infinite measures of all space; and thought it to be You, and placed it in its heart; and had again become the temple of its own idol, to You abominable. But after You had soothed my head, unknown to me, and closed mine eyes that they should not behold vanity, I ceased somewhat of my former self, and my frenzy was lulled to sleep; and I awoke in You, and saw You infinite, but in another way, and this sight was not derived from the flesh.

15. *How there is truth and falsehood in the creatures*

And I looked back on other things; and I saw that they owed their being to You; and were all bounded in You, but in a different way; not as being in space, but because You contain all things in Your hand in Your truth; and all things are true so far as they exist, nor is there any falsehood, unless when that is thought to exist, which does not exist. And I saw that all things did harmonize, not with their places only, but with their seasons. And that You, who alone are eternal, did not begin to work after innumerable spaces of times spent; for that all spaces of times, both which have passed, and which shall pass, neither go nor come but through You, working and abiding.

16. *All things are good, though to some things not fit*

And I perceived and found it nothing strange, that bread which is pleasant to a healthy palate is loathsome to one distempered: and to sore eyes light is offensive, which to the clear-sighted is delightful. And Your righteousness displeases the wicked; much more the viper and reptiles, which You have created good, fitting in with the inferior portions of Your creation, with which the very wicked also fit in; and that the more, by how much they be unlike You; but with the superior creatures, by how much they become more like to You. And I enquired what iniquity was, and found it not to be a substance, but the perversion of the will, turned aside from the highest substance, which is You, O God, towards these lower things, and casting out its bowels, and puffed up outwardly.

17. *What things hinder us of God's knowledge*

And I wondered that I now loved You, and not a phantasm instead of You. Yet did I not press on to enjoy my God; but was borne up to You by Your beauty, and soon borne down from You by mine own weight, sinking with sorrow into these inferior things. And this weight was my carnal habits. Yet dwelt there with me a remembrance of You; nor did I any way doubt that there was one to whom I might hold fast, but that I was not yet such as to hold fast to You: for that the body which is corrupted presses down the soul, and the earthly tabernacle weighs down the mind that muses upon many things. And most certain I was, that Your invisible works from the creation of the world are clearly seen, being understood by the things that are made, even Your eternal power and Godhead. For examining whence it was that I admired the beauty of bodies celestial or terrestrial; and what aided me in judging soundly on things mutable, and pronouncing, This ought to be thus, this not; examining, I say, whence it was that I so judged, seeing I did so judge, I had found the unchangeable and true eternity of truth above my changeable mind. And thus by degrees I passed from bodies to the soul, which through the bodily senses perceives; and thence to its inward faculty, to which the bodily senses represent things external, whitherto reach the faculties of beasts; and thence again to the reasoning faculty, to which what is received from the senses of the body is referred to be judged. Which finding itself also to be in me a thing variable, raised itself up to its own understanding, and drew away my thoughts from the power of habit, withdrawing itself from those troops of contradictory phantasms; that so it might find what that light was whereby it was bedewed, when, without all doubting, it cried out, that the unchangeable was to be preferred to the changeable; whence also it knew that unchangeable which, unless it had in some way known, it had had no sure ground to prefer it to the changeable. And thus with the flash of one trembling glance it arrived at that which is. And then I saw Your invisible things understood by the things which are made. But I could not fix my gaze thereon; and my infirmity being struck back, I was thrown again on my wonted habits, carrying along with me only a loving memory thereof, and a longing for what I had, as it were, perceived the odor of, but was not yet able to feed on.

18. *Christ alone is the way to salvation*

Then I sought a way of obtaining strength sufficient to enjoy
You; and found it not, until I embraced that mediator betwixt
God and men, the man Christ Jesus, who is over all, God blessed
for evermore, calling unto me, saying, I am the way, the truth, and
the life, and mingling with my flesh that food which I was unable
to receive. For, the word was made flesh, that Your wisdom,
whereby You created all things, might provide milk for our infant
state. For I did not hold to my Lord Jesus Christ, I, humbled, to
the humble; nor knew I yet whereto His infirmity would guide
us. For Your word, the eternal truth, far above the higher parts of
Your creation, raises up the subdued unto Itself: but in this lower
world built for Itself a lowly habitation of our clay, whereby to
abase from themselves such as would be subdued, and bring them
over to Himself; allaying their swelling, and fomenting their love;
to the end they might go on no further in self-confidence, but
rather consent to become weak, seeing before their feet the
Divinity weak by taking our coats of skin; and wearied, might cast
themselves down upon it, and it rising, might lift them up.

19. *What he thought of Christ's incarnation*

But I thought otherwise; conceiving only of my Lord Christ as
of a man of excellent wisdom, whom no one could be equalled
unto; especially, for that being wonderfully born of a virgin, He
seemed, in conformity therewith, through the Divine care for us,
to have attained that great eminence of authority, for an example
of despising things temporal for the obtaining of immortality. But
what mystery there lay in 'The word was made flesh', I could not
even imagine. Only I had learnt out of what is delivered to us in
writing of Him that He did eat, and drink, sleep, walk, rejoiced in
spirit, was sorrowful, discoursed; that flesh did not hold fast by
itself unto Your word, but with the human soul and mind. All
know this who know the unchangeableness of Your word, which
I now knew, as far as I could, nor did I at all doubt thereof. For,
now to move the limbs of the body by will, now not, now to be
moved by some affection, now not, now to deliver wise sayings
through human signs, now to keep silence, belong to soul and
mind subject to variation. And should these things be falsely
written of Him, all the rest also would risk the charge, nor would

there remain in those books any saving faith for mankind. Since then they were written truly, I acknowledged a perfect man to be in Christ; not the body of a man only, nor, with the body, a sensitive soul without a rational, but actual man; whom, not only as being a form of truth, but for a certain great excellence of human nature and a more perfect participation of wisdom, I judged to be preferred before others. But Alypius imagined the Catholics to believe God to be so clothed with flesh, that besides God and flesh, there was no soul at all in Christ, and did not think that a human mind was ascribed to Him. And because he was well persuaded that the actions recorded of Him could only be performed by a vital and a rational creature, he moved the more slowly towards the Christian faith. But understanding afterwards that this was the error of the Apollinarian heretics, he joyed in and was conformed to the Catholic faith. But somewhat later, I confess, did I learn how in that saying, The word was made flesh, the Catholic truth is distinguished from the falsehood of Photinus. For the rejection of heretics makes the tenets of Your church and sound doctrine to stand out more clearly. For there must also be heresies, that the approved may be made manifest among the weak.

20. *Of divers books of the Platonists*

But having then read those books of the Platonists, and thence been taught to search for incorporeal truth, I saw Your invisible things, understood by those things which are made; and though cast back, I perceived what that was which through the darkness of my mind I was hindered from contemplating, being assured that You were, and were infinite, and yet not diffused in space, finite or infinite; and that You truly are, who are the same ever, in no part nor motion varying; and that all other things are from You, on this most sure ground alone, that they are. Of these things I was assured, yet too unsure to enjoy You. I prated as one well skilled; but had I not sought Your way in Christ our Saviour, I had proved to be, not skilled, but killed. For now I had begun to wish to seem wise, being filled with mine own punishment, yet I did not mourn, but rather scorn, puffed up with knowledge. For where was that charity building upon the foundation of humility, which is Christ Jesus? Or when should these books teach me it?

Upon these, I believe, You therefore willed that I should fall,
before I studied Your scriptures, that it might be imprinted on
my memory how I was affected by them; and that afterwards
when my spirits were tamed through Your books, and my
wounds touched by Your healing fingers, I might discern and
distinguish between presumption and confession; between those
who saw whither they were to go, yet saw not the way, and the
way that leads not to behold only but to dwell in the beatific
country. For had I first been formed in Your holy scriptures, and
had You in the familiar use of them grown sweet unto me, and
had I then fallen upon those other volumes, they might perhaps
have withdrawn me from the solid ground of piety, or, had I
continued in that healthful frame which I had thence imbibed, I
might have thought that it might have been obtained by the
study of those books alone.

21. *What he found in the holy scriptures,*
which was not in the Platonists

Most eagerly then did I seize that venerable writing of Your spirit;
and chiefly the apostle Paul. Whereupon those difficulties vanished
away, wherein he once seemed to me to contradict himself, and
the text of his discourse not to agree with the testimonies of the
Law and the Prophets. And the face of that pure word appeared to
me one and the same; and I learned to rejoice with trembling. So I
began; and whatsoever truth I had read in those other books, I
found here amid the praise of Your grace; that whoso sees, may
not so glory as if he had not received, not only what he sees, but
also the power to see it (for what has he, which he has not
received?), and that he may be not only admonished to behold
You, who are ever the same, but also healed, that he may hold
You; and that he who cannot see afar off, may yet walk on the
way, whereby he may arrive, and behold, and hold You. For,
though a man be delighted with the law of God after the inner
man, what shall he do with that other law in his members which
wars against the law of his mind, and brings him into captivity to
the law of sin which is in his members? For You are righteous, O
Lord, but we have sinned and committed iniquity, and have done
wickedly, and Your hand is grown heavy upon us, and we are
justly delivered over unto that ancient sinner, the king of death;

because he persuaded our will to be like his will whereby he abode not in Your truth. What shall wretched man do? Who shall deliver him from the body of his death, but only Your grace, through Jesus Christ our Lord, whom You have begotten co-eternal, and formed in the beginning of Your ways, in whom the prince of this world found nothing worthy of death, yet killed he Him; and the handwriting, which was against us, was blotted out? This those writings contain not. Those pages present not the image of this piety, the tears of confession, Your sacrifice, a troubled spirit, a broken and a contrite heart, the salvation of the people, the bridal city, the earnest of the Holy Ghost, the cup of our redemption. No man sings there, Shall not my soul be submitted unto God? For of Him comes my salvation. For He is my God and my salvation, my guardian, I shall no more be moved. No one there hears Him call, Come unto Me, all ye that labour. They scorn to learn of Him, because He is meek and lowly in heart; for these things have You hid from the wise and prudent, and have revealed them unto babes. For it is one thing, from the mountain's shaggy top to see the land of peace, and to find no way thither; and in vain to essay through ways unpassable, opposed and beset by fugitives and deserters, under their captain the lion and the dragon: and another to keep on the way that leads thither, guarded by the host of the heavenly general; where they spoil not who have deserted the heavenly army; for they avoid it, as very torment. These things did wonderfully sink into my bowels, when I read that least of Your apostles, and had meditated upon Your works, and trembled exceedingly.

Book 8

1. *How being inflamed with the love of heavenly things, he goes to Simplicianus*

O my God, let me with thanksgiving remember, and confess unto You Your mercies on me. Let my bones be bedewed with Your love, and let them say unto You, Who is like unto You, O Lord? You have broken my bonds in sunder, I will offer unto You the sacrifice of thanksgiving. And how You have broken them, I will declare; and all who worship You, when they hear this, shall say, Blessed be the Lord, in heaven and in earth, great and wonderful is his name. Your words had stuck fast in my heart, and I was hedged round about on all sides by You. Of Your eternal life I was now certain, though I saw it in a figure and as through a glass. Yet I had ceased to doubt that there was an incorruptible substance, whence was all other substance; nor did I now desire to be more certain of You, but more steadfast in You. But for my temporal life, all was wavering, and my heart had to be purged from the old leaven. The way, the Saviour Himself, well pleased me, but as yet I shrunk from going through its straitness. And You did put into my mind, and it seemed good in my eyes, to go to Simplicianus, who seemed to me a good servant of Yours; and Your grace shone in him. I had heard also that from his very youth he had lived most devoted unto You. Now he was grown into years; and by reason of so great age spent in such zealous following of Your ways, he seemed to me likely to have learned much experience; and so he had. Out of which store I wished that he would tell me (setting before him my anxieties) which were the fittest way for one in my case to walk in Your paths.

For, I saw the church full; and one went this way, and another that way. But I was displeased that I led a secular life; yea now that my desires no longer inflamed me, as of old, with hopes of honor and profit, a very grievous burden it was to undergo so heavy a bondage. For, in comparison of Your sweetness, and the beauty of Your house which I loved, those things delighted me no longer. But still I was enthralled with the love of woman; nor did the apostle forbid me to marry, although he advised me to something better, chiefly wishing that all men were as himself was. But I being weak, chose the more indulgent place; and because of this alone, was tossed up and down in all beside, faint and wasted with withering cares, because in other matters I was constrained against my will to conform myself to a married life, to which I was given up and enthralled. I had heard from the mouth of the truth, that there were some eunuchs which had made themselves eunuchs for the kingdom of heaven's sake: but, says he, let him who can receive it, receive it. Surely vain are all men who are ignorant of God, and could not out of the good things which are seen, find out Him who is good. But I was no longer in that vanity; I had surmounted it; and by the common witness of all Your creatures had found You our creator, and Your word, God with You, and together with You one God, by whom You created all things. There is yet another kind of ungodly, who knowing God, glorified Him not as God, neither were thankful. Into this also had I fallen, but Your right hand upheld me, and took me thence, and You placed me where I might recover. For You have said unto man, Behold, the fear of the Lord is wisdom, and, Desire not to seem wise; because they who affirmed themselves to be wise, became fools. But I had now found the goodly pearl, which, selling all that I had, I ought to have bought, and I hesitated.

2. How Victorinus, the famous orator, was converted

To Simplicianus then I went, the father of Ambrose (a bishop now) in receiving Your grace, and whom Ambrose truly loved as a father. To him I related the mazes of my wanderings. But when I mentioned that I had read certain books of the Platonists, which Victorinus, sometime rhetoric professor of Rome (who had died a Christian, as I had heard), had translated into Latin, he testified his joy that I had not fallen upon the writings of other philosophers, full of fallacies and deceits, after the rudiments of this world, whereas the Platonists many ways led to the belief in God and His word. Then to exhort me to the humility of Christ, hidden from the wise, and revealed to little ones, he spoke of Victorinus himself, whom while at Rome he had most intimately known: and of him he related what I will not conceal. For it contains great praise of Your grace, to be confessed unto You, how that aged man, most learned and skilled in the liberal sciences, and who had read and weighed so many works of the philosophers; the instructor of so many noble senators, who also, as a monument of his excellent discharge of his office, had (which men of this world esteem a high honor) both deserved and obtained a statue in the Roman forum; he, to that age a worshipper of idols, and a partaker of the sacrilegious rites, to which almost all the nobility of Rome were given up, and had inspired the people with the love of

> Anubis, barking deity, and all
> The monster gods of every kind, who fought
> 'Gainst Neptune, Venus, and Minerva:

whom Rome once conquered, but now adored, all which the aged Victorinus had with thundering eloquence so many years defended – he now blushed not to be the child of Your Christ, and the new-born babe of Your fountain; submitting his neck to the yoke of humility, and subduing his forehead to the reproach of the cross.

O Lord, Lord, which have bowed the heavens and come down, touched the mountains and they did smoke, by what means did You convey Yourself into that breast? He used to read (as Simplicianus said) the holy scripture, most studiously sought and searched into all the Christian writings, and said to Simplicianus (not openly, but privately and as a friend), Understand that I am already a Christian. Whereto he answered, I will not believe it, nor will I rank you among Christians, unless I see you in the Church of Christ. The other, in banter, replied, Do walls then make Christians? And this he often said, that he was already a Christian; and Simplicianus as often made the same answer, and the conceit of the 'walls' was by the other as often renewed. For he feared to offend his friends, proud daemon-worshippers, from the height of whose Babylonian dignity, as from cedars of Libanus, which the Lord had not yet broken down, he supposed the weight of enmity would fall upon him. But after that by reading and earnest thought he had gathered firmness, and feared to be denied by Christ before the holy angels, should he now be afraid to confess Him before men, and appeared to himself guilty of a heavy offence, in being ashamed of the sacraments of the humility of Your word, and not being ashamed of the sacrilegious rites of those proud daemons, whose pride he had imitated and their rites adopted, he became bold-faced against vanity, and shame-faced towards the truth, and suddenly and unexpectedly said to Simplicianus (as himself told me), Go we to the church; I wish to be made a Christian. But he, not containing himself for joy, went with him. And having been admitted to the first sacrament and become a catechumen, not long after he further gave in his name, that he might be regenerated by baptism, Rome wondering, the Church rejoicing. The proud saw, and were wroth; they gnashed with their teeth, and melted away. But the Lord God was the hope of Your servant, and he regarded not vanities and lying madness.

To conclude, when the hour was come for making profession of his faith (which at Rome they who are about to approach to Your grace, deliver from an elevated place, in the sight of all the faithful, in a set form of words committed to memory), the presbyters, he said, offered Victorinus (as was done to such as seemed likely through bashfulness to be alarmed) to make his profession more privately: but he chose rather to profess his salvation in the presence of the holy multitude. 'For it was not salvation that he taught in rhetoric, yet that he had publicly professed: how much less then ought he, when pronouncing Your word, to dread Your meek flock, who, when delivering his own words, had not feared a mad multitude!' When, then, he went up to make his profession, all, as they knew him, whispered his name one to another with the voice of congratulation. And who there knew him not? And there ran a low murmur through all the mouths of the rejoicing multitude, Victorinus! Victorinus! Sudden was the burst of rapture, that they saw him; suddenly were they hushed that they might hear him. He pronounced the true faith with an excellent boldness, and all wished to draw him into their very heart; yea by their love and joy they drew him thither, such were the hands wherewith they drew him.

3. *That God and his angels do rejoice the more,*
at the conversion of a greater sinner

Good God! what takes place in man, that he should more rejoice
at the salvation of a soul despaired of, and freed from greater peril,
than if there had always been hope of him, or the danger had been
less? For so You also, merciful Father, do more rejoice over one
penitent than over ninety-nine just persons that need no repent-
ance. And with much joyfulness do we hear, so often as we hear
with what joy the sheep which had strayed is brought back upon
the shepherd's shoulder, and the groat is restored to Your treasury,
the neighbours rejoicing with the woman who found it; and the
joy of the solemn service of Your house forces to tears, when in
Your house it is read of Your younger son, that he was dead, and
lives again; had been lost, and is found. For You rejoice in us, and
in Your holy angels, holy through holy charity. For You are ever
the same; for all things which abide not the same nor for ever,
You for ever know in the same way.

What then takes place in the soul, when it is more delighted
at finding or recovering the things it loves, than if it had never
lost them? Yea, and other things witness hereunto; and all things
are full of witnesses, crying out, 'So is it.' The conquering
commander triumphs; yet had he not conquered unless he had
fought; and the more peril there was in the battle, so much the
more joy is there in the triumph. The storm tosses the sailors,
threatens shipwreck; all wax pale at approaching death; sky and
sea are calmed, and they are exceeding joyed, as having been
exceeding afraid. A friend is sick, and his pulse threatens danger;
all who long for his recovery are sick in mind with him. He is
restored, though as yet he walks not with his former strength; yet
there is such joy, as was not, when before he walked sound and
strong. Yea, the very pleasures of human life men acquire by
difficulties, not those only which fall upon us unlooked for, and
against our wills, but even by self-chosen, and pleasure-seeking
trouble. Eating and drinking have no pleasure, unless there
precede the pinching of hunger and thirst. Men, given to drink,
eat certain salt meats, to procure a troublesome heat, which the
drink allaying, causes pleasure. It is also ordered that the affianced
bride should not at once be given, lest the husband should hold
cheap her whom, as betrothed, he sighed not after.

This law holds in foul and accursed joy; this in permitted and lawful joy; this in the very purest perfection of friendship; this, in him who was dead, and lived again; had been lost and was found. Everywhere the greater joy is ushered in by the greater pain. What means this, O Lord my God, whereas You are everlastingly joy to Yourself, and some things around You evermore rejoice in You? What means this, that this portion of things thus ebbs and flows alternately displeased and reconciled? Is this their allotted measure? Is this all You have assigned to them, whereas from the highest heavens to the lowest earth, from the beginning of the world to the end of ages, from the angel to the worm, from the first motion to the last, You set each in its place, and realize each in their season, every thing good after its kind? Woe is me! how high are You in the highest, and how deep in the deepest! You never depart, and we scarcely return to You.

4. *Why we are more to rejoice in the conversion of a great sinner*

Up, Lord, and do; stir us up, and recall us; kindle and draw us; inflame, grow sweet unto us, let us now love, let us run. Do not many, out of a deeper hell of blindness than Victorinus, return to You, approach, and are enlightened, receiving that light, which they who receive, receive power from You to become Your sons? But if they be less known to the nations, even they that know them, joy less for them. For when many joy together, each also has more exuberant joy for that they are kindled and inflamed one by the other. Again, because those known to many, influence the more towards salvation, and lead the way with many to follow. And therefore do they also who preceded them much rejoice in them, because they rejoice not in them alone. For far be it, that in Your tabernacle the persons of the rich should be accepted before the poor, or the noble before the ignoble; seeing rather You have chosen the weak things of the world to confound the strong; and the base things of this world, and the things despised have You chosen, and those things which are not, that You might bring to nothing things that are. And yet even that least of Your apostles, by whose tongue You sounded forth these words, when through his warfare, Paulus the proconsul, his pride conquered, was made to pass under the easy yoke of Your Christ, and became a provincial of the great King; he also for his former name Saul, was pleased to be called Paul, in testimony of so great a victory. For the enemy is more overcome in one, of whom he has more hold; by whom he has hold of more. But the proud he has more hold of, through their nobility; and by them, of more through their authority. By how much the more welcome then the heart of Victorinus was esteemed, which the devil had held as an impregnable possession, the tongue of Victorinus, with which mighty and keen weapon he had slain many; so much the more abundantly ought Your sons to rejoice, for that our King has bound the strong man, and they saw his vessels taken from him and cleansed, and made meet for Your honor; and become serviceable for the Lord, unto every good work.

5. *What hindered his conversion*

But when that man of Yours, Simplicianus, related to me this of Victorinus, I was on fire to imitate him; for to this very end had he related it. But when he had subjoined also, how in the days of the emperor Julian a law was made, whereby Christians were forbidden to teach the liberal sciences or oratory; and how he, obeying this law, chose rather to give over the wordy school than Your word, by which You make eloquent the tongues of the dumb; he seemed to me not more resolute than blessed, in having thus found opportunity to wait on You only. Which thing I was sighing for, bound as I was, not with another's irons, but by my own iron will. My will the enemy held, and thence had made a chain for me, and bound me. For of a forward will, was a lust made; and a lust served became custom; and custom not resisted, became necessity. By which links, as it were, joined together (whence I called it a chain) a hard bondage held me enthralled. But that new will which had begun to be in me, freely to serve You, and to wish to enjoy You, O God, the only assured pleasantness, was not yet able to overcome my former wilfulness, strengthened by age. Thus did my two wills, one new and the other old, one carnal, the other spiritual, struggle within me; and by their discord, undid my soul.

Thus I understood, by my own experience, what I had read, how the flesh lusts against the spirit and the spirit against the flesh. Myself verily either way; yet more myself, in that which I approved in myself, than in that which in myself I disapproved. For in this last, it was now for the more part not myself, because in much I rather endured against my will, than acted willingly. And yet it was through me that custom had obtained this power of warring against me, because I had come willingly, whither I willed not. And who has any right to speak against it, if just punishment follow the sinner? Nor had I now any longer my former plea, that I therefore as yet hesitated to be above the world and serve You, for that the truth was not altogether ascertained to me; for now it too was. But I still under service to the earth, refused to fight under Your banner, and feared as much to be freed of all encumbrances, as we should fear to be encumbered with it.

Thus with the baggage of this present world was I held down pleasantly, as in sleep: and the thoughts wherein I meditated on You were like the efforts of such as would awake, who yet, overcome with a heavy drowsiness, are again drenched therein. And as no one would sleep for ever, and in all men's sober judgment waking is better, yet a man for the most part, feeling a heavy lethargy in all his limbs, defers to shake off sleep, and though half displeased, yet, even after it is time to rise, with pleasure yields to it, so was I assured that much better were it for me to give myself up to Your charity, than to give myself over to mine own cupidity; but though the former course satisfied me and gained the mastery, the latter pleased me and held me mastered. Nor had I anything to answer You calling to me, Awake, you that sleep, and arise from the dead, and Christ shall give You light. And when You did on all sides show me that what You said was true, I, convicted by the truth, had nothing at all to answer, but only those dull and drowsy words, Anon, anon, Presently, Leave me but a little. But 'Presently, presently', had no present, and my 'little while' went on for a long while; in vain I delighted in Your law according to the inner man, when another law in my members rebelled against the law of my mind, and led me captive under the law of sin which was in my members. For the law of sin is the violence of custom, whereby the mind is drawn and holden, even against its will; but deservedly, for that it willingly fell into it. Who then should deliver me thus wretched from the body of this death, but Your grace only, through Jesus Christ our Lord?

6. *Ponticianus relates the life of Saint Antony*

And how You did deliver me out of the bonds of desire, where-with I was bound most straitly to carnal concupiscence, and out of the drudgery of worldly things, I will now declare, and confess unto Your name, O Lord, my helper and my redeemer. Amid increasing anxiety, I was doing my wonted business, and daily sighing unto You. I attended Your church, whenever free from the business under the burden of which I groaned. Alypius was with me, now after the third sitting released from his law business, and awaiting to whom to sell his counsel, as I sold the skill of speaking, if indeed teaching can impart it. Nebridius had now, in consideration of our friendship, consented to teach under Vere-cundus, a citizen and a grammarian of Milan, and a very intimate friend of us all; who urgently desired, and by the right of friend-ship challenged from our company, such faithful aid as he greatly needed. Nebridius then was not drawn to this by any desire of advantage (for he might have made much more of his learning had he so willed), but as a most kind and gentle friend, he would not be wanting to a good office, and slight our request. But he acted herein very discreetly, shunning to become known to personages great according to this world, avoiding the distraction of mind thence ensuing, and desiring to have it free and at leisure, as many hours as might be, to seek, or read, or hear something concerning wisdom.

Upon a day then, Nebridius being absent (I recollect not why), there came to see me and Alypius, one Pontitianus, our country-man so far as being an African, in high office in the emperor's court. What he would with us, I know not, but we sat down to converse, and it happened that upon a table for some game, before us, he observed a book, took, opened it, and contrary to his expectation, found it the apostle Paul; for he had thought it one of those books which I was wearing myself in teaching. Whereat smiling, and looking at me, he expressed his joy and wonder that he had on a sudden found this book, and this only before my eyes. For he was a Christian, and baptized, and often bowed himself before You our God in the church, in frequent and continued prayers. When then I had told him that I bestowed very great pains upon those scriptures, a conversation arose (suggested by his account) on Antony the Egyptian monk: whose name was in high reputation among Your servants, though to that hour unknown to us. Which when he discovered, he dwelt the more upon that subject, informing and wondering at our ignorance of one so eminent. But we stood amazed, hearing Your wonderful works most fully attested, in times so recent, and almost in our own, wrought in the true faith and church Catholic. We were all amazed: we, that they were so great, and he, that they had not reached us.

Thence his discourse turned to the flocks in the monasteries, and their holy ways, a sweet-smelling savor unto You, and the fruitful deserts of the wilderness, whereof we knew nothing. And there was a monastery at Milan, full of good brethren, without the city walls, under the fostering care of Ambrose, and we knew it not. He went on with his discourse, and we listened in intent silence. He told us then how one afternoon at Triers, when the emperor was taken up with the games at the Circus, he and three others, his companions, went out to walk in gardens near the city walls, and there as they happened to walk in pairs, one went apart with him, and the other two wandered by themselves; and these, in their wanderings, lighted upon a certain cottage, inhabited by certain of Your servants, poor in spirit, of whom is the kingdom of heaven, and there they found a little book containing the life of Antony. This one of them began to read, admire, and kindle at it; and as he read, to meditate on taking up such a life, and giving over his secular service to serve You. (These two were of those whom they style agents for the public affairs.) Then suddenly, filled with a holy love, and a sober shame, in anger with himself he cast his eyes upon his friend, saying, 'Tell me, I pray You, what would we attain by all these labours of ours? What aim we at? What serve we for? Can our hopes in court rise higher than to be the emperor's favorites? And in this, what is there not brittle, and full of perils? And by how many perils arrive we at a greater peril? And when do we arrive thither? But a friend of God, if I wish it, I can become now at once.' So spoke he. And in pain with the travail of a new life, he turned his eyes again upon the book, and read on, and was changed inwardly, where You saw, and his mind was stripped of the world, as soon appeared. For as he read, and rolled up and down the waves of his heart, he stormed at himself a while, then discerned, and determined on a better course; and now being Yours, said to his friend, 'Now have I broken loose from those our hopes, and am resolved to serve God; and this, from this hour, in this place, I begin upon. If you like not to imitate me, oppose not.' The other answered, he would hold fast to him, to partake so glorious a reward, so glorious a service. Thus both being now Yours, were building the tower at the necessary cost, the forsaking all that they had, and following You. Then Pontitianus and the other with him, that had walked in other parts of the garden, came in search of them to the same place; and finding them, reminded them to return, for the day was now far spent. But they relating their resolution and purpose, and how that will was begun and settled in them, begged them, if they would not join, not to molest them. But the others, though nothing altered from their former selves, did yet bewail themselves (as he affirmed), and piously congratulated them, recommending themselves to their prayers; and so, with hearts lingering on the earth, went away to the palace. But the other two, fixing their heart on heaven, remained in the cottage. And both had affianced brides, who when they heard hereof, also dedicated their virginity unto God.

7. *He was out of love with himself upon this story*

Such was the story of Pontitianus; but You, O Lord, while he was speaking, did turn me round towards myself, taking me from behind my back where I had placed me, unwilling to observe myself; and setting me before my face, that I might see how foul I was, how crooked and defiled, bespotted and ulcerous. And I beheld and stood aghast; and whither to flee from myself I found not. And if I sought to turn mine eye from off myself, he went on with his relation, and You again did set me over against myself, and thrusted me before my eyes, that I might find out mine iniquity, and hate it. I had known it, but made as though I saw it not, winked at it, and forgot it.

But now, the more ardently I loved those whose healthful affections I heard of, that they had resigned themselves wholly to You to be cured, the more did I abhor myself, when compared with them. For many of my years (some twelve) had now run out with me since my nineteenth, when, upon the reading of Cicero's *Hortensius*, I was stirred to an earnest love of wisdom; and still I was deferring to reject mere earthly felicity, and give myself to search out that, whereof not the finding only, but the very search, was to be preferred to the treasures and kingdoms of the world, though already found, and to the pleasures of the body, though spread around me at my will. But I − wretched, most wretched − in the very commencement of my early youth, had begged chastity of You, and said, Give me chastity and continency, only not yet. For I feared lest You should hear me soon, and soon cure me of the disease of concupiscence, which I wished to have satisfied, rather than extinguished. And I had wandered through crooked ways in a sacrilegious superstition, not indeed assured thereof, but as preferring it to the others which I did not seek religiously, but opposed maliciously.

And I had thought that the reason I deferred from day to day to reject the hopes of this world, and follow You only, was because there did not appear anything certain, whither to direct my course. And now was the day come wherein I was to be laid bare to myself, and my conscience was to upbraid me. 'Where are you now, my tongue? You said that for an uncertain truth you liked not to cast off the baggage of vanity; now, it is certain, and yet that burden still oppresses You, while they who neither have so worn themselves out with seeking it, nor for ten years and more have been thinking thereon, have had their shoulders lightened, and received wings to fly away.' Thus was I gnawed within, and exceedingly confounded with a horrible shame, while Pontitianus was so speaking. And he having brought to a close his tale and the business he came for, went his way; and I into myself. What said I not against myself? With what scourges of condemnation lashed I not my soul, that it might follow me, striving to go after You! Yet it drew back; refused, but excused not itself. All arguments were spent and confuted; there remained a mute shrinking; and she feared, as she would death, to be restrained from the flux of that custom, whereby she was wasting to death.

8. *What he did in the garden*

Then in this great contention of my inward dwelling, which I had strongly raised against my soul, in the chamber of my heart, troubled in mind and countenance, I turned upon Alypius. What ails us? I exclaim: What is it? What heard you? The unlearned start

up and take heaven by force, and we with our learning, see where
we wallow in flesh and blood! Are we ashamed to follow, because
others are gone before, and yet not ashamed not to follow at all?
Some such words I uttered, and my fever of mind tore me away
from him, while he, gazing on me in astonishment, kept silence.
For it was not my wonted tone; and my forehead, cheeks, eyes,
color, tone of voice, spoke my mind more than the words I
uttered. A little garden there was to our lodging, which we had
the use of, as of the whole house; for the master of the house, our
host, was not living there. Thither had the tumult of my breast
hurried me, where no man might hinder the hot contention
wherein I had engaged with myself, until it should end as You
knew, but I knew not. Only I was healthfully distracted and
dying, yet full of life; knowing what evil thing I was, but not
knowing what good thing I was shortly to become. I retired then
into the garden, and Alypius followed, step by step. For his
presence did not lessen my privacy; and how could he forsake me
so disturbed? We sat down as far removed as might be from the
house. I was troubled in spirit, most vehemently indignant that I
entered not into Your will and covenant, O my God, which all
my bones cried out unto me to enter, and praised it to the skies.
And therein we enter not by ships, or chariots, or feet, no, not
even so far as I had come from the house to that place where we
were sitting. For, not to approach only, but to go right in, was
nothing else but to will to go, to will resolutely and thoroughly;
not to turn and toss, this way and that, a maimed and half-divided
will, struggling, with one part sinking as another rose.

Lastly, in the very fever of my irresoluteness, I made with my
body many such motions as men sometimes would, but cannot,
if either they have not the limbs, or these be bound with bands,
weakened with infirmity, or any other way hindered. Thus, if I
tore my hair, beat my forehead, if locking my fingers I clasped
my knee, I willed, I did it. But I might have willed, and not done
it, if the power of motion in my limbs had not obeyed. So many
things then I did, when 'to will' was not in itself 'to be able';
and I did not what both I longed incomparably more to do, and
which soon after, when I should will, I should be able to do;
because soon after, when I should will, I should will thoroughly.
For in these things the ability was one with the will, and to will

was to do; and yet was it not done: and more easily did my body obey the weakest willing of my soul, in moving its limbs at its nod, than the soul obeyed itself to accomplish in the will alone this its momentous will.

9. *Why the mind is so slow to goodness*

Whence is this freak of nature? And to what end? Let Your mercy gleam that I may ask, if so be the secret penalties of men, and those darkest pangs of the sons of Adam, may perhaps answer me. Whence is this freak of nature? And to what end? The mind commands the body, and it obeys instantly; the mind commands itself, and is resisted. The mind commands the hand to be moved; and such readiness is there, that command is scarce distinct from obedience. Yet the mind is mind, the hand is body. The mind commands the mind, its own self, to will, and yet it does not. Whence this freak of nature? And to what end? It commands itself, I say, to will, and would not command, unless it willed, and what it commands is not done. But it wills not entirely: therefore does it not command entirely. For it commands only so far as it wills: and the thing commanded is not done, only so far as it wills not. For the will commands that there be a will; not another, but itself. But it does not command entirely, therefore what it commands, is not. For were the will entire, it would not even command it to be, because it would already be. It is therefore no freak of nature partly to will, partly to not will, but a disease of the mind, that it does not wholly rise, borne up by truth, borne down by custom. And therefore are there two wills, for that one of them is not entire: and what the one lacks, the other has.

10. *The will of man is various*

Let them perish from Your presence, O God, as perish vain talkers and seducers of the soul, who after observing that in deliberating there are two wills, affirm that there are two minds in us of two kinds, one good, the other evil. Themselves are truly evil, when they hold these evil things; and themselves shall become good when they hold the truth and assent unto the truth, that Your apostle may say to them, You were at one time darkness, but now light in the Lord. But they, wishing to be light, not in the Lord, but in themselves, imagining the nature of the soul to be that

which God is, are made more gross darkness through a dreadful
arrogancy; for that they went back farther from You, the true
light that enlightened every man that comes into the world.
Take heed what you say, and blush for shame: draw near unto
Him and be enlightened, and your faces shall not be ashamed.
When I myself was deliberating upon serving the Lord my God
now, as I had long purposed, it was I who willed, I who did not
will, I, I myself. I neither willed entirely, nor entirely did not
will. Therefore was I at strife with myself, and rent asunder by
myself. And this rent befell me against my will, and yet indicated,
not the presence of another mind, but the punishment of my
own. Therefore it was no more I that wrought it, but sin that
dwelt in me; the punishment of a sin more freely committed, in
that I was a son of Adam.

For if there be so many contrary natures as there be conflicting
wills, there shall now be not two only, but many. If a man
deliberate whether he should go to their conventicle or to the
theatre, these Manichees cry out, Behold, here are two natures:
one good, draws this way; another bad, draws back that way. For
whence else is this hesitation between conflicting wills? But I say
that both be bad: that which draws to them, as that which draws
back to the theatre. But they do not believe that will to be other
than good, which draws to them. What then if one of us should
deliberate, and amid the strife of his two wills be in a strait,
whether he should go to the theatre or to our church? Would not
these Manichees also be in a strait what to answer? For either they
must confess (which they would rather not) that the will which
leads to our church is good, as well as theirs, who have received
and are held by the mysteries of theirs: or they must suppose two
evil natures, and two evil souls conflicting in one man, and it will
not be true, what they say, that there is one good and another bad;
or they must be converted to the truth, and no more deny that
where one deliberates, one soul fluctuates between contrary wills.

Let them no more say then, when they perceive two conflicting
wills in one man, that the conflict is between two contrary souls,
of two contrary substances, from two contrary principles, one
good, and the other bad. For You, O true God, do disprove,
check, and convict them; as when, both wills being bad, one
deliberates whether he should kill a man by poison or by the

sword; whether he should seize this or that estate of another's, when he cannot both; whether he should purchase pleasure by luxury, or keep his money by covetousness; whether he go to the circus or the theatre, if both be open on one day; or thirdly, to rob another's house, if he have the opportunity; or, fourthly, to commit adultery, if at the same time he have the means thereof also; all these meeting together in the same juncture of time, and all being equally desired, which cannot at one time be acted: for they rend the mind amid four, or even (amid the vast variety of things desired) more, conflicting wills, nor do they yet allege that there are so many divers substances. So also in wills which are good. For I ask them, is it good to take pleasure in reading the apostle? Or good to take pleasure in a sober psalm? Or good to discourse on the gospel? They will answer to each, It is good. What then if all give equal pleasure, and all at once? Do not divers wills distract the mind, while he deliberates which he should rather choose? Yet are they all good, and are at variance till one be chosen, whither the one entire will may be borne, which before was divided into many. Thus also when, above, eternity delights us, and the pleasure of temporal good holds us down below, it is the same soul which wills not this or that with an entire will; and therefore is rent asunder with grievous perplexities, while out of truth it sets this first, but out of habit sets not that aside.

11. *The combat in him betwixt the spirit and the flesh*

Thus soul-sick was I, and tormented, accusing myself much more severely than my wont, rolling and turning me in my chain, till that were wholly broken, whereby I now was but just held, but still was held. And You, O Lord, pressed upon me in my inward parts by a severe mercy, redoubling the lashes of fear and shame, lest I should again give way, and not bursting that same slight remaining tie, it should recover strength, and bind me the faster. For I said with myself, Be it done now, be it done now. And as I spoke, I all but enacted it: I all but did it, and did it not: yet sunk not back to my former state, but kept my stand hard by, and took breath. And I essayed again, and wanted somewhat less of it, and somewhat less, and all but touched, and laid hold of it; and yet came not at it, nor touched nor laid hold of it; hesitating to die to death and to live to life: and the worse whereto I was inured, prevailed more with me than the better whereto I was unused: and the very moment wherein I was to become other than I was, the nearer it approached me, the greater horror did it strike into me; yet did it not strike me back, nor turned me away, but held me in suspense.

The very toys of toys, and vanities of vanities, my ancient mistresses, still held me; they plucked my fleshy garment, and whispered softly, Do you cast us off? And from that moment shall we no more be with You for ever? And from that moment shall not this or that be lawful for You for ever? And what was it which they suggested in that 'this or that' of mine, what did they suggest, O my God? Let Your mercy turn it away from the soul of Your servant. What defilements did they suggest! What shame! And now I much less than half heard them, and not openly showing themselves and contradicting me, but muttering as it were behind my back, and privily plucking me, as I was departing, but to look back on them. Yet they did retard me, so that I hesitated to burst and shake myself free from them, and to spring over whither I was called; a violent habit saying to me, Think you, you can live without them?

But now it spoke very faintly. For on that side whither I had set my face, and whither I trembled to go, there appeared unto me the chaste dignity of continency, serene, yet not relaxedly, gay, honestly alluring me to come and doubt not; and stretching forth to receive and embrace me, her holy hands full of multitudes of good examples: there were so many young men and maidens here, a multitude of youth and every age, grave widows and aged virgins; and Continence herself in all, not barren, but a fruitful mother of children of joys, by You her husband, O Lord. And she smiled on me with a persuasive mockery, as she would say, Can not you what these youths, what these maidens can? Or can they either in themselves, and not rather in the Lord their God? The Lord their God gave me unto them. Why stand you in yourself, and so stand not? Cast yourself upon Him, fear not. He will not withdraw Himself that you should fall; cast yourself fearlessly upon Him. He will receive, and will heal You. And I blushed exceedingly, for that I yet heard the muttering of those toys, and hung in suspense. And she again seemed to say, Stop your ears against those your unclean members on the earth, that they may be mortified. They tell you of delights, but not as does the law of the Lord your God. This controversy in my heart was self against self only. But Alypius sitting close by my side, in silence waited the issue of my unwonted emotion.

12. *How he was converted by a voice*

But when a deep consideration had from the secret bottom of my soul drawn together and heaped up all my misery in the sight of my heart, there arose a mighty storm, bringing a mighty shower of tears. Which that I might pour forth wholly, in its natural expressions, I rose from Alypius: solitude was suggested to me as fitter for the business of weeping; so I retired so far that even his presence could not be a burden to me. Thus was it then with me, and he perceived something of it; for something I suppose I had spoken, wherein the tones of my voice appeared choked with weeping, and so had risen up. He then remained where we were sitting, most extremely astonished. I cast myself down I know not how, under a certain fig-tree, giving full vent to my tears; and the floods of mine eyes gushed out an acceptable sacrifice to You. And, not indeed in these words, yet to this purpose, spoke I much unto You: And You, O Lord, how long? How long, Lord, will You be angry, for ever? Remember not our former iniquities, for I felt that I was held by them. I sent up these sorrowful words: How long, how long, 'tomorrow, and tomorrow'? Why not now? Why is there not this hour an end to my uncleanness?

So was I speaking and weeping in the most bitter contrition of my heart, when, lo! I heard from a neighbouring house a voice, as of boy or girl, I know not, chanting, and oft repeating, Take up and read; Take up and read. Instantly, my countenance altered, I began to think most intently whether children were wont in any kind of play to sing such words: nor could I remember ever to have heard the like. So checking the torrent of my tears, I arose; interpreting it to be no other than a command from God to open the book, and read the first chapter I should find. For I had heard of Antony, that coming in during the reading of the gospel, he received the admonition, as if what was being read was spoken to him: Go, sell all that you have, and give to the poor, and you shall have treasure in heaven, and come and follow me: and by such oracle he was forthwith converted unto You. Eagerly then I returned to the place where Alypius was sitting; for there had I laid the volume of the apostle when I arose thence. I seized, opened, and in silence read that section on which my eyes first fell: Not in rioting and drunkenness, not in chambering and wantonness, not in strife and envying; but put ye on the Lord Jesus Christ, and make not provision for the flesh, in concupiscence. No further would I read; nor needed I: for instantly at the end of this sentence, by a light as it were of serenity infused into my heart, all the darkness of doubt vanished away.

Then putting my finger between, or some other mark, I shut the volume, and with a calmed countenance made it known to Alypius. And what was wrought in him, which I knew not, he thus showed me. He asked to see what I had read: I showed him; and he looked even further than I had read, and I knew not what followed. This followed: Him that is weak in the faith, receive; which he applied to himself, and disclosed to me. And by this admonition was he strengthened; and by a good resolution and purpose, and most corresponding to his character, wherein he did always very far differ from me, for the better, without any turbulent delay he joined me. Thence we go in to my mother; we tell her; she rejoices: we relate in order how it took place; she leaps for joy, and triumphs, and blesses You, who are able to do above that which we ask or think; for she perceived that You had given her more for me, than she was wont to beg by her pitiful and most sorrowful groanings. For you converted me unto Yourself, so that I sought neither wife, nor any hope of this world, standing in that rule of faith, where You had showed me unto her in a vision, so many years before. And You did convert her mourning into joy, much more plentiful than she had desired, and in a much more precious and purer way than she required before, by having grandchildren of my body.

Book 9

1. He praises God's goodness; and acknowledges
his own wretchedness

O Lord, I am Your servant; I am Your servant, and the son of Your handmaid: You have broken my bonds in sunder. I will offer to You the sacrifice of praise. Let my heart and my tongue praise You; yea, let all my bones say, O Lord, who is like unto You? Let them say; and answer You me, and say unto my soul, I am your salvation. Who am I, and what am I? What evil have not been either my deeds, or if not my deeds, my words, or if not my words, my will? But You, O Lord, are good and merciful, and Your right hand had respect unto the depth of my death, and from the bottom of my heart emptied that abyss of corruption. And this Your whole gift was, not to will what I willed, but to will what You willed. But where through all those years, and out of what low and deep recess was my free-will called forth in a moment, whereby to submit my neck to Your easy yoke, and my shoulders unto Your light burden, O Christ Jesus, my helper and my redeemer? How sweet did it at once become to me, to be without the sweetnesses of those toys! and what I feared to be parted from, was now a joy to part with. For You did cast them forth from me, You true and highest sweetness. You cast them forth, and for them entered in Yourself, sweeter than all pleasure, though not to flesh and blood; brighter than all light, but more hidden than all depths, higher than all honor, but not to those high in their own conceits. Now was my soul free from the biting cares of canvassing and getting, and weltering in filth, and scratching off the itch of lust. And my infant tongue spoke freely to You, my brightness, and my riches, and my health, the Lord my God.

2. *He gives over his teaching of rhetoric*

And I resolved in Your sight, not tumultuously to tear, but gently to withdraw, the service of my tongue from the marts of lip-labour: that the young, students not in Your law, nor in Your peace, but in lying dotages and law-skirmishes, should no longer buy at my mouth arms for their madness. And very seasonably, it now wanted but very few days unto the holiday of the vintage, and I resolved to endure them, then in a regular way to take my leave, and having been purchased by You, no more to return for sale. Our purpose then was known to You; but to men, other than our own friends, was it not known. For we had agreed among ourselves not to let it out abroad to any: although to us, now ascending from the valley of tears, and singing that song of degrees, You had given sharp arrows, and destroying coals against the subtle tongue, which as though advising for us, would thwart, and would out of love devour us, as it does its meat.

You had pierced our hearts with Your charity, and we carried Your words as it were fixed in our entrails: and the examples of Your servants, whom from black You had made bright, and from dead, alive, being piled together in the receptacle of our thoughts, kindled and burned up that our heavy torpor, that we should not sink down to the abyss; and they fired us so vehemently, that all the blasts of subtle tongues of denial might only inflame us the more fiercely, not extinguish us. Nevertheless, because for Your name's sake which You have hallowed throughout the earth, this our vow and purpose might also find some to commend it, it seemed like ostentation not to wait for the vacation now so near, but to quit beforehand a public profession, which was before the eyes of all; so that all looking on this act of mine, and observing how near was the time of vintage which I wished to anticipate, would talk much of me, as if I had desired to appear some great one. And what end had it served me, that people should form judgment and dispute upon my purpose, and that our good should be evil spoken of.

Moreover, it had at first troubled me that in this very summer my lungs began to give way, amid too great literary labour, and to have difficulty breathing deeply, and by the pain in my chest to show that they were injured, and to refuse any full or lengthened speaking; this had troubled me, for it almost constrained me of necessity to lay down that burden of teaching, or, if I could be cured and recover, at least to intermit it. But when the full wish for leisure arose, and was fixed in me, that I might see how that You are the Lord, You, my God, know I began even to rejoice that I had this secondary, and that not pretended, excuse, which might something moderate the offence taken by those who, for their sons' sake, wished me never to have the freedom of Your sons. Full then of such joy, I endured till that interval of time were run; it may have been some twenty days, yet they were endured manfully; endured, for the covetousness which aforetime bore a part of this heavy business, had left me, and I remained alone, and had been overwhelmed, had not patience taken its place. Perchance, some of Your servants, my brethren, may say that I sinned in this, that with a heart fully set on Your service, I suffered myself to sit even one hour in the chair of lies. Nor would I be contentious. But have not You, O most merciful Lord, pardoned and remitted this sin also, with my other most horrible and deadly sins, in the holy water?

3. *Verecundus lends them his country house*

Verecundus was worn down with care about this our blessedness, for that being held back by bonds, whereby he was most straitly bound, he saw that he should be severed from us. For himself was not yet a Christian, his wife one of the faithful; and yet hereby, more rigidly than by any other chain, was he let and hindered from the journey which we had now essayed. For he would not, he said, be a Christian on any other terms than on those he could not. However, he offered us courteously to remain at his country-house so long as we should stay there. You, O Lord, shall reward him in the resurrection of the just, seeing You have already given him the lot of the righteous. For although, in our absence, being now at Rome, he was seized with bodily sickness, and therein being made a Christian, and one of the faithful, he departed this life, yet had You mercy not on him only, but on us also: lest remembering the exceeding kindness of our friend towards us, yet unable to number him among Your flock, we should be agonized with intolerable sorrow. Thanks unto You, our God, we are Yours: Your suggestions and consolations tell us, faithful in promises, You now requite Verecundus for his country-house of

Cassiacum, where from the fever of the world we reposed in You, with the eternal freshness of Your Paradise: for that You have forgiven him his sins upon earth, in that rich mountain, that mountain which yields milk, Your own mountain.

He then had at that time sorrow, but Nebridius joy. For although he also, not being yet a Christian, had fallen into the pit of that most pernicious error, believing the flesh of Your Son to be a phantom: yet emerging thence, he believed as we did; not as yet endued with any sacraments of Your church, but a most ardent searcher out of truth. Whom, not long after our conversion and regeneration by Your baptism, being also a faithful member of the church Catholic, and serving You in perfect chastity and continence amongst his people in Africa, his whole house having through him first been made Christian, You did release from the flesh; and now he lives in Abraham's bosom. Whatever that be, which is signified by that bosom, there lives my Nebridius, my sweet friend, and Your child, O Lord, adopted of a freed man: there he lives. For what other place is there for such a soul? There he lives, whereof he asked much of me, a poor inexperienced man. Now lays he not his ear to my mouth, but his spiritual mouth unto Your fountain, and drinks as much as he can receive, wisdom in proportion to his thirst, endlessly happy. Nor do I think that he is so inebriated therewith, as to forget me; seeing You, Lord, whom he drinks, are mindful of us. So were we then, comforting Verecundus, who sorrowed, as far as friendship permitted, that our conversion was of such sort; and exhorting him to become faithful, according to his measure, namely, of a married estate; and awaiting Nebridius to follow us, which, being so near, he was all but doing: and so, lo! those days rolled by at length; for long and many they seemed, for the love I bore to the easeful liberty, that I might sing to You, from my inmost marrow, My heart has said unto You, I have sought Your face: Your face, Lord, will I seek.

4. *What things he wrote with Nebridius*

Now was the day come wherein I was in deed to be freed of my rhetoric professorship, whereof in thought I was already freed. And it was done. You did rescue my tongue, whence You had before rescued my heart. And I blessed You, rejoicing; retiring with all mine to the villa. What I there did in writing, which was now enlisted in Your service, though still, in this breathing-time as it were, panting from the school of pride, my books may witness, as well what I debated with others, as what with myself alone, before You: what with Nebridius, who was absent, my letters bear witness. And when shall I have time to rehearse all Your great benefits towards us at that time, especially when hasting on to yet greater mercies? For my remembrance recalls me, and pleasant is it to me, O Lord, to confess to You, by what inward goads You tamed me; and how You have evened me, lowering the mountains and hills of my high imaginations, straightening my crookedness, and smoothing my rough ways; and how You also subdued the brother of my heart, Alypius, unto the name of Your only begotten, our Lord and Saviour Jesus Christ, which he would not at first vouchsafe to have inserted in our writings. For rather would he have them savor of the lofty cedars of the Schools, which the Lord has now broken down, than of the wholesome herbs of the church, the antidote against serpents.

Oh, in what accents spoke I unto You, my God, when I read the psalms of David, those faithful songs, and sounds of devotion, which allow of no swelling spirit, as yet a catechumen, and a novice in Your real love, resting in that villa, with Alypius a catechumen, my mother holding fast to us, in female garb with masculine faith, with the tranquillity of age, motherly love, Christian piety! Oh, what accents did I utter unto You in those psalms, and how was I by them kindled towards You, and on fire to rehearse them, if possible, through the whole world, against the pride of mankind! And yet they are sung through the whole world, nor can any hide himself from Your heat. With what vehement and bitter sorrow was I angered at the Manichees! and again I pitied them, for they knew not those sacraments, those medicines, and were mad against the antidote which might have recovered them of their madness. How I would they had then been somewhere near me, and without my knowing that they were there, could have beheld my countenance, and heard my words, when I read the fourth psalm in that time of my rest, and how that psalm wrought upon me: When I called, the God of my righteousness heard me; in tribulation You enlarged me. Have mercy upon me, O Lord, and hear my prayer. Would that what I uttered on these words, they could hear, without my knowing whether they heard, lest they should think I spoke it for their sakes! Because in truth neither should I speak the same things, nor in the same way, if I perceived that they heard and saw me; nor if I spoke them would they so receive them, as when I spoke by and for myself before You, out of the natural feelings of my soul.

I trembled for fear, and again kindled with hope, and with rejoicing in Your mercy, O Father; and all issued forth both by mine eyes and voice, when Your good spirit turning unto us, said, O you sons of men, how long slow of heart? Why do you love vanity, and seek after lying? For I had loved vanity, and sought after lying. And You, O Lord, had already magnified Your holy one, raising Him from the dead, and setting Him at Your right hand, whence from on high He should send His promise, the Comforter, the spirit of truth. And He had already sent Him, but I knew it not; He had sent Him, because He was now magnified, rising again from the dead, and ascending into heaven. For till then, the Spirit was not yet given, because Jesus was not yet glorified. And the prophet cries out, How long, slow of heart? Why do you love vanity, and seek after lying? Know this, that the Lord has magnified His holy one. He cries out, How long? He cries out, Know this: and I so long, not knowing, loved vanity, and sought after lying: and therefore I heard and trembled, because it was spoken unto such as I remembered myself to have been. For in those phantoms which I had held for truths, was there vanity and lying; and I spoke aloud many things earnestly and forcibly, in the bitterness of my remembrance. Which would they had heard, who yet love vanity and seek after lying! They would perchance have been troubled, and have vomited it up; and You would hear them when they cried unto You; for by a true death in the flesh did He die for us, who now intercedes unto You for us.

I further read, Be angry, and sin not. And how was I moved, O my God, who had now learned to be angry at myself for things past, that I might not sin in time to come! Yea, to be justly angry; for that it was not another nature of a people of darkness which sinned for me, as they say who are not angry at themselves, and treasure up wrath against the day of wrath, and of the revelation of Your just judgment. Nor were my good things now without, nor sought with the eyes of flesh in that earthly sun; for they that would have joy from without soon become vain, and waste themselves on things seen and temporal, and in their famished thoughts do lick their very shadows. Oh that they were wearied out with their famine, and said, Who will show us good things? And we would say, and they hear, The light of Your countenance is sealed upon us. For we are not that light which enlightens every man, but we are enlightened by You; that having been sometimes darkness, we may be light in You. Oh that they could see the inner eternal, which having tasted, I was grieved that I could not show it them, so long as they brought me their heart in their eyes roving abroad from You, while they said, Who will show us good things? For there, where I was angry within myself in my chamber, where I was inwardly pricked, where I had sacrificed, slaying my old man and commencing the purpose of a new life, putting my trust in You – there had You begun to grow sweet unto me, and had put gladness in my heart. And I cried out, as I read this outwardly, finding it inwardly. Nor would I be multiplied with worldly goods; wasting away time, and wasted by time; whereas I had in Your eternal simple essence other corn, and wine, and oil.

And with a loud cry of my heart I cried out in the next verse, O in peace, O for the self-same! O what said he, I will lay me down and sleep, for who shall hinder us, when comes to pass that saying which is written, Death is swallowed up in victory? And You surpassingly are the self-same, who are not changed; and in You is rest which forgets all toil, for there is none other with You, nor are we to seek those many other things, which are not what You are: but You, Lord, alone have made me dwell in hope. I read, and kindled; nor found I what to do to those deaf and dead, of whom myself had been, a pestilent person, a bitter and a blind bawler against those writings, which are honeyed with the honey of heaven, and lightsome with Your own light: and I was consumed with zeal at the enemies of this scripture.

When shall I recall all which passed in those feast-days? Yet neither have I forgotten, nor will I pass over the severity of Your scourge, and the wonderful swiftness of Your mercy. You did then torment me with pain in my teeth; which when it had

come to such height that I could not speak, it came into my heart
to desire all my friends present to pray for me to You, the God
of all manner of health. And this I wrote on wax, and gave it
them to read. Presently so soon as with humble devotion we
had bowed our knees, that pain went away. But what pain? Or
how went it away? I was affrighted, O my Lord, my God; for
from infancy I had never experienced the like. And the the nod
of Your head was deeply conveyed to me, and rejoicing in faith,
I praised Your name. And that faith suffered me not to be at
ease about my past sins, which were not yet forgiven me by
Your baptism.

5. *Ambrose directs him what books to read*

The holiday of the vintage ended, I gave notice to the people of
Milan to provide their scholars with another master to sell words
to them; both because I had made choice to serve You, and
because my difficulty of breathing and pain in my chest made
me unequal to that profession. And by letters I signified to Your
prelate, the holy man Ambrose, my former errors and present
desires, begging his advice what of Your scriptures I had best read,
to become readier and fitter for receiving so great grace. He
recommended Isaiah the Prophet: I believe, because he above
the rest more clearly foreshows the gospel and the calling of
the gentiles. But I, not understanding the first lesson in him, and
imagining the whole to be like it, laid it by, to be resumed when
better practiced in our Lord's own words.

6. *He is baptized at Milan*

Thence, when the time was come wherein I was to put forward
my name, we left the country and returned to Milan. It pleased
Alypius also to be with me born again in You, being already
clothed with the humility befitting Your sacraments; and a most
valiant tamer of the body, so as, with unwonted boldness, to wear
out the frozen ground of Italy with his bare feet. We joined with
us the boy Adeodatus, born after the flesh, of my sin. Excellently
had You made him. He was not quite fifteen, and in wit surpassed
many grave and learned men. I confess unto You Your gifts, O
Lord my God, creator of all, and abundantly able to reform our
deformities: for I had no part in that boy, but the sin. For that we

brought him up in Your discipline, it was You, none else, had inspired us with it. I confess unto You Your gifts. There is a book of ours entitled *The Master*; it is a dialogue between him and me. You know that all there ascribed to the person conversing with me were his ideas, in his sixteenth year. Much besides, and yet more admirable, I found in him. That talent struck awe into me. And who but You could be the workmaster of such wonders? Soon did You take his life from the earth: and I now remember him with an easier mind, fearing nothing for his childhood or youth, or his whole self. Him we joined with us, our contemporary in grace, to be brought up in Your discipline: and we were baptized, and anxiety for our past life vanished from us. Nor was I sated in those days with the wondrous sweetness of considering the depth of Your counsels concerning the salvation of mankind. How did I weep, in Your hymns and canticles, touched to the quick by the voices of Your sweet-attuned church! The voices flowed into mine ears, and the truth distilled into my heart, whence the affections of my devotion overflowed, and tears ran down, and happy was I therein.

7. *A persecution in the church miraculously diverted*

Not long had the Church of Milan begun to use this kind of consolation and exhortation, the brethren zealously joining with harmony of voice and hearts. For it was a year, or not much more, that Justina, mother to the emperor Valentinian, a child, persecuted Your servant Ambrose, in favor of her heresy, to which she was seduced by the Arians. The devout people kept watch in the church, ready to die with their bishop Your servant. There my mother Your handmaid, bearing a chief part of those anxieties and watchings, lived for prayer. We, yet unwarmed by the heat of Your spirit, still were stirred up by the sight of the amazed and disquieted city. Then it was first instituted that after the manner of the Eastern Churches, hymns and psalms should be sung, lest the people should wax faint through the tediousness of sorrow: and from that day to this the custom is retained, divers (yea, almost all) Your congregations, throughout other parts of the world, following herein.

Then did You by a vision discover to Your forenamed bishop where the bodies of Gervasius and Protasius the martyrs lay hid (whom You had in Your secret treasury stored uncorrupted so many years), whence You might seasonably produce them to repress the fury of a woman, but an empress. For when they were discovered and dug up, and with due honor translated to the Ambrosian Basilica, not only they who were vexed with unclean spirits (the devils confessing themselves) were cured, but a certain man who had for many years been blind, a citizen, and well known to the city, asking and hearing the reason of the people's confused joy, sprang forth desiring his guide to lead him thither. Led thither, he begged to be allowed to touch with his handkerchief the bier of Your saints, whose death is precious in Your sight. Which when he had done, and put to his eyes, they were forthwith opened. Thence did the fame spread, thence Your praises glowed, shone; thence the mind of that enemy, though not turned to the soundness of believing, was yet turned back from her fury of persecuting. Thanks to You, O my God. Whence and whither have You thus led my remembrance, that I should confess these things also unto You? Which great though they be, I had passed by in forgetfulness. Yet even then, when the odor of Your ointments was so fragrant, did we not run after You. Therefore did I more weep among the singing of Your hymns, formerly sighing after You, and at length breathing in You, as far as the breath may enter into this our house of grass.

8. *The conversion of Euodius. A discourse of his mother*

You that make men to dwell of one mind in one house, did join with us Euodius also, a young man of our own city. Who while taking part in the hurly-burly of public life, was before us converted to You and baptized: and quitting his day-to-day warfare, girded himself to Yours. We were together, about to dwell together in our devout purpose. We sought where we might serve You most usefully, and were together returning to Africa: whitherward being as far as Ostia, my mother departed this life. Much I omit, as hastening much. Receive my confessions and thanksgivings, O my God, for innumerable things whereof I am silent. But I will not omit whatsoever my soul would bring forth concerning that Your handmaid, who brought me forth, both in the flesh, that I might be born to this temporal light, and in heart, that I might be born to light eternal. Not her gifts, but Yours in her, would I speak of; for neither did she make nor educate herself. You created her; nor did her father and mother know what a one should come from them. And the sceptre of Your Christ, the discipline of Your only Son, in a Christian house, a good member of Your Church, educated her in Your fear. Yet for her good discipline was she wont to commend not so much her mother's diligence, as that of a certain decrepit maid-servant, who had carried her father when a child, as little ones used to be carried at the backs of elder girls. For which reason, and for her great age, and excellent conversation, was she, in that Christian family, well respected by its heads. Whence also the charge of her master's daughters was entrusted to her, to which she gave diligent heed, restraining them earnestly, when necessary, with a holy severity, and teaching them with a grave discretion. For, except at those hours wherein they were most temperately fed at their parents' table, she would not suffer them, though parched with thirst, to drink even water; preventing an evil custom, and adding this wholesome advice: 'You drink water now, because you have not wine in your power; but when you come to be married, and be made mistresses of cellars and cupboards, you will scorn water, but the custom of drinking will abide.' By this method of instruction, and the authority she had, she reined in the greediness of childhood, and moulded their very thirst to such an excellent moderation that what they should not, that they would not.

And yet (as Your handmaid told me her son) there had crept upon her a love of wine. For when (as the manner was) she, as though a sober maiden, was bidden by her parents to draw wine out of the hogshed, holding the vessel under the opening, before she poured the wine into the flagon, she sipped a little with the tip of her lips; for more her instinctive feelings refused. For this she did, not out of any desire of drink, but out of the exuberance of youth, whereby it boils over in playful freaks, which in youthful spirits are wont to be kept under by the gravity of their elders. And thus by adding to that little, daily littles (for whoso despises little things shall fall by little and little), she had fallen into such a habit as greedily to drink off her little cup brim-full almost of wine. Where was then that discreet old woman, and that her earnest countermanding? Would anything avail against a secret disease, if Your healing hand, O Lord, watched not over us? Father, mother, and governors absent, You present, who created,

who call, who also by those set over us, work something towards
the salvation of our souls, what did You then, O my God? How
did You cure her? How heal her? Did You not out of another soul
bring forth a hard and a sharp taunt, like a lancet out of Your
secret store, and with one touch remove all that foul stuff? For a
maid-servant with whom she used to go to the cellar, falling to
words (as it happens) with her little mistress, when alone with her,
taunted her with this fault, with most bitter insult, calling her
wine-bibber. With which taunt she, stung to the quick, saw the
foulness of her fault, and instantly condemned and forsook it. As
flattering friends pervert, so reproachful enemies mostly correct.
And You repay them, not for what through them You do, but for
what themselves purposed. For she in her anger sought to vex her
young mistress, not to amend her; and did it in private, either for
that the time and place of the quarrel so found them; or lest her
mistress also should be angry, for discovering it thus late. But You,
Lord, Governor of all in heaven and earth, who turn to Your
purposes the deepest currents, and the ruled turbulence of the tide
of times, did by the very unhealthiness of one soul heal another;
lest any, when he observes this, should ascribe it to his own
power, even when another, whom he wished to be reformed, is
reformed through words of his.

9. His mother Monnica's carriage towards her husband; a description of a rare wife

Brought up thus modestly and soberly, and made subject rather by
You to her parents, than by her parents to You, so soon as she was
of marriageable age, being bestowed upon a husband, she served
him as her lord; and did her best to win him unto You, preaching
You unto him by her conversation; by which You ornamented
her, making her reverently amiable, and admirable unto her husband. And she so endured the wronging of her bed as never to
have any quarrel with her husband thereon. For she looked for
Your mercy upon him, that believing in You, he might be made
chaste. But besides this, he was fervid, as in his affections, so in
anger: but she had learnt not to resist an angry husband, not in
deed only, but not even in word. Only when he was smoothed
and tranquil, and in a temper to receive it, she would give an
account of her actions, if haply he had overhastily taken offence.

In a word, while many matrons, who had milder husbands, yet bore even in their faces marks of shame, would in familiar talk blame their husbands' lives, she would blame them for their gossip, giving them, as in jest, earnest advice: 'That from the time they heard the marriage writings read to them, they should account them as indentures, whereby they were made servants; and so, remembering their condition, ought not to set themselves up against their lords.' And when they, knowing what a choleric husband she endured, marvelled that it had never been heard, nor by any token perceived, that Patricius had beaten his wife, or that there had been any domestic difference between them, even for one day, and confidentially asking the reason, she taught them her practice above mentioned. Those wives who followed her advice found it good, and returned thanks; those who followed it not, were oppressed, and suffered.

Her mother-in-law also, at first by whisperings of evil servants incensed against her, she so overcame by attention and persevering endurance and meekness, that she of her own accord revealed to her son the meddling tongues whereby the domestic peace betwixt her and her daughter-in-law had been disturbed, asking him to correct them. Then, when out of respect for his mother, and for the well-ordering of the family, he had with stripes corrected those reported to him, at her will who had discovered them, she promised the like reward to any who, with a view to pleasing her, should speak ill of her daughter-in-law to her: and none now venturing, they lived together with a remarkable sweetness of mutual kindness.

This great gift also you bestowed, O my God, my mercy, upon that good handmaid of Yours, in whose womb You created me, that between any disagreeing and discordant parties where she was able, she showed herself such a peacemaker, that hearing on both sides most bitter things, such as swelling and undigested anger often breaks out into, when the crudities of enmities are breathed out in sour discourses to a present friend against an absent enemy, she never would disclose anything of the one unto the other, but what might tend to their reconcilement. A small good this might appear to me, did I not to my grief know numberless persons, who through some horrible and wide-spreading contagion of sin, not only disclose to persons mutually angered things said in anger, but add withal things never spoken, whereas to humane humanity, it ought to seem a light thing not to foment or increase ill will by ill words, unless one study withal by good words to quench it. Such was she, with You, her most inward instructor, teaching her in the school of the heart.

Finally, her own husband, towards the very end of his earthly life, did she gain unto You; nor had she to complain of that in him as a believer, which before he was a believer she had borne from him. She was also the servant of Your servants; whosoever of them knew her, did in her much praise and honor and love You; for that through the witness of the fruits of a holy conversation they perceived Your presence in her heart. For she had been the wife of one man, had requited her parents, had governed her house piously, was well reported of for good works, had brought up children, so often travailing in birth of them, as she saw them swerving from You. Lastly, of all of us Your servants, O Lord (whom on occasion of Your own gift You suffer to speak), she so took care of us, who before her sleeping in You lived united together, having received the grace of Your baptism, as though she had been mother of us all; so served us, as though she had been child to us all.

10. *Of a conference he had with his mother about the kingdom of heaven*

The day now approaching whereon she was to depart this life (which day You well knew, though we knew not), it came to pass, You by Your secret ways, as I believe, so ordering it, that she and I stood alone, leaning in a certain window, which looked into the garden of the house where we now lay, at Ostia; where removed from the din of men, we were gaining strength for the voyage, after the fatigues of a long journey. We were discoursing then together, alone, very sweetly; and forgetting those things which are behind, and reaching forth unto those things which are before, we were enquiring between ourselves in the presence of the truth, which You are, of what sort the eternal life of the saints was to be, which eye has not seen, nor ear heard, nor has it entered into the heart of man. But yet we gasped with the mouth of our heart, after those heavenly streams of Your fountain, the fountain of life, which is with You; that being bedewed thence according to our capacity, we might in some sort meditate upon so high a mystery.

And when our discourse was brought to that point, that the very highest delight of the earthly senses, in the very purest material light, was, in respect of the sweetness of that life, not only not worthy of comparison, but not even of mention; we raising up ourselves with a more glowing affection towards the thing itself, did by degrees pass through all things bodily, even the very heaven whence sun and moon and stars shine upon the earth; yea, we were soaring higher yet, by inward musing, and discourse, and admiring of Your works; and we came to our own minds, and went beyond them, that we might arrive at that region of never-failing plenty, where You feed Israel for ever with the food of truth, and where life is the wisdom by which all these things are made, both things that have been, and things that shall be. This wisdom is not made, but is as she has been, and so shall she be ever; yea rather, 'to have been' and 'to be going to be' are not in her, but only 'to be', seeing she is eternal. For 'to have been' and 'to be going to be', are not eternal. And while we were discoursing and panting after her, we slightly touched on her with the whole effort of our heart; and we sighed, and there, bound to it, we leave the first fruits of the spirit; and returned to vocal expressions of our mouth, where the word spoken has beginning and end. And what is like unto Your word, our Lord, which endures in itself without becoming old, and makes all things new?

We were saying then: If to any the tumult of the flesh were hushed, hushed the images of earth, and waters, and air, hushed also the pole of heaven, yea the very soul be hushed to herself, and by not thinking on self surmount self; hushed all dreams and imaginary revelations, every tongue and every sign, and whatso-ever exists only in transition, since for anyone who can hear, all these say, We made not ourselves, but He made us that abides for ever – if then having uttered this, they too should be hushed, having roused our ears to Him who made them, and He alone speak, not by them but by Himself, that we may hear His word, not through any tongue of flesh, nor angel's voice, nor sound of thunder, nor in the dark riddle of a similitude, but might hear Him whom in these things we love, might hear His very self without these (as we two now strained ourselves, and in swift thought touched on that eternal wisdom which abides over all) – could this be continued on, and other visions of kind far unlike be withdrawn, and this one ravish, and absorb, and wrap up its beholder amid these inward joys, so that life might be for ever like that one moment of understanding which now we sighed after; is not this, Enter into your Master's joy? And when shall that be? When we shall all rise again, though we shall not all be changed?

Such things was I speaking, and even if not in this very manner, and these same words, yet, Lord, You know that in that day when we were speaking of these things, and this world with all its delights became, as we spoke, contemptible to us, my mother said, Son, for mine own part I have no further delight in anything in this life. What I do here any longer, and why I am here, I know not, now that my hopes in this world are accomplished. One thing there was for which I desired to linger for a while in this life, that I might see You a Catholic Christian before I died. My God has done for me more than I aked, in that I now see you withal, despising earthly happiness, become His servant: what have I to do I here?

11. *Of the ecstasy and death of his mother*

What answer I made her unto these things, I remember not. For scarce five days after, or not much more, she fell sick of a fever; and in that sickness one day she fell into a swoon, and was for a while withdrawn from these visible things. We hastened round her; but she was soon brought back to her senses; and looking on me and my brother standing by her, said to us enquiringly, 'Where was I?' And then looking fixedly on us, with grief amazed: 'Here,' says she, 'shall you bury your mother.' I held my peace and refrained weeping; but my brother spoke something, wishing for her, as the happier lot, that she might die, not in a strange place, but in her own land. Whereat she, with anxious look, checking him with her eyes, for that he still savored such things, and then looking upon me: 'Behold,' says she, 'what he says': and soon after to us both, 'Lay,' she says, 'this body anywhere; let not the care for that any way disquiet you: this only I request, that you would remember me at the Lord's altar, wherever you be.' And having delivered this sentiment in what words she could, she held her peace, being exercized by her growing sickness.

But I, considering Your gifts, You unseen God, which You instil into the hearts of Your faithful ones, whence wondrous fruits do spring, did rejoice and give thanks to You, recalling what I before knew, how careful and anxious she had ever been as to her place of burial, which she had provided and prepared for herself by the body of her husband. For because they had lived in great harmony together, she also wished (so little can the human mind embrace things divine) to have this addition to that happiness, and to have it remembered among men, that after her pilgrimage beyond the seas, what was earthly of this united pair had been permitted to be united beneath the same earth. But when this emptiness had through the fullness of Your goodness begun to cease in her heart, I knew not, and rejoiced admiring what she had so disclosed to me; though indeed in that our discourse also in the window, when she said, 'What do I here any longer?' there appeared no desire of dying in her own country. I heard afterwards also, that when we were now at Ostia, she with a mother's confidence, when I was absent, one day discoursed with certain of my friends about the contempt of this life, and the blessing of death: and when they were amazed at such courage which You had given to a woman, and asked, 'Whether she were not afraid to leave her body so far from her own city?' she replied, 'Nothing is far to God; nor was it to be feared lest at the end of the world, He should not recognize whence He were to raise me up.' On the ninth day then of her sickness, and the fifty-sixth year of her age, and the three-and-thirtieth of mine, was that religious and holy soul freed from the body.

12. *He laments his mother's death*

I closed her eyes; and there flowed withal a mighty sorrow into my heart, which was overflowing into tears; mine eyes at the same time, by the violent command of my mind, drank up their fountain wholly dry; and woe was me in such a strife! But when she breathed her last, the boy Adeodatus burst out into a loud lament; then, checked by us all, held his peace. In like manner also a childish feeling in me, which was, through my heart's youthful voice, finding its vent in weeping, was checked and silenced. For we thought it not fitting to solemnize that funeral with tearful lament and groanings; for thereby do they for the most part express grief for the departed, as though unhappy, or altogether dead; whereas she was neither unhappy in her death, nor altogether dead. Of this we were assured on good grounds, the testimony of her good conversation and her faith unfeigned.

What then was it which did grievously pain me within, but a fresh wound wrought through the sudden wrench of that most sweet and dear custom of living together? I joyed indeed in her testimony, when, in that her last sickness, mingling her endearments with my acts of duty, she called me 'dutiful', and mentioned, with great affection of love, that she never had heard any harsh or reproachful sound uttered by my mouth against her. But yet, O my God, who made us, what comparison is there betwixt that honor that I paid to her, and her slavery for me? Being then forsaken of so great comfort in her, my soul was wounded, and that life rent asunder as it were, which, of hers and mine together, had been made but one.

The boy then being stilled from weeping, Euodius took up the psalter, and began to sing, our whole house answering him, the psalm, I will sing of mercy and judgments to You, O Lord. But hearing what we were doing, many brethren and religious women came together; and whilst they (whose office it was) made ready for the burial, as the manner is, I (in a part of the house, where I might properly), together with those who thought not fit to leave me, discoursed upon something fitting the time; and by this balm of truth assuaged that torment, known to You, they unknowing and listening intently, and conceiving me to be without all sense of sorrow. But in Your ears, where none of them heard, I blamed the weakness of my feelings, and refrained my flood of grief, which gave way a little unto me; but again came, as with a tide, yet not so as to burst out into tears, nor to change of countenance; still I knew what I was keeping down in my heart. And being very much displeased that these human things had such power over me, which in the due order and appointment of our natural condition must needs come to pass, with a new grief I grieved for my grief, and was thus worn by a double sorrow.

And behold, the corpse was carried to the burial; we went and returned without tears. For neither in those prayers which we poured forth unto You, when the sacrifice of our ransom was offered for her, when now the corpse was by the grave's side, as the manner there is, previous to its being laid therein, did I weep even during those prayers; yet was I the whole day in secret heavily sad, and with troubled mind prayed You, as I could, to heal my sorrow, yet You did not; impressing, I believe, upon my memory by this one instance, how strong is the bond of all habit, even upon a soul which now feeds upon no deceiving word. It seemed also good to me to go and bathe, having heard that the bath had its name (*balneum*) from the Greek *balaneion*, for that it drives sadness from the mind. And this also I confess unto Your mercy, Father of the fatherless, that I bathed, and was the same as before I bathed. For the bitterness of sorrow could not exude out of my heart. Then I slept, and woke up again, and found my grief not a little softened; and as I was alone in my bed, I remembered those true verses of Your Ambrose. For You are the

> Maker of all, the Lord
> And ruler of the height,
> Who, robing day in light, have poured
> Soft slumbers o'er the night,
> That to our limbs the power
> Of toil may be renewed,
> And hearts be raised that sink and cower,
> And sorrows be subdued.

And then by little and little I recovered my former thoughts of Your handmaid, her holy conversation towards You, her holy tenderness and observance towards us, whereof I was suddenly deprived: and I was minded to weep in Your sight, for her and for myself, in her behalf and in my own. And I gave way to the tears which I before restrained, to overflow as much as they desired; reposing my heart upon them; and it found rest in them, for it was in Your ears, not in those of man, who would have scornfully interpreted my weeping. And now, Lord, in writing I confess it unto You. Read it who will, and interpret it how he will: and if he finds sin therein, that I wept my mother for a small portion of an hour (the mother who for the time was dead to mine eyes, who had for many years wept for me that I might live in Your eyes), let him not deride me; but rather, if he be one of large charity, let him weep himself for my sins unto You, the Father of all the brethren of Your Christ.

13. *He prays for his dead mother*

But now, with a heart cured of that wound, wherein it might seem blameworthy for an earthly feeling, I pour out unto You, our God, in behalf of that Your handmaid, a far different kind of tears, flowing from a spirit shaken by the thoughts of the dangers of every soul that dies in Adam. And although she having been quickened in Christ, even before her release from the flesh, had lived to the praise of Your name for her faith and conversation; yet dare I not say that from what time You regenerated her by baptism, no word issued from her mouth against Your Commandment. Your Son, the Truth, has said, Whosoever shall say unto his brother, You fool, shall be in danger of hell fire. And woe be even unto the commendable life of men, if, laying aside mercy, You should examine it. But because You are not extreme in enquiring after sins, we confidently hope to find some place with You. But whosoever reckons up his real merits to You, what reckons he up to You but Your own gifts? O that men would know themselves to be men; and that he that glories would glory in the Lord.

I therefore, O my praise and my life, God of my heart, laying aside for a while her good deeds, for which I give thanks to You with joy, do now beseech You for the sins of my mother. Hearken unto me, I entreat You, by the medicine of our wounds, Him who hung upon the tree, and now sitting at Your right hand makes intercession to You for us. I know that she dealt mercifully, and from her heart forgave her debtors their debts; do You also forgive her debts, whatever she may have contracted in so many years, since the water of salvation. Forgive her, Lord, forgive, I beseech You; enter not into judgment with her. Let Your mercy be exalted above Your justice, since Your words are true, and You have promised mercy unto the merciful; which You granted those to be, who will have mercy where You will have mercy; and will show compassion where You have shown compassion.

And I believe, You have already done what I ask; but accept, O Lord, the free-will offerings of my mouth. For she, the day of her dissolution now at hand, took no thought to have her body sumptuously wound up, or embalmed with spices; nor desired she a choice monument, or to be buried in her own land. These things she ordered us not; but desired only to have her name commemorated at Your altar, which she had served without intermission of one day: whence she knew the holy sacrifice to be dispensed, by which the hand-writing that was against us is blotted out; through which the enemy was triumphed over, who summing up our offences, and seeking what to lay to our charge, found nothing in Him, in whom we conquer. Who shall restore to Him the innocent blood? Who repay Him the price wherewith He bought us, and so take us from Him? Unto the sacrament of which our ransom, Your handmaid bound her soul by the bond of faith. Let none sever her from Your protection: let neither the lion nor the dragon interpose himself by force or fraud. For she will not answer that she owes nothing, lest she be convicted and seized by the crafty accuser: but she will answer that her sins are forgiven her by Him, to whom none can repay that price which He, who owed nothing, paid for us.

May she rest then in peace with the husband before and after whom she had never any; whom she obeyed, with patience bringing forth fruit unto You, that she might win him also unto You. And inspire, O Lord my God, inspire Your servants my brethren, Your sons my masters, whom with voice and heart and pen I serve, that so many as shall read this, may at Your altar remember Monnica Your handmaid, with Patricius, her sometime husband, by whose bodies You brought me into this life, how I know not. May they with devout affection remember my parents in this transitory light, my brethren under You our Father in our Catholic mother, and my fellow-citizens in that eternal Jerusalem which Your pilgrim people sigh after from their exodus, even unto their return thither. That so my mother's last request of me may through my *Confessions*, more than through my prayers, be through the prayers of many, more abundantly fulfilled to her.

Book 10

1. *The confessions of the heart*

Let me know You, O Lord, who know me: let me know You, as I am known. Power of my soul, enter into it, and fit it for You, that You may have and hold it without spot or wrinkle. This is my hope, therefore do I speak; and in this hope do I rejoice, when I rejoice healthfully. Other things of this life are the less to be sorrowed for, the more they are sorrowed for; and the more to be sorrowed for, the less men sorrow for them. For behold, You love the truth, and he that does it, comes to the light. This would I do in my heart before You in confession: and in my writing, before many witnesses.

2. *Secret things are known unto God*

And from You, O Lord, unto whose eyes the abyss of man's conscience is naked, what could be hidden in me though I would not confess it? For I should hide You from me, not me from You. But now, for that my groaning is witness, that I am displeased with myself, You shine out, and are pleasing, and beloved, and longed for; that I may be ashamed of myself, and renounce myself, and choose You, and neither please You nor myself, but in You. To You therefore, O Lord, am I open, whatever I am; and with what fruit I confess unto You, I have said. Nor do I it with words and sounds of the flesh, but with the words of my soul, and the cry of the thought which Your ear knows. For when I am evil, then to confess to You is nothing else than to be displeased with myself; but when holy, nothing else than not to ascribe it to myself: because You, O Lord, bless the godly, but first You justifiy him when ungodly. My confession then, O my God, in Your sight, is made silently, and not silently. For in sound, it is silent; in affection, it cries aloud. For neither do I utter anything right unto men, which You have not before heard from me; nor do You hear any such thing from me, which You have not first said unto me.

3. *The confessions of our ill deeds, what it helps us*

What then have I to do with men, that they should hear my confessions – as if they could heal all my infirmities – a race, curious to know the lives of others, slothful to amend their own? Why seek they to hear from me what I am, who will not hear from You what themselves are? And how know they, when from myself they hear of myself, whether I say true, seeing no man knows what is in man, but the spirit of man which is in him? But if they hear from You of themselves, they cannot say, The Lord lies. For what is it to hear from You of themselves, but to know themselves? And who knows and says, It is false, unless he himself lies? But because charity believes all things (that is, among those whom knitting unto itself it makes one), I also, O Lord, will in such wise confess unto You, that men may hear, to whom I cannot demonstrate whether I confess truly; yet they believe me, whose ears charity opens unto me.

But do You, my inmost physician, make plain unto me what fruit I may reap by doing it. For the confessions of my past sins, which You have forgiven and covered, that You might bless me in You, changing my soul by faith and Your sacrament, when read and heard, stir up the heart, that it sleep not in despair and say 'I cannot', but awake in the love of Your mercy and the sweetness of Your grace, whereby whoso is weak, is strong, when by it he became conscious of his own weakness. And the good delight to hear of the past evils of such as are now freed from them, not because they are evils, but because they have been and are not. With what fruit then, O Lord my God, to whom my conscience daily confesses, trusting more in the hope of Your mercy than in her own innocency, with what fruit, I pray, do I by this book confess to men also in Your presence what I now am, not what I have been? For that other fruit I have seen and spoken of. But what I now am, at the very time of making these confessions, divers desire to know, who have or have not known me, who have heard from me or of me; but their ear is not at my heart where I am, whatever I am. They wish then to hear me confess what I am within; whither neither their eye, nor ear, nor

understanding can reach; they wish it, as ready to believe – but
will they know? For charity, whereby they are good, tells them
that in my confessions I lie not; and she in them, believes me.

4. *Of the great fruit of confession*

But for what fruit would they hear this? Do they desire to joy with
me, when they hear how near, by Your gift, I approach unto
You? And to pray for me, when they shall hear how much I am
held back by my own weight? To such will I discover myself. For
it is no mean fruit, O Lord my God, that by many thanks should
be given to You on our behalf, and You be by many entreated for
us. Let the brotherly mind love in me what You teach is to be
loved, and lament in me what You teach is to be lamented. Let a
brotherly, not a stranger, mind; not that of the foreign children,
whose mouth talks of vanity, and their right hand is a right hand of
iniquity, but that brotherly mind which when it approves, rejoices
for me, and when it disapproves, is sorry for me; because whether
it approves or disapproves, it loves me. To such will I discover
myself: they will breathe freely at my good deeds, sigh for my ill.
My good deeds are Your appointments, and Your gifts; my evil
ones are my offences, and Your judgments. Let them breathe
freely at the one, sigh at the other; and let hymns and weeping go
up into Your sight, out of the hearts of my brethren, Your censers.
And do You, O Lord, he pleased with the incense of Your holy
temple, have mercy upon me according to Your great mercy for
Your own name's sake; and no ways forsaking what You have
begun, perfect my imperfections.

This is the fruit of my confessions of what I am, not of what I
have been, to confess this, not before You only, in a secret exultation with trembling, and a secret sorrow with hope; but in the ears
also of the believing sons of men, sharers of my joy, and partners
in my mortality, my fellow-citizens, and fellow-pilgrims, who are
gone before, or are to follow on, companions of my way. These
are Your servants, my brethren, whom You will to be Your sons;
my masters, whom You command me to serve, if I would live
with You and from You. But this Your word were little did it
only command by speaking, and not go before in performing. This
then I do in deed and word, this I do under Your wings; in over
great peril, were not my soul subdued unto You under Your wings,

and my infirmity known unto You. I am a little one, but my Father ever lives, and my guardian is sufficient for me. For He is the same who begat me, and defends me: and You Yourself are all my good; You, Almighty, who are with me, yea, before I am with You. To such then whom You command me to serve will I discover, not what I have been, but what I now am and what I yet am. But neither do I judge myself. Thus therefore I would be heard.

5. *That man knows not himself thoroughly: and knows not God but in a glass darkly*

For You, Lord, do judge me: because, although no man knows the things of a man, but the spirit of a man which is in him, yet is there something of man, which not even the spirit of man that is in him, itself knows. But You, Lord, know all of him, because You have made him. Yet I, though in Your sight I despise myself, and account myself dust and ashes, yet know I something of You, which I know not of myself. And truly, now we see through a glass darkly, as yet not face to face. So long therefore as I be absent from You, I am more present with myself than with You; yet know I You, that no harm can be done to You; as for me, what temptations I can resist, and what I cannot, I know not. And there is hope, because You are faithful, who will not suffer us to be tempted above that we are able; but will with the temptation also make a way to escape, that we may be able to bear it. I will confess then what I know of myself, I will confess also what I know not of myself. And that because what I do know of myself, I know by Your shining upon me; and what I know not of myself, so long know I not it, until my darkness be made as the noon-day in Your countenance.

6. *What God is, and how known*

Not with doubting, but with assured consciousness, do I love You, Lord. You struck my heart with Your word, and I loved You. Yea also heaven, and earth, and all that therein is, behold, on every side they bid me love You; nor cease to say so unto all, to leave them no excuse. But more deeply will You have mercy on whom You will have mercy, and will have compassion on whom You have had compassion: else in deaf ears do the heaven and the earth speak Your praises. But what do I love, when I love You? Not beauty of bodies, nor the fair harmony of time, nor the brightness of the light, so gladsome to our eyes, nor sweet melodies of varied songs, nor the fragrant smell of flowers and ointments and spices, not manna and honey, not limbs acceptable to embracements of flesh. None of these I love, when I love my God; and yet I love a kind of light, and melody, and fragrance, and meat, and embracement when I love my God, the light, melody, fragrance, meat, embracement of my inner man: where there shines unto my soul what space cannot contain, and there sounds what time bears not away, and there smells what breathing disperses not, and there tastes what eating diminishes not, and there clings what satiety divorces not. This is it which I love when I love my God.

And what is this? I asked the earth, and it answered me, I am not it; and the things which are in the earth confessed the same. I asked the sea and the deeps, and the living creeping things, and they answered, We are not your god, seek above us. I asked the moving air; and the whole air with its inhabitants answered, Anaximenes is wrong, I am not god. I asked the heavens, sun, moon, stars, Neither are we (say they) the God whom you seek. And I replied unto all the things which encompass the door of my flesh: You have told me of my God, that you are not He; tell me something of Him. And they cried out with a loud voice, He made us. My thought was my questioning, and their appearance was their answer. And I turned myself unto myself, and said to myself, Who are you? And I answered, A man. And behold, in me there present themselves to me soul and body, one without, the other within. By which of these ought I to seek my God? I had sought Him in the body from earth to heaven, so far as I could send messengers, the beams of mine eyes. But the better is the inner, for to it as presiding and judging, all the bodily messengers reported the answers of heaven and earth, and all things therein, who said, We are not God, but He himself made us. These things did my inner man know by the ministry of the outer: I the inner knew them; I, the mind, through the senses of my body. I asked the whole frame of the world about my God; and it answered me, I am not he, but he made me.

Is not this corporeal figure apparent to all whose senses are perfect? Why then speaks it not the same to all? Animals small and great see it, but they cannot ask it, because no reason is set over their senses to judge on what they report. But men can ask, so that the invisible things of God are clearly seen, being understood by the things that are made; but by love of them, they are made subject unto them: and subjects cannot judge. Nor yet do the creatures answer such as ask, unless they can judge; nor yet do they change their voice (i.e. their appearance) if one man merely sees, while another sees and asks, so as to appear one way to one man, and another way to another; but appearing the same way to both, it is dumb to one, and speaks to the other; yea rather it speaks to all, but only they understand, who compare its voice received from without, with the truth within. For truth says unto me, Neither heaven, nor earth, nor any other body is your God. This, their very nature declares. And they see: a mass is less in part than in the whole. Now you, my soul, are my better part: to you I speak; for you quicken the mass of my body, giving it life, which no body can give to body: but your God is indeed to you the life of your life.

7. *God is not to be found by any ability in our bodies*

What then do I love, when I love my God? Who is He above the head of my soul? By my very soul will I ascend to Him. I will pass beyond that power whereby I am united to my body, and fill its whole frame with life. Nor can I by that power find my God; for so horse and mule that have no understanding might find Him; seeing it is the same power, whereby even their bodies live. But another power there is, not that only whereby I animate, but that too whereby I imbue with sense my flesh, which the Lord has framed for me: commanding the eye not to hear, and the ear not to see; but the eye, that through it I should see, and the ear, that through it I should hear; and to the other senses severally, in their own peculiar seats and offices; which I, the one mind, do make use of in my various actions. I will pass beyond this power of mine also; for this also have the horse and mule, for they also perceive through the body.

8. *The force of the memory*

I will pass then beyond this power of my nature also, rising by degrees unto Him who made me. And I come to the fields and spacious palaces of my memory, where are the treasures of innumerable images, brought into it from things of all sorts perceived by the senses. There is stored up, whatsoever besides we think, either by enlarging or diminishing, or any other way varying those things which the sense has come to; and whatever else has been committed and laid up, which forgetfulness has not yet swallowed up and buried. When I enter there, I demand whatever I choose to be brought forth; some things come instantly; others must be longer sought after, which are fetched, as it were, out of some inner receptacle; others rush out in troops, and while one thing is desired and required, they start forth, as who should say, Is it perchance I? These I drive away with the hand of my heart, from the face of my remembrance; until what I wish for be unveiled, and appear in sight, out of its secret place. Other things come up readily, in unbroken order, as they are called for, those in front making way for the following; and as they make way, they are hidden from sight, ready to come when I will. All which takes place when I repeat a thing by heart.

There are all things preserved distinctly and under general heads, each having entered by its own avenue: as light, and all colors and forms of bodies, by the eyes; by the ears, all sorts of sounds; all smells, by the avenue of the nostrils; all tastes, by the mouth; and by the sensation of the whole body, what is hard or soft, hot or cold, smooth or rough, heavy or light, either outwardly or inwardly to the body. All these the memory receives in her numberless secret and inexpressible windings, to be forthcoming, and brought out at need; each entering in by his own gate, and there laid up. Nor yet do the things themselves enter in; only the images of the things perceived are there in readiness, for thought to recall. Which images, how they are formed, who can tell, though it does plainly appear by which sense each has been brought in and stored up? For even while I dwell in darkness and silence, in my memory I can produce colors, if I will, and distinguish betwixt black and white, and what others I will: nor yet do sounds break in and disturb the image drawn in by my eyes, which I am reviewing, though they also are there, lying dormant, and laid up, as it were, apart. For these too I call for, and forthwith they appear. And though my tongue be still, and my throat mute, so can I sing as much as I will; nor do those images of colors, which notwithstanding be there, intrude themselves and interrupt, when another store is called for, which flowed in by the ears. So the other things, piled in and up by the other senses, I recall at my pleasure. Yea, I distinguish the breath of lilies from violets, though smelling nothing; and I prefer honey to sweet wine, smooth before rough, at the time neither tasting nor handling, but remembering only.

These things do I within, in that vast court of my memory. For there are present with me, heaven, earth, sea, and whatever I could think on therein, besides what I have forgotten. There also meet I with myself, and recall myself, and when, where, and what I have done, and under what feelings. There is everything I remember, either from my own experience, or from hearsay. Out of the same store do I myself with the past continually combine other and yet other likenesses of things which I have experienced, or, from what I have experienced, have believed: and thence again infer future actions, events and hopes, and all these again I reflect on, as present. 'I will do this or that,' say I to myself, in that great receptacle of my mind, stored with the images of things so many and so great, 'and this or that will follow.' 'O that this or that might be!' 'God avert this or that!' So speak I to myself: and when I speak, the images of all I speak of are present, out of the same treasury of memory; nor would I speak of any thereof, were the images wanting.

Great is this force of memory, too great, O my God; a large and boundless chamber! Who ever sounded the bottom thereof? Yet is this a power of mine, and belongs unto my nature; nor do I myself comprehend all that I am. Therefore is the mind too narrow to contain itself. And where should that be, which it contains not of itself? Is it without it, and not within? How then does it not comprehend itself? A wonderful admiration surprises me, amazement seizes me upon this. And men go abroad to admire the heights of mountains, the mighty billows of the sea, the broad tides of rivers, the compass of the ocean, and the circuits of the stars, and pass themselves by; nor wonder that when I spoke of all these things, I did not see them with mine eyes, yet could not have spoken of them, unless I then actually saw the mountains, billows, rivers, stars which I had seen, and that ocean which I believe to be, inwardly in my memory, and that, with the same vast spaces between, as if I saw them abroad. Yet did not I by seeing draw them into myself, when with mine eyes I beheld them; nor are they themselves with me, but their images only. And I know by what sense of the body each was impressed upon me.

9. *The memory of divers sciences*

Yet these are not all that the unmeasurable capacity of my memory retains. Here also is everything I have learnt, and not yet forgotten, of the liberal sciences; removed as it were to some inner place, which is yet no place: nor are they the images thereof, but the things themselves. For, what literature is, what the art of disputing, how many kinds of questions there be, whatsoever of these I know, so exists in my memory, as that I have not taken in the image and left out the thing, or that it has sounded and passed away like a voice fixed on the ear by that impress, whereby it might be recalled, as if it sounded, when it no longer sounded; or as a smell while it passes and evaporates into air affects the sense of smell, whence it conveys into the memory an image of itself, which remembering, we renew, or as meat, which verily in the belly has now no taste, and yet in the memory still in a manner tastes; or as anything which the body by touch perceives, and which when removed from us, the memory still conceives. For those things are not transmitted into the memory, but their images only are with an admirable swiftness caught up, and stored as it were in wondrous cabinets, and thence wonderfully by the act of remembering, brought forth.

10. *Our senses convey things into our memory*

But now when I hear that there are three kinds of questions: Whether the thing be? What it is? Of what kind it is? I do indeed hold the images of the sounds of which those words be composed; I know that those sounds passed through the air with a noise, and now are not. But the actual things signified by those sounds, I never reached with any sense of my body, nor ever discerned them otherwise than in my mind; yet in my memory have I laid up not their images, but themselves. Which how they entered into me, let them say if they can; for I have gone over all the avenues of my flesh, but cannot find by which they entered. For the eyes say, those images were colored, we reported of them. The ears say, they made a sound, then it was we who drew attention to them.

The nostrils say, If they smell, they passed through us. The taste says, Unless they have a flavor, ask me not. The touch says, If it have not size, I handled it not; if I handled it not, I gave no notice of it. From where, and how, did these things enter into my memory? I know not how. For when I learned them, I gave not credit to another man's mind, but recognized them in mine; and approving them for true, I commended them to it, laying them up as it were, whence I might bring them forth when I willed. In my heart then they were, even before I learned them, but in my memory they were not. Where then? Or wherefore, when they were spoken, did I acknowledge them, and say, So is it, it is true, unless that they were already in the memory, but so thrown back and buried as it were in deeper recesses, that had not the suggestion of another drawn them forth I had perchance been unable to conceive of them?

11. *The forms of things are in the soul*

Wherefore we find, that to learn these things whereof we imbibe not the images by our senses, but perceive within by themselves, without images, as they are, is nothing else, but by conception to receive, and by marking to take heed that those things which the memory did before contain at random and unarranged, be laid up at hand as it were in that same memory where before they lay unknown, scattered and neglected, and so readily occur to the mind familiarized to them. And how many things of this kind does my memory bear which have been already found out, and as I said, placed as it were at hand, which we are said to have learned and come to know which were I for some short space of time to cease to call to mind, they are again so buried, and glide back, as it were, into the deeper recesses, that they must again, as if new, be thought out thence, for other abode they have none: but they must be drawn together again, that they may be known; that is to say, they must as it were be collected together from their dispersion: whence the word 'cogitation' is derived. For *cogo* (collect) and *cogito* (re-collect) have the same relation to each other as *ago* and *agito*, *facio* and *factito*. But the mind has appropriated to itself this word (cogitation), so that, not what is 'collected' any how, but what is 'recollected', i.e., brought together, in the mind, is properly said to be cogitated, or thought upon.

12. *The memory of mathematicians*

The memory contains also the reasons and laws innumerable of numbers and dimensions, none of which has any bodily sense impressed; seeing they have neither color, nor sound, nor taste, nor smell, nor touch. I have heard the sound of the words whereby when discussed they are denoted: but the sounds are other than the things. For the sounds are other in Greek than in Latin; but the things are neither Greek, nor Latin, nor any other language. I have seen the lines of architects, the very finest, like a spider's thread; but those are still different, they are not the images of those lines which the eye of flesh showed me: anyone knows them, who without any conception whatsoever of a body, recognises them within himself. I have indeed perceived the numbers, with all the senses of my body, which we can count; but those numbers wherewith we number are different; they are not images of those others, and therefore they do exist. Let him who sees them not, deride me for saying these things, and I will pity him, while he derides me.

13. *The memory of memory*

All these things I remember, and I remember how I learnt them. Many things also most falsely objected against them have I heard, and remember; which though they be false, yet is it not false that I remember them; and I remember also that I have distinguished betwixt those truths and these falsehoods objected to them. And I perceive that the present distinguishing of these things is different from remembering that I often distinguished them, when I often thought upon them. I both remember that I often understood these things; and what I now distinguish and understand, I lay up in my memory, that hereafter I may remember that I did understand now. So then I remember also to have remembered; just as later, if I recall that I was now able to remember these things, I shall certainly recall it by the force of memory.

14. *How, when we are not glad, we call to mind things that have made us glad*

The same memory contains also the affections of my mind, not in the same manner that my mind itself contains them, when it feels them; but far otherwise, according to a power of its own. For without rejoicing I remember myself to have joyed; and without sorrow do I recollect my past sorrow. And what I once feared, I review without fear; and without desire call to mind a past desire. Sometimes, on the contrary, I remember with joy my past sorrow, and with sorrow, joy. Which is not wonderful, as to the body; for mind is one thing, body another. If I therefore with joy remember some past pain of body, it is not so wonderful. But now seeing this very memory itself is mind (for when we give a thing in charge, to be kept in memory, we say, See that you keep it in mind; and when we forget, we say, It did not come to mind, and, It slipped my mind, calling the memory itself the mind); this being so, how is it that when with joy I remember my past sorrow, the mind has joy, the memory has sorrow; the mind upon the joyfulness which is in it, is joyful, yet the memory upon the sadness which is in it, is not sad? Does the memory perchance not belong to the mind? Who will say so? The memory then is, as it were, the belly of the mind; and joy and sadness, like sweet and bitter food, which, when committed to the memory, are as it were passed into the belly, where they may be stowed, but cannot taste. It is absurd to imagine these to be alike; and yet are they not utterly unlike.

But, behold, out of my memory I bring it, when I say there be four perturbations of the mind, desire, joy, fear, sorrow; and whatsoever I can dispute thereon, by dividing each into its subordinate species, and by defining it, I find in my memory what to say, and thence do I bring it: yet am I not disturbed by any of these perturbations, when by calling them to mind, I remember them; yea, and before I recalled and brought them back, they were there; and that is why they could, by recollection, thence be brought. Perchance, then, as meat is by chewing the cud brought up out of the belly, so by recollection these out of the memory. Why then does not the disputer, thus recollecting, taste in the mouth of his musing the sweetness of joy, or the bitterness of sorrow? Is the comparison unlike in this, because not in all respects like? For who would willingly speak thereof, if so oft as we name grief or fear, we should be compelled to be sad or fearful? And yet we could not speak of them, if we did not find in our memory, not only the sounds of the names according to the images impressed by the senses of the body, but notions of the very things themselves which we never received by any avenue of the body, but which the mind itself perceiving by the experience of its own passions, committed to the memory, or the memory of itself retained, without them being committed unto it.

15. *We remember absent things also*

But whether by images or no, who can readily say? Thus, I name a stone, I name the sun, the things themselves not being present to my senses, but their images to my memory. I name a bodily pain, yet it is not present with me, when nothing aches: yet unless its image were present to my memory, I should not know what to say thereof, nor in discoursing distinguish pain from pleasure. I name bodily health; being sound in body, the thing itself is present with me; yet, unless its image also were present in my memory, I could by no means recall what the sound of this name should signify. Nor would the sick, when health were named, recognize what were spoken, unless the same image were by the force of memory retained, although the thing itself were absent from the body. I name numbers whereby we number; and not their images, but themselves are present in my memory. I name the image of the sun, and that image is present in my memory. For I recall not the image of its image, but the image itself is present to me, calling it to mind. I name memory, and I recognize what I name. And where do I recognize it, but in the memory itself? Is it also present to itself by its image, and not by itself?

16. *There is a memory of forgetfulness also*

What, when I name forgetfulness, and withal recognize what I name? Whence should I recognize it, did I not remember it? I speak not of the sound of the name, but of the thing which it signifies: which if I had forgotten, I could not recognize what that sound signifies. When then I remember memory, memory itself is, through itself, present with itself: but when I remember forgetfulness, there are present both memory and forgetfulness; memory whereby I remember, forgetfulness which I remember. But what is forgetfulness, but the privation of memory? How then is that present for me to remember, which when present I cannot remember? But if what we remember we hold in memory, whereas with forgetfulness, if we did not remember it, we could never when we hear the name recognize the thing thereby signified, then forgetfulness is retained by memory. It is there to stop us forgetting, though when it is there, we do forget. It is to be understood from this that forgetfulness, when we remember it, is not present to the memory by itself but by its image: because if it were present by itself, it would not cause us to remember, but to forget. Who now shall search this out? Who shall comprehend how it is?

Lord, I truly toil therein, yea and toil in myself; I am become a heavy soil requiring overmuch sweat of the brow. For we are not now searching out the regions of heaven, or measuring the distances of the stars, or enquiring the balancings of the earth. It is I myself who remember, I the mind. It is not so wonderful, if what I myself am not, be far from me. But what is nearer to me than myself? And lo, the force of mine own memory is not understood by me, though I cannot so much as name myself without it. For what shall I say, when it is clear to me that I remember forgetfulness? Shall I say that that is not in my memory, which I remember? Or shall I say that forgetfulness is for this purpose in my memory, that I might not forget? Both were most absurd. What third way is there? How can I say that the image of forgetfulness is retained by my memory, not forgetfulness itself, when I remember it? How could I say this either, seeing that when the image of anything is impressed on the memory, the thing itself must needs be first present, whence that image may be impressed? For thus do I remember Carthage, thus all places where I have been, thus men's faces whom I have seen, and things reported by the other senses; thus the health or sickness of the body. For when these things were present, my memory received from them images, which being present with me, I might look on and bring back in my mind, when I remembered them in their absence. If then this forgetfulness is retained in the memory through its image, not through itself, then plainly itself was once present, that its image might be taken. But when it was present, how did it write its image in the memory, seeing that forgetfulness by its presence effaces even what it finds already noted? And yet, in whatever way, although that way be past conceiving and explaining, yet certain am I that I remember forgetfulness itself also, whereby what we remember is effaced.

17. *A threefold power of memory*

Great is the power of memory, a fearful thing, O my God, a deep and boundless manifoldness; and this thing is the mind, and this am I myself. What am I then, O my God? What nature am I? A life various and manifold, and exceeding immense. Behold in the plains and caves and caverns of my memory, innumerable and innumerably full of innumerable kinds of things, either through images, as all bodies; or by actual presence, as the arts; or by certain notions or impressions, as the affections of the mind, which, even when the mind does not feel, the memory retains, while yet whatsoever is in the memory is also in the mind — over all these do I run, I fly; I dive on this side and on that, as far as I can, and there is no end. So great is the force of memory, so great the force of life, even in the mortal life of man. What shall I do then, O You my true life, my God? I will pass even beyond this power of mine which is called memory: yea, I will pass beyond it, that I may approach unto You, O sweet Light. What say You to me? See, I am mounting up through my mind towards You who abide above me. Yea, I now will pass beyond this power of mine which is called memory, desirous to touch You, from whatever direction You may be touched; and to hold fast to You, from whatever direction one may hold fast to You. For even beasts and birds have memory; else could they not return to their dens and nests, nor many other things they are used to: nor indeed could they be used to anything, but by memory. I will pass then beyond memory also, that I may arrive at Him who has separated me from the four-footed beasts and made me wiser than the fowls of the air. I will pass beyond memory also, and where shall I find You, You truly good and certain sweetness? And where shall I find You? If I find You without my memory, then do I not retain You in my memory. And how shall I find You, if I remember You not?

18. *Of the remembrance*

For the woman that had lost her groat, and sought it with a light; unless she had remembered it, she had never found it. For when it was found, whence should she know whether it were the same, unless she remembered it? I remember to have sought and found many a thing; and this I thereby know, that when I was seeking any of them, and was asked, Is this it? Is that it? so long said I

No, until that were offered me which I sought. Which had I not remembered (whatever it were) though it were offered me, yet should I not find it, because I could not recognize it. And so it ever is, when we seek and find any lost thing. Notwithstanding, when anything is by chance lost from the sight, not from the memory (as any visible body), yet its image is still retained within, and it is sought until it be restored to sight; and when it is found, it is recognized by the image which is within: nor do we say that we have found what was lost, unless we recognize it; nor can we recognize it, unless we remember it. This was indeed lost to the eyes, but retained in the memory.

19. *What remembrance is*

But what when the memory itself loses anything, as falls out when we forget and seek that we may recollect? Where in the end do we search, but in the memory itself? And there, if one thing be perchance offered instead of another, we reject it, until what we seek meets us; and when it does, we say, This is it; which we should not unless we recognized it, nor recognize it unless we remembered it. Certainly then we had forgotten it. Or, the whole had not escaped us, but the lost part was sought for by the part whereof we had hold; in that the memory felt that it did not carry on together all which it was wont, and maimed, as it were, by the curtailment of its ancient habit, demanded the restoration of what it missed? For instance, if we see or think of someone known to us, and having forgotten his name, try to recover it; whatever else occurs, connects itself not therewith, because it was not wont to be thought upon together with him, and therefore is rejected, until that present itself, whereon the knowledge reposes equably as its wonted object. And whence does that present itself, but out of the memory itself? For even when we recognize it, on being reminded by another, it is thence it comes. For we do not believe it as something new, but, upon recollection, allow what was named to be right. But were it utterly blotted out of the mind, we should not remember it, even when reminded. For we have not as yet utterly forgotten that, which we remember ourselves to have forgotten. What then we have utterly forgotten, though lost, we cannot even seek after.

20. *All men desire blessedness*

How then do I seek You, O Lord? For when I seek You, my God, I seek a happy life. I will seek You, that my soul may live. For my body lives by my soul; and my soul by You. How then do I seek a happy life, seeing I have it not, until I can say, where I ought to say it, It is enough? How seek I it? By remembrance, as though I had forgotten it, remembering that I had forgotten it? Or, desiring to learn it as a thing unknown, either never having known, or so forgotten it, as not even to remember that I had forgotten it? Is not a happy life what all will, and no one altogether wills it not? Where have they known it, that they so will it? Where seen it, that they so love it? Truly we have it, how, I know not. Yea, there is another way, wherein when one has it, then is he happy; and there are, who are blessed, in hope. These have it in a lower kind, than they who have it in very deed; yet are they better off than such as are happy neither in deed nor in hope. Yet even these, had they it not in some sort, would not so will to be happy, which that they do will, is most certain. They have known it then, I know not how, and so have it by some sort of knowledge, what, I know not, and am perplexed whether it be in the memory, which if it be, then we have been happy once; whether all severally, or in that man who first sinned, in whom also we all died, and from whom we are all born with misery, I now enquire not; but only, whether the happy life be in the memory? For neither should we love it, did we not know it. We hear the name, and we all confess that we desire the thing; for we are not delighted with the mere sound. For when a Greek hears it in Latin, he is not delighted, not knowing what is spoken; but we Latins are delighted, as would he too, if he heard it in Greek; because the thing itself is neither Greek nor Latin, which Greeks and Latins, and men of all other tongues, long for so earnestly. Known therefore it is to all, for if they could with one voice be asked, do they wish to be happy? they would answer without hesitation, they do. And this could not be, unless the thing itself whereof it is the name were retained in their memory.

21. *We also remember what we never had*

But is it in the way I remember Carthage, I who have seen it? No. For a happy life is not seen with the eye, because it is not a body. As we remember numbers then? No. For these, he that has in his knowledge, seeks not further to attain unto; but a happy life we have in our knowledge, and therefore love it, and yet still desire to attain it, that we may be happy. As we remember eloquence then? No. For although upon hearing this name also, some call to mind the thing, who still are not yet eloquent, and many who desire to be so, whence it appears that it is in their knowledge; yet these have by their bodily senses observed others to be eloquent, and been delighted, and desire to be the like (though indeed they would not be delighted but for some inward knowledge thereof, nor wish to be the like, unless they were thus delighted); whereas a happy life, we do by no bodily sense experience in others. As then we remember joy? Perchance; for my joy I remember, even when sad, as a happy life, when unhappy; nor did I ever with bodily sense see, hear, smell, taste, or touch my joy; but I experienced it in my mind, when I rejoiced; and the knowledge of it stuck fast in my memory, so that I have the power to recall it with disgust sometimes, at others with longing, according to the nature of the things, wherein I remember myself to have joyed. For even from foul things have I been immersed in a sort of joy; which now recalling, I detest and execrate; otherwhiles in good and honest things, which I recall with longing, although perchance no longer present; and therefore with sadness I recall former joy.

Where then and when did I experience my happy life, that I should remember, and love, and long for it? Nor is it I alone, or some few besides, but we all would fain be happy; which, unless by some certain knowledge we knew, we should not with so certain a will desire. But how is this, that if two men be asked whether they would go to the wars, one, perchance, would answer that he would, the other, that he would not; but if they were asked whether they would be happy, both would instantly without any doubting say they would; and for no other reason would the one go to the wars, and the other not, but to be happy. Is it perchance that as one looks for his joy in this thing, another in that, all agree in their desire of being happy, as they would (if they were asked) that they wished to have joy, and this joy they call a happy life? Although then one obtains this joy by one means, another by another, all have one end, which they strive to attain, namely, joy. Which being a thing which all must say they have experienced, it is therefore found in the memory, and recognized whenever the name of a happy life is mentioned.

22. *True joy, is this blessed life*

Far be it, Lord, far be it from the heart of Your servant who here confesses unto You, far be it, that, be the joy what it may, I should therefore think myself happy. For there is a joy which is not given to the ungodly, but to those who love You for Your own sake, whose joy You Yourself are. And this is the happy life, to rejoice to You, of You, for You; this is it, and there is no other. For they who think there is another, pursue some other and not the true joy. Yet is not their will turned away from some semblance of joy.

23. *A blessed life; what, and where, it is*

It is not certain then that all wish to be happy, inasmuch as they who wish not to joy in You, which is the only happy life, do not truly desire the happy life. Or do all men desire this, but because the flesh lusts against the spirit, and the spirit against the flesh, that they cannot do what they would, they fall upon that which they can, and are content therewith; because, what they are not able to do, they do not will so strongly as would suffice to make them able? For I ask anyone, had he rather joy in truth, or in falsehood? They will as little hesitate to say, in the truth, as to say, that they desire to be happy, for a happy life is joy in the truth: for this is a joying in You, who are the truth, O God my light, health of my countenance, my God. This is the happy life which all desire; this life which alone is happy, all desire; to joy in the truth all desire. I have met with many that would deceive; who would *be* deceived, no one. Where then did they know this happy life, save where they know the truth also? For they love it also, since they would not be deceived. And when they love a happy life, which is no other than joying in the truth, then also do they love the truth; which yet they would not love, were there not some notice of it in their memory. Why then joy they not in it? Why are they not happy? Because they are more strongly taken up with other things which have more power to make them miserable, than that which they so faintly remember to make them happy. For there is yet a little light in men; let them walk, let them walk, that the darkness overtake them not.

But why does truth bring forth hatred, and the man of Yours, preaching the truth, become an enemy to them? Whereas a happy life is loved, which is nothing else but joying in the truth; unless that truth is in that kind loved, that they who love anything else would gladly have that which they love to be the truth: and because they do not want to be deceived, will not be convinced that they are so? Therefore do they hate the truth for that thing's sake which they loved instead of the truth. They love truth when she enlightens, they hate her when she reproves them. For since they do not want to be deceived, but do want to deceive, they love her when she reveals herself unto them, and hate her when she reveals them. Whence she shall so repay them, that they who would not be made manifest by her, she both against their will makes manifest, and herself becomes not manifest unto them. Thus, thus, yea thus does the mind of man, thus blind and sick, foul and ill-favored, wish to be hidden; but that anything should be hidden from it, it wills not. Its reward is the contrary: that itself is not hidden from the truth, but the truth is hid from it. Yet even thus miserable, it had rather joy in truths than in falsehoods. Happy then will it be, when, no distraction interposing, it shall joy in that only truth, by whom all things are true.

24. *That the memory contains God too*

See what a space I have gone over in my memory seeking You, O Lord; and I have not found You, outside it. Nor have I found anything concerning You, but what I have kept in memory, ever since I learnt You. For since I learnt You, I have not forgotten You. For where I found truth, there found I my God, the truth itself; which since I learnt, I have not forgotten. Since then I learnt You, You reside in my memory; and there do I find You, when I call You to remembrance, and delight in You. These be my holy delights, which You have given me in Your mercy, having regard to my poverty.

25. *In what degree of the memory God is found*

But where in my memory do You reside, O Lord, where do You reside there? What manner of lodging have You framed for Yourself? What manner of sanctuary have You built Yourself? You have given this honor to my memory, to reside in it; but in what quarter of it You reside, that am I considering. For in thinking on You, I passed beyond such parts of it as the beasts also have, for I found You not there among the images of corporeal things: and I came to those parts to which I committed the affections of my mind, nor found You there. And I entered into the very seat of my mind (which it has in my memory, inasmuch as the mind remembers itself also), neither were You there: for as You are not a corporeal image, nor the affection of a living being (as when we rejoice, condole, desire, fear, remember, forget, or the like); so neither are You the mind itself; because You are the Lord God of the mind; and all these are changed, but You remain unchangeable over all, and yet have vouchsafed to dwell in my memory, since I learnt You. And why seek I now in what place thereof You dwell, as if there were places therein? Sure I am, that in it You dwell, since I have remembered You ever since I learnt You, and there I find You, when I call You to remembrance.

26. *Whereabouts God is to be found*

Where then did I find You, that I might learn You? For You were not in my memory, before I learned You. Where then did I find You, that I might learn You, but in You above me? Place there is none; we go backward and forward, and there is no place. Everywhere, O truth, do You give audience to all who ask counsel of You, and at once answer all, though they ask Your counsel on manifold matters. Clearly do You answer, though all do not clearly hear. All consult You on what they will, though they hear not always what they will. He is Your best servant who looks not so much to hear that from You which himself wills, as rather to will that which he hears from You.

27. *How God draws us to himself*

Too late I loved You, O You beauty of ancient days, yet ever new! Too late I loved You! And behold, You were within, and I abroad, and there I searched for You; deformed I, plunging amid those fair forms which You had made. You were with me, but I was not with You. Things held me far from You, which, unless they were in You, were not at all. You called, and shouted, and burst my deafness. You flashed, shone, and scattered my blindness.

You breathed odors, and I drew in breath and now pant for You. I tasted, and do now hunger and thirst. You touched me, and I burned for Your peace.

28. *The misery of this life*

When I shall with my whole self hold fast to You, I shall nowhere have sorrow or labour; and my life shall wholly live, as wholly full of You. But now since whom You fill, You lift up, because I am not full of You I am a burden to myself. Lamentable joys strive with joyous sorrows: and on which side is the victory, I know not. Woe is me! Lord, have pity on me. My evil sorrows strive with my good joys; and on which side is the victory, I know not. Woe is me! Lord, have pity on me. Woe is me! Lo! I hide not my wounds; You are the physician, I the sick; You merciful, I miserable. Is not the life of man upon earth all trial? Who wishes for troubles and difficulties? You command them to be endured, not to be loved. No man loves what he endures, though he love to endure. For though he rejoices that he endures, he had rather there were nothing for him to endure. In adversity I long for prosperity, in prosperity I fear adversity. What middle place is there betwixt these two, where the life of man is not all trial? Woe to the prosperities of the world, once and again, through fear of adversity, and corruption of joy! Woe to the adversities of the world, once and again, and the third time, from the longing for prosperity, and because adversity itself is a hard thing, and lest it shatter endurance. Is not the life of man upon earth all trial, without any interval?

29. *Our hope is all in God*

And all my hope is nowhere but in Your exceeding great mercy. Give what You order, and order what You will. You command us continency; and when I knew, says one, that no man can be continent, unless God give it, this also was a part of wisdom to know whose gift she is. By continency verily are we bound up and brought back into One, whence we were dissipated into many. For too little does he love You, who loves anything with You, which he loves not for You. O love, who ever burn and never consume! O charity, my God, kindle me. You order continency: give me what You order, and order what You will.

30. *The deceitfulness of dreams*

Truly You order me continency from the lust of the flesh, the
lust of the eyes, and the ambition of the world. You order
continency from concubinage; and for wedlock itself, You have
counselled something better than what You have permitted. And
since You gave it, it was done, even before I became a dispenser
of Your sacrament. But there yet live in my memory (whereof I
have much spoken) the images of such things as my ill custom
there fixed; which haunt me, strengthless when I am awake: but
in sleep, not only so as to give pleasure, but even to obtain assent,
and what is very like reality. Yea, so far prevails the illusion of the
image, in my soul and in my flesh, that, when asleep, false visions
persuade to that which when waking, the true cannot. Am I not
then myself, O Lord my God? And yet there is so much difference betwixt myself and myself, within that moment wherein I
pass from waking to sleeping, or return from sleeping to waking!
Where is reason then, which, awake, resists such suggestions?
And should the things themselves be urged on it, it remains
unshaken. Is it clasped up with the eyes? Is it lulled asleep with
the senses of the body? And whence is it that often even in sleep
we resist, and mindful of our purpose, and abiding most chastely
in it, yield no assent to such enticements? And yet so much
difference there is, that when it happens otherwise, upon waking
we return to peace of conscience: and by this very difference
discover that we did not do, which yet we are sorry was in some
way done in us.

Are You not mighty, God almighty, so as to heal all the diseases
of my soul, and by Your more abundant grace to quench even the
impure motions of my sleep! You will increase, Lord, Your gifts
more and more in me, that my soul may follow me to You,
disentangled from the birdlime of concupiscence; that it rebel not
against itself, and even in dreams not only not commit those
debasing corruptions through images of sense, even to pollution of
the flesh, but not even to consent unto them. For that nothing of
this sort should have the very least influence over the pure affections even of a sleeper, not even such as a thought would restrain –
to work this, not only in this life, but also in this age, is not hard
for the almighty, You who are able to do above all that we ask or
think. But what I yet am in this kind of my evil, have I confessed

unto my good Lord; rejoicing with trembling, in that which You have given me, and bemoaning that wherein I am still imperfect; hoping that You will perfect Your mercies in me, even to perfect peace, which my outward and inward man shall have with You, when death shall be swallowed up in victory.

31. *The temptation of eating and drinking*

There is another evil of the day, which I would were sufficient for it. For by eating and drinking we repair the daily decays of our body, until You destroy both belly and meat, when You shall slay my emptiness with a wonderful fullness, and clothe this incorruptible with an eternal incorruption. But now the necessity is sweet unto me, against which sweetness I fight, that I be not taken captive, and carry on a daily war by fastings; often bringing my body into subjection, and my pains are driven away by pleasure. For hunger and thirst are in a manner pains; they burn and kill like a fever, unless the medicine of nourishments come to our aid. Which since it is at hand through the consolations of Your gifts, whereby land and water and air serve our weakness, our calamity is termed gratification.

This have You taught me, that I should set myself to take food as physic. But while I am passing from the discomfort of emptiness to the content of replenishing, in the very passage the snare of concupiscence besets me. For that passing, is pleasure, nor is there any other way to pass thither, whither we needs must pass. And health being the cause of eating and drinking, there joins itself as an attendant a dangerous pleasure, which mostly endeavors to go before it, so that I may for her sake do what I say I do, or wish to do, for health's sake. Nor have each the same measure; for what is enough for health, is too little for pleasure. And oft it is uncertain, whether it be the necessary care of the body which is yet asking for sustenance, or whether a voluptuous and deceiving greediness is proffering its services. In this uncertainty the unhappy soul rejoices, and therein prepares an excuse to shield itself, glad that it is not apparent what suffices for the moderation of health, that under the cloak of health it may disguise the business of gratification. These temptations I daily endeavor to resist, and I call on Your right hand, and to You do I refer my perplexities; because I have as yet no settled counsel herein.

I hear the voice of my God commanding, Let not your hearts be overcharged with surfeiting and drunkenness. Drunkenness is far from me; You will have mercy, that it come not near me. But full feeding sometimes creeps upon Your servant; You will have mercy, that it may be far from me. For no one can be continent unless You give it. Many things You give us, when we pray for them; and what good soever we have received before we prayed, from You we received it; yea to the end we might afterwards know this, did we before receive it. Drunkard was I never, but drunkards have I known made sober by You. From You then it was, that they who never were such, should not so be, as from You it was, that they who have been, should not so be for ever; and from You it was, that both might know from whom it was. I heard another voice of Yours, Go not after your lusts, and from your pleasure turn away. Yea by Your favor have I heard that which I have much loved, Neither if we eat, shall we abound; neither if we eat not, shall we lack; which is to say, neither shall the one make me plenteous, nor the other miserable. I heard also another, For I have learned in whatsoever state I am, therewith to be content; I know how to abound, and how to suffer need. I can do all things through Christ that strengthens me. Behold a soldier of the heavenly camp, not the dust which we are. But remember, Lord, that we are dust, and that of dust You have made man; and he was lost and is found. Nor could he of himself do this, because he whom I so loved, saying this through the in-breathing of Your inspiration, was of the same dust. I can do all things (says he) through Him that strengthens me. Strengthen me, that I can. Give what You order, and order what You will. He confesses to have received, and when he glories, he glories in the Lord. Another have I heard begging that he might receive. Take from me (says he) the desires of the belly; whence it it is apparent, O my holy God, that it is Your gift, when that is done which You command to be done.

You have taught me, good Father, that to the pure, all things are pure; but that it is evil unto the man that eats with offence; and, that every creature of Yours is good, and nothing to be refused, which is received with thanksgiving; and that meat commends us not to God; and, that no man should judge us in meat or drink; and, that he which eats, let him not despise him that eats not; and let not him that eats not, judge him that eats. These things have I learned, thanks be to You, praise to You, my God, my teacher, knocking at my ears, enlightening my heart; deliver me out of all temptation. I fear not uncleanness of meat, but the uncleanness of lusting. I know that Noah was permitted to eat all kind of flesh that was good for food; that Elijah was fed with flesh that endued with an admirable abstinence, was not polluted by feeding on living creatures, locusts. I know also that Esau was deceived by lusting for lentils; and that David blamed himself for desiring a draught of water; and that our King was tempted, not concerning flesh, but bread. And therefore the people in the wilderness also deserved to be reproved, not for desiring flesh, but because, in the desire of food, they murmured against the Lord.

Placed then amid these temptations, I strive daily against concupiscence in eating and drinking. For it is not of such nature that I can settle on cutting it off once for all, and never touching it afterward, as I could of concubinage. The bridle of the throat then is to be held attempered between slackness and stiffness. And who is he, O Lord, who is not some whit transported beyond the limits of necessity? Whoever he is, he is a great one; let him make Your name great. But I am not such, for I am a sinful man. Yet do I too magnify Your name; and He makes intercession to You for my sins who has overcome the world, numbering me among the weak members of His body; because Your eyes have seen that of Him which is imperfect, and in Your book shall all be written.

32. *Of our delight in smelling*

With the allurements of smells, I am not much concerned. When absent, I do not miss them; when present, I do not refuse them, yet ever ready to be without them. So I seem to myself; perchance I am deceived. For that also is a mournful darkness whereby my abilities within me are hidden from me; so that my mind making enquiry into herself of her own powers, ventures not readily to believe herself; because even what is in it is mostly hidden, unless experience reveal it. And no one ought to be secure in that life, the whole whereof is called a trial, whether he who has been able to become better from worse, may not also be able of better to be made worse. Our only hope, only confidence, only assured promise is Your mercy.

33. *The pleasures taken in hearing*

The delights of the ear had more firmly entangled and subdued me; but You did loosen and free me. Now, in those melodies which Your words breathe soul into, when sung with a sweet and attuned voice, I do a little repose; yet not so as to be held thereby, but that I can disengage myself when I will. But with the words which are their life and whereby they find admission into me, they seek in my affections a place of some estimation, and I can scarcely assign them one suitable. For at one time I seem to myself to give them more honor than is seemly, feeling our minds to be more holily and fervently raised unto a flame of devotion, by the holy words themselves when thus sung, than when not; and feeling that the several affections of our spirit, by a sweet variety, have their own proper measures in the voice and singing, by some hidden correspondence wherewith they are stirred up. But this content-ment of the flesh, to which the soul must not be given over to be enervated, does oft beguile me, the sense not so waiting upon reason as patiently to follow her; but having been admitted merely for her sake, it strives even to run before her, and lead her. Thus in these things I sin unawares, but afterwards am aware of it.

At other times, over-anxiously shunning this very deception, I err in too great strictness; and sometimes to that degree, as to wish the whole melody of sweet music which is used to David's Psalter, banished from my ears, and the Church's too; and that mode seems to me safer, which I remember to have been often told me of Athanasius, Bishop of Alexandria, who made the reader of the psalm utter it with so slight inflection of voice, that it was nearer speaking than singing. Yet again, when I remember the tears I shed at the psalmody of Your church, in the beginning of my recovered faith; and how at this time I am moved, not with the singing, but with the things sung, when they are sung with a clear voice and modulation most suitable, I acknowledge the great use of this institution. Thus I fluctuate between peril of pleasure and approved wholesomeness; inclined the rather (though not as pro-nouncing an irrevocable opinion) to approve of the usage of singing in the church; that so by the delight of the ears the weaker minds may rise to the feeling of devotion. Yet when it befalls me to be more moved with the voice than the words sung, I acknow-ledge a sin worthy of punishment, and then had rather not hear music. See now my state; weep with me, and weep for me, you who regulate your feelings within, from which good actions follow. You who do not act, these things touch not you. But You, O Lord my God, hearken; behold, and see, and have mercy and heal me, You, in whose presence I have become a problem to myself; and that is my infirmity.

34. *The enticements coming in by the eyes*

There remains the pleasure of these eyes of my flesh, on which to make my confessions in the hearing of the ears of Your temple, those brotherly and devout ears; and so to conclude the temptations of the lust of the flesh, which yet assail me, groaning earnestly, and desiring to be clothed with my heavenly habitation. The eyes love fair and varied forms, and bright and soft colors. Let not these occupy my soul; let God rather occupy it, who made these things (and very good they are, too), yet is He my good, not they. And these affect me, waking, the whole day, nor is any rest given me from them, as there is, in silence, from musical, and sometimes from all, voices. For this queen of colors, the light, bathing all which we behold, wherever I am through the day, gliding by me in varied forms, soothes me when engaged on other things, and not observing it. And so strongly does it entwine itself, that if it be suddenly withdrawn, it is with longing sought for, and if absent long, saddens the mind.

O you light, which Tobias saw, when, these eyes closed, he taught his son the way of life; and himself went before with the feet of charity, never swerving. Or which Isaac saw, when his fleshly eyes being heavy and closed by old age, his reward was, not to bless his sons by recognizing them, but by blessing to recognize them. Or which Jacob saw, when he also, blind through great age, with illumined heart, in the persons of his sons shed light on the different races of the future people, in them foresignified; and laid his hands, mystically crossed, upon his grandchildren by Joseph, not as their father by his outward eye corrected them, but as himself inwardly discerned. This is the light, it is one, and all are one, who see and love it. But that corporeal light whereof I spoke, seasons the life of this world for her blind lovers, with an enticing and dangerous sweetness. But they who know how to praise You for it, O all-creating Lord, take it up in Your hymns, and are not taken up with it in their sleep. Such would I be. These seductions of the eyes I resist, lest my feet wherewith I walk upon Your way be ensnared; and I lift up mine invisible eyes to You, that You would pluck my feet out of the snare. You do ever and anon pluck them out, for they are ensnared. You cease not to pluck them out, while I often entangle myself in the snares on all sides laid; because You that keep Israel shall neither slumber nor sleep.

What innumerable toys, made by divers arts and manufactures, in our apparel, shoes, utensils and all sorts of works, in pictures also and divers images (and these far exceeding all necessary and moderate use and all pious meaning) have men added to tempt their own eyes withal; outwardly following what themselves make, inwardly forsaking Him by whom themselves were made, and destroying that which themselves have been made! But I, my God and my glory, do hence also sing a hymn to You, and do consecrate praise to Him who consecrates me, because those beautiful patterns which through men's souls are conveyed into their cunning hands, come from that beauty which is above our souls, which my soul day and night sighs after. But the framers and followers of the outward beauties derive thence the rule of judging of them, but not of using them. And He is there, though they perceive Him not, that so they might not wander, but keep their strength for You, and not scatter it abroad upon pleasurable weariness. And I, though I speak and see this, entangle my steps with these outward beauties; but You pluck me out, O Lord, You pluck me out; because Your loving-kindness is before my eyes. For I am taken miserably, and You pluck me out mercifully; sometimes not perceiving it, when I had but lightly lighted upon them; otherwhiles with pain, because I had stuck fast in them.

35. Of our curiosity in knowing

To this is added another form of temptation more manifoldly dangerous. For besides that concupiscence of the flesh which consists in the delight of all senses and pleasures, wherein its slaves, who go far from You, waste and perish, the soul has, through the same senses of the body, a certain vain and curious desire, veiled under the title of knowledge and learning, not of delighting in the flesh, but of making experiments through the flesh. The seat whereof being in the appetite of knowledge, and sight being the sense chiefly used for attaining knowledge, it is in divine language called the lust of the eyes. For to see, belongs properly to the eyes; yet we use this word of the other senses also, when we employ them in seeking knowledge. For we do not say, hark how it flashes, or smell how it glows, or taste how it shines, or feel how it gleams; for all these are said to be seen. And yet we say not only, see how it shines, which the eyes alone can perceive; but also, see how it sounds, see how it smells, see how it tastes, see how hard it is. And so the general experience of the senses, as was said, is called the lust of the eyes, because the office of seeing, wherein the eyes hold the prerogative, the other senses by way of similitude take to themselves, when they make search after any knowledge.

But by this may more evidently be discerned, wherein pleasure and wherein curiosity is the object of the senses; for pleasure seeks objects beautiful, melodious, fragrant, savory, soft; but curiosity, for trial's sake, the contrary as well, not for the sake of suffering annoyance, but out of the lust of making trial and knowing them. For what pleasure is there in seeing in a mangled carcase what will make you shudder? And yet if it be lying near, they flock thither, to be made sad, and to turn pale. Even in sleep they are afraid to see it. As if when awake, anyone forced them to see it, or any report of its beauty drew them thither! Thus also in the other senses, which it were long to go through. From this disease of curiosity are all those strange sights exhibited in the theatre. Hence men go on to search out those powers of nature which are not beyond our powers), which to know profits not, and wherein men desire nothing but to know. Hence also, if with that same end of perverted knowledge magical arts be employed. Hence also in religion itself, God is made trial of, when signs and wonders are demanded of Him, not desired for any good end, but merely to satisfy curiosity.

In this so vast wilderness, full of snares and dangers, behold many of them I have cut off, and thrust out of my heart, as You have granted me the power to do, O God of my salvation. And yet when dare I say, since so many things of this kind buzz on all sides about our daily life − when dare I say that nothing of this sort engages my attention, or causes in me an idle interest? True, the theatres do not now carry me away, nor care I to know the courses of the stars, nor did my soul ever consult ghosts departed;

all sacrilegious mysteries I detest. From You, O Lord my God, to whom I owe humble and single-hearted service, by what artifices and suggestions does the enemy prompt me to ask for some sign! But I beseech You by our King, and by our pure and holy country, Jerusalem, that as any consenting thereto is far from me, so may it ever be further and further. But when I pray You for the salvation of any, my end and intention is far different. You give and will give me to follow You willingly, doing what You will.

Notwithstanding, in how many most petty and contemptible things our curiosity is daily tempted, and how often we give way, who can recount? How often do we begin as if we were tolerating people telling vain stories, lest we offend the weak; then by degrees we take interest therein! I go not now to the circus to see a dog coursing a hare; but in the field, if passing, that coursing peradventure will distract me even from some weighty thought, and draw me after it: not that I turn aside the body of my beast, yet still incline my mind thither. And unless You, having made me see my infirmity did speedily admonish me either through the sight itself by some contemplation to rise towards You, or altogether to despise and pass it by, I dully stand fixed therein. Or what about a lizard catching flies, or a spider entangling them rushing into her nets, as oft-times takes my attention when I am sitting at home? Is the thing different, because they are but small creatures? I go on from them to praise You the wonderful creator and orderer of all, but this does not first draw my attention. It is one thing to rise quickly, another not to fall. And of such things is my life full; and my one hope is Your wonderful great mercy. For when our heart becomes the receptacle of such things, and is overcharged with throngs of this abundant vanity, then are our prayers also thereby often interrupted and distracted, and whilst in Your presence we direct the voice of our heart to Your ears, this so great concern is broken off by the rushing in of I know not what idle thoughts.

36. The sin of pride

Shall we then account this also among things of slight concern? Shall anything bring us back to hope, save Your complete mercy, since You have begun to change us? And You know how far You have already changed me, who first healed me of the lust of vindicating myself, that so You might forgive all the rest of my iniquities, and heal all my infirmities, and redeem life from corruption, and crown me with mercy and pity, and satisfy my desire with good things: who did curb my pride with Your fear, and tame my neck to Your yoke. And now I bear it and it is light unto me, because so have You promised, and have made it; and verily so it was, and I knew it not, when I feared to take it.

But, O Lord, You alone Lord without pride, because You are the only true Lord, who have no lord; has this third kind of temptation also ceased from me, or can it cease through this whole life? To wish, namely, to be feared and loved of men, for no other end, but that we may have a joy therein which is no joy? A miserable life this and a foul boastfulness! Hence especially it comes that men do neither purely love nor fear You. And therefore do You resist the proud, and give grace to the humble: yea, You thunder down upon the ambitions of the world, and the foundations of the mountains tremble. Because now certain offices of human society make it necessary to be loved and feared of men, the adversary of our true blessedness lays hard at us, everywhere spreading his snares of 'well-done, well-done'; that greedily catching at them, we may be taken unawares, and sever our joy from Your truth, and set it in the deceivingness of men; and be pleased at being loved and feared, not for Your sake, but in Your stead: and thus having been made like him, he may have us for his own, not in the bands of charity, but in the bonds of punishment: who purposed to set his throne in the north, that dark and chilled they might serve him, pervertedly and crookedly imitating You. But we, O Lord, behold we are Your little flock; possess us as Yours, stretch Your wings over us, and let us fly under them. Be You our glory; let us be loved for You, and Your word feared in us. Who would be praised of men when You blame, will not be defended of men when You judge; nor delivered when You condemn. But when – not the sinner is praised in the desires of his soul, nor he blessed who does ungodlily, but – a man is praised for some gift which You have given him, and he rejoices more at the praise for himself than that he has the gift for which he is praised, he indeed is praised, while You criticize; better is he who praised than he who is praised. For the one took pleasure in the gift of God in man; the other was better pleased with the gift of man, than of God.

37. *Praise and dispraise, how they move us*

By these temptations we are assailed daily, O Lord; without ceasing are we assailed. Our daily furnace is the tongue of men. And in this way also You command us continence. Give what You order, and order what You will. You know on this matter the groans of my heart, and the floods of mine eyes. For I cannot learn how far I am more cleansed from this plague, and I much fear my secret sins, which Your eyes know, mine do not. For in other kinds of temptations I have some sort of means of examining myself; in this, scarce any. For, in refraining my mind from the pleasures of the flesh and idle curiosity, I see how much I have attained to, when I do without them; foregoing, or not having them. For then I ask myself how much more or less troublesome it is to me not to have them? After all, riches, which are desired, that they may serve to some one or two or all of the three concupiscences, if the soul cannot discern whether, when it has them, it despises them, they may be cast aside, that so it may prove itself. But to be without praise, and therein essay our powers, must we live ill, yea so abandonedly and atrociously, that no one should know without detesting us? What greater madness can be said or thought? But if praise normally, and rightly, accompanies a good life and good works, we ought as little to forego its company, as good life itself. Yet I know not whether I can well or ill be without anything, unless it be absent.

What then do I confess unto You in this kind of temptation, O Lord? What, but that I am delighted with praise, but with truth itself more than with praise? For were it proposed to me, whether I would rather be frenzied in error on all things, and praised by all men, or, being consistent and most settled in the truth, be blamed by all, I see which I should choose. Yet fain would I that the approbation of another should not even increase my joy for any good in me. Yet I own, it does increase it, and not so only, but dispraise does diminish it. And when I am troubled at this my misery, an excuse occurs to me, which of what value it is, You God know, for it leaves me uncertain. For since You have commanded us not continency alone, that is, from what things to refrain our love, but righteousness also, that is, whereon to bestow it, and have willed us to love not You only, but our neighbour also; often, when pleased with intelligent praise, I seem to myself

to be pleased with the proficiency or towardliness of my neighbour, or to be grieved for evil in him, when I hear him dispraise
either what he understands not, or what is good. For sometimes I
am grieved at my own praise, either when those things be praised
in me, in which I mislike myself, or even lesser and slight goods
are more esteemed than they ought. But again how do I know
whether the reason I am thus affected is because I would not have
him who praises me differ from me about myself; not as being
influenced by concern for him, but because those same good
things which please me in myself, please me more when they
please another also? For somehow I am not praised when my
judgment of myself is not praised; forasmuch as either those things
are praised, which displease me; or those more, which please me
less. Am I then doubtful of myself in this matter?

Behold, in You, O truth, I see that I ought not to be moved at
my own praises, for my own sake, but for the good of my neighbour. And whether it be so with me, I know not. For herein I
know less of myself than of You. I beseech now, O my God,
discover to me myself also, that I may confess unto my brethren,
who are to pray for me, wherein I find myself maimed. Let me
examine myself again more diligently. If in my praise I am moved
with the good of my neighbour, why am I less moved if another be
unjustly dispraised than if it be myself? Why am I more stung by
reproach cast upon myself, than at that cast upon another, with the
same injustice, before me? Am I unaware of this also? Or is it at last
that I deceive myself, and do not own the truth before You in my
heart and tongue? This madness put far from me, O Lord, lest mine
own mouth be to me the sinner's oil to make fat my head.

38. *Virtue is endangered by vain-glory*

I am poor and needy; yet better, while in hidden groanings I
displease myself, and seek Your mercy, until what is lacking in my
defective state be renewed and perfected, till it reaches that peace
which the eye of the proud knows not. Yet the word which
comes out of the mouth, and deeds known to men, bring with
them a most dangerous temptation through the love of praise:
which, to establish a certain excellency of our own, solicits and
collects men's suffrages. It tempts, even when it is reproved by
myself in myself, on the very ground that it is reproved; and often

glories more vainly of the very contempt of vain-glory; and so it is
no longer contempt of vain-glory, whereof it glories; for it does
not contemn when it glories.

39. *Of self-love*

Within also, within is another evil, arising out of a like temptation;
whereby men become vain, pleasing themselves in themselves,
though they please not, or displease, or care not to please others.
But pleasing themselves, they much displease You, not only taking pleasure in things not good, as if good, but in Your good
things, as though their own; or even if as Yours, yet as though for
their own merits; or even if as though from Your grace, yet not
with brotherly rejoicing, but envying that grace to others. In all
these and the like perils and travails, You see the trembling of my
heart; and I rather feel my wounds to be cured by You, than not
inflicted by me.

40. *His striving against sin*

Where have You not walked with me, O truth, teaching me what
to beware, and what to desire, when I referred to You what I
could discover here below, and consulted You? With my outward
senses, as I might, I surveyed the world, and observed the life,
which my body has from me, and these my senses. Thence
entered I the recesses of my memory, those manifold and spacious
chambers, wonderfully furnished with innumerable stores; and I
considered, and stood aghast; being able to discern nothing of
these things without You, and finding none of them to be You.
Nor was I myself, who found out these things, who went over
them all, and laboured to distinguish and to value every thing
according to its dignity, taking some things upon the report of my
senses, questioning about others which I felt to be mingled with
myself, numbering and distinguishing the reporters themselves, and
in the large treasure-house of my memory revolving some things,
storing up others, drawing out others. Nor yet was it I myself when
I did this, (i.e. was it my power whereby I did it), neither were
You that power, for You are the abiding light, which I consulted
concerning all these, whether they were, what they were, and how
to be valued; and I heard You directing and commanding me; and
this I often do, this delights me, and as far as I may be freed from

necessary duties, unto this pleasure have I recourse. Nor in all the things which I run over consulting You can I find any safe place for my soul, but in You; whither my scattered members may be gathered, and nothing of me depart from You. And sometimes You admit me to an affection, very unusual, in my inmost soul; rising to a strange sweetness, which if it were perfected in me, I know not what in it would not belong to the life to come. But through my miserable encumbrances I sink down again into these lower things, and am swept back by former custom, and am held, and greatly weep, but am greatly held. So much does the burden of a bad custom weigh us down. Here I can stay, but would not; there I would, but cannot; both ways, miserable.

41. *God and a lie cannot stand together*

Thus then have I considered the sicknesses of my sins in that threefold concupiscence, and have called Your right hand to my help. For with a wounded heart have I beheld Your brightness, and stricken back I said, Who can attain thither? I am cast away from the sight of Your eyes. You are the truth who preside over all, but I through my covetousness would not indeed forego You, but would with You possess a lie; as no man would in such wise speak falsely, as himself to be ignorant of the truth. So then I lost You, because You vouchsafe not to be possessed with a lie.

42. *Angels cannot be our mediators*

Whom could I find to reconcile me to You? Was I to have recourse to angels? By what prayers? By what sacraments? Many endeavoring to return unto You, and of themselves unable, have, as I hear, tried this, and fallen into the desire of curious visions, and been accounted worthy to be deluded. For they, being high-minded, sought You by the pride of learning, swelling out rather than smiting upon their breasts, and so by the agreement of their heart, drew unto themselves the princes of the air, the fellow-conspirators of their pride, by whom, through magical influences, they were deceived, seeking a mediator, by whom they might be purged, and there was none. For the devil it was, transforming himself into an angel of light. And it much enticed proud flesh, that he had no body of flesh. For they were mortal, and sinners; but you, Lord, to whom they proudly sought to be reconciled, are immortal, and without sin. But a mediator between God and man must have something like to God, something like to men; lest being in both like to man, he should be far from God: or if in both like God, too unlike man: and so not be a mediator. That deceitful mediator then, by whom in Your secret judgments pride deserved to be deluded, has one thing in common with man, that is sin; another he would seem to have in common with God; and not being clothed with the mortality of flesh, would vaunt himself to be immortal. But since the wages of sin is death, this has he in common with men, that with them he should be condemned to death.

43. *Christ alone is the all-sufficient intercessor*

But the true mediator, whom in Your secret mercy You have showed to the humble, and sent, that by His example also they might learn that same humility, that mediator between God and man, the man Christ Jesus, appeared betwixt mortal sinners and the immortal just one; mortal with men, just with God: that because the wages of righteousness is life and peace, He might by a righteousness conjoined with God make void that death of sinners, now made righteous, which He willed to have in common with them. Hence He was showed forth to holy men of old; that so they, through faith in His passion to come, as we through faith of it passed, might be saved. For as man, He was a mediator; but as the word, not in the middle between God and man, because equal to God, and God with God, and together one God.

How have You loved us, good Father, who spared not Your only Son, but delivered Him up for us ungodly! How have You loved us, for whom He that thought it no robbery to be equal with You, was made subject even to the death of the cross, He alone, free among the dead, having power to lay down His life, and power to take it again: for us to You both victor and victim, and therefore victor, because the victim; for us to You priest and sacrifice, and therefore priest because the sacrifice; making us to You, of servants, sons by being born of You, and serving us. Well then is my hope strong in Him, that You will heal all my infirmities, by Him who sits at Your right hand and makes intercession for us; else should I despair. For many and great are my infirmities, many they are, and great; but Your medicine is mightier. We might imagine that Your word was far from any union with man, and despair of ourselves, unless He had been made flesh and dwelt among us.

Affrighted with my sins and the burden of my misery, I had cast in my heart, and had purposed to flee to the wilderness: but You forbade me, and strengthened me, saying, The reason Christ died for all, was that they which live may now no longer live unto themselves, but unto Him that died for them. See, Lord, I cast my care upon You, that I may live, and consider wondrous things out of Your law. You know my unskilfulness, and my infirmities; teach me, and heal me. He, Your only Son, in whom are hid all the treasures of wisdom and knowledge, has redeemed me with His blood. Let not the proud speak evil of me; because I meditate on my ransom, and eat and drink, and poor as I am, ask and desire to be satisfied from Him, amongst those that eat and are satisfied, and they shall praise the Lord who seek Him.

Book 11

1. *Why we confess unto God who knows all*

Lord, since eternity is Yours, are You ignorant of what I say to You? Or do You see in time, what passes in time? Why then do I lay in order before You so many relations? Not, of a truth, that You might learn them through me, but to stir up mine own and my readers' devotions towards You, that we may all say, Great is the Lord, and greatly to be praised. I have said already, and again will say, for love of Your love do I this. For we pray also, and yet truth has said, Your Father knows what you have need of, before you ask. It is then our affections which we lay open unto You, confessing our own miseries, and Your mercies upon us, that You may free us wholly, since You have begun, that we may cease to be wretched in ourselves, and be blessed in You; seeing You have called us, to become poor in spirit, and meek, and mourners, and hungering and athirst after righteousness, and merciful, and pure in heart, and peace-makers. See, I have told You many things, as I could and as I would, because You wished first that I should confess unto You, my Lord God. For You are good, for Your mercy endures for ever.

2. *He asks to be delivered from his sins and errors, and to be guided unto true knowledge*

But how shall I suffice with the tongue of my pen to utter all Your exhortations, and all Your terrors, and comforts, and guidances, whereby You brought me to preach Your word, and dispense Your sacrament to Your people? And if I suffice to utter them in order, the drops of time are precious with me; and long have I burned to meditate in Your law, and therein to confess to You my skill and unskilfulness, the daybreak of Your enlightening, and the remnants of my darkness, until infirmity be swallowed up by strength. And I would not have anything besides steal away those hours which I find free from the necessities of refreshing my body and the powers of my mind, and of the service which we owe to men, or which though we owe not, we yet pay.

O Lord my God, give ear unto my prayer, and let Your mercy hearken unto my desire: because it is anxious not for myself alone, but would serve brotherly charity; and You see my heart, that so it is. I would sacrifice to You the service of my thought and tongue; do You give me, what I may offer You. For I am poor and needy, You rich to all that call upon You; who, free from care, do care for us. Circumcise from all rashness and all lying both my inward and outward lips: let Your scriptures be my pure delights: let me not be deceived in them, nor deceive out of them. Lord, hearken and pity, O Lord my God, light of the blind, and strength of the weak; yea also light of those that see, and strength of the strong; hearken unto my soul, and hear it crying out of the depths. For if Your ears be not with us in the depths also, whither shall we go? Whither cry? The day is Yours, and the night is Yours; at Your beck the moments flee by. Grant thereof a space for our meditations in the hidden things of Your law, and close it not against us who knock. For not in vain would You have the darksome secrets of so many pages written; nor are those forests without their harts which retire therein and range and walk; feed, lie down, and ruminate. Perfect me, O Lord, and reveal them unto me. Behold, Your voice is my joy; Your voice exceeds the abundance of pleasures. Give what I love: for I do love; and this have You given: forsake not Your own gifts, nor despise Your green herb that thirsts. Let me confess unto You whatsoever I shall find in Your books, and hear the voice of praise, and drink You in, and meditate on the wonderful things out of Your law; even from the beginning, wherein You made the heaven and the earth, unto the everlasting reigning of Your holy city with You.

Lord, have mercy on me, and hear my desire. For it is not, I deem, of the earth, not of gold and silver, and precious stones, or gorgeous apparel, or honors and offices, or the pleasures of the flesh, or necessaries for the body and for this life of our pilgrimage: all which shall be added unto those that seek Your kingdom and Your righteousness. Behold, O Lord my God, wherein is my desire. The wicked have told me of delights, but not such as Your law, O Lord. Behold, wherein is my desire. Behold, Father, behold, and see and approve; and be it pleasing in the sight of Your mercy, that I may find grace before You, that the inward parts of Your words be opened to me knocking. I beseech by our Lord Jesus Christ Your Son, the man of Your right hand, the son of man, whom You have established for Yourself, as Your mediator and ours, through whom You sought us, not seeking You, but sought us, that we might seek You – Your word, through whom You made all things, and among them, me also – Your only-begotten, through whom You called to adoption the believing people, and therein me also – I beseech You by Him, who sits at Your right hand, and intercedes with You for us, in whom are hidden all the treasures of wisdom and knowledge. These do I seek in Your books. Of Him did Moses write; This says Himself; this says the truth.

3. *He desires to understand the holy scriptures*

I would hear and understand, how, In the beginning You made the heaven and earth. Moses wrote this, wrote and departed, passed hence from You to You; nor is he now before me. For if he were, I would hold him and ask him, and beseech him by You to open these things unto me, and would lay the ears of my body to the sounds bursting out of his mouth. And should he speak Hebrew, in vain will it strike on my senses, nor would anything of it touch my mind; but if Latin, I should know what he said. But whence should I know, whether he spoke truth? Yea, and if I knew this also, should I know it from him? Truly within me, within, in the chamber of my thoughts, truth, neither Hebrew nor Greek nor Latin nor barbarian, without organs of voice or tongue, or sound of syllables, would say, It is truth, and I forthwith should say confidently to that man of Yours, You say truly. Since then I cannot enquire of him, You, You I beseech, O truth, full of whom he spoke truth, You, my God, I beseech, forgive my sins; and You, who gave him Your servant to speak these things, give to me also to understand them.

4. *The creatures proclaim God to be their creator*

Behold, the heavens and the earth are; they proclaim that they were created, for they change and vary. Whereas whatsoever has not been made, and yet is, has nothing in it which before it had not (which is to change, and vary). They proclaim also, that they made not themselves: 'the reason we are, is because we have been made; we were not therefore, before we were, so as to make ourselves.' Now the evidence of the thing, is the voice of the speakers. You therefore, Lord, made them; who are beautiful, for they are beautiful; who are good, for they are good; who are, for they are; yet are they not so beautiful, nor so good, nor are they so, as You their creator are; compared with whom, they are neither beautiful nor good, nor are. This we know, thanks to You. And our knowledge, compared with Your knowledge, is ignorance.

5. *How the world was made of nothing*

But how did You make the heaven and the earth? And what was the engine of Your so mighty fabric? For it was not as a human artificer, forming one body from another, according to the discretion of his mind, which can in some way invest with such a form, as it sees in itself by its inward eye. And whence should he be able to do this, unless You had made that mind? He invests with a form what already exists, and has a being, as clay, or stone, or wood, or gold, or the like. And whence should they be, had not You appointed them? You made the artificer his body, You the mind commanding the limbs, You the matter whereof he makes anything; You the apprehension whereby to take in his art, and see within what he does without; You the sense of his body, whereby, as by an interpreter, he may from mind to matter, convey that which he does, and report to his mind what is done; that it within may consult the truth, which presides over itself, whether it be well done or no. All these praise You, the creator of all. But how do You make them? How, O God, did You make heaven and earth? Verily, neither in the heaven, nor in the earth, did You make heaven and earth; nor in the air, or waters, seeing these also belong to the heaven and the earth; nor in the whole world did You make the whole world; because there was no place where to make it, before it was made, that it might be. Nor did You hold anything in Your hand, whereof to make heaven and earth. For whence should You have this, which You had not made, thereof to make anything? For what is, but because You are? Therefore You spoke, and they were made, and in Your word You made them.

6. *What manner of Word the world was created by*

But how did You speak? In the way that the voice came out of
the cloud, saying, This is my beloved Son? For that voice passed
by and passed away, began and ended; the syllables sounded and
passed away, the second after the first, the third after the second,
and so forth in order, until the last after the rest, and silence after
the last. Whence it is abundantly clear and plain that the motion
of a creature expressed it, itself temporal, serving Your eternal
will. And these Your words, created for a time, the outward ear
reported to the intelligent soul, whose inward ear lay listening
to Your eternal word. But she compared these words sounding
in time, with that Your eternal word in silence, and said, It is
different, far different. These words are far beneath me, nor are
they, because they flee and pass away; but the word of my Lord
abides above me for ever. If then in sounding and passing words
You said that heaven and earth should be made, and so made
heaven and earth, there was a corporeal creature before heaven
and earth, by whose motions in time that voice might take his
course in time. But there was nothing corporeal before heaven
and earth; or if there were, surely You had, without such a
passing voice, created that, whereof to make this passing voice,
by which to say, Let the heaven and the earth be made. For
whatsoever that were, whereof such a voice were made, unless it
were made by You, it could not be at all. By what word then did
You speak, that a body might be made, whereby these words
again might be made?

7. *The Son of God is the word co-eternal with the Father*

You call us then to understand the word, God, with You God,
which is spoken eternally, and by it are all things spoken eternally.
For what was spoken was not spoken successively, one thing
concluded that the next might be spoken, but all things together
and eternally. Else have we time and change; and not a true
eternity nor true immortality. This I know, O my God, and give
thanks. I know, I confess to You, O Lord, and with me there
knows and blesses You, whoso is not ungrateful for certain truth.
We know, Lord, we know; since inasmuch as anything is not
which was, and is, which was not, so far forth it dies and arises.
Nothing then of Your word does give place or replace, because

it is truly immortal and eternal. And therefore unto the word co-eternal with You You do at once and eternally say all that You do say; and whatever You say shall be made is made; nor do You make, otherwise than by saying; and yet are not all things made together, or everlasting, which You make by saying.

8. *The word of God is our teacher in everything*

Why, I beseech You, O Lord my God? I see it in a way; but how to express it, I know not, unless it be, that whatsoever begins to be, and leaves off to be, begins then, and leaves off then, when in Your eternal reason it is known, that it ought to begin or leave off; in which reason nothing begins or leaves off. This is Your word, which is also 'the beginning, because also it speaks unto us'. Thus in the gospel He speaks through the flesh; and this sounded out-wardly in the ears of men, that it might be believed and sought inwardly, and found in the eternal verity; where the good and only Master teaches all His disciples. There, Lord, hear I Your voice speaking unto me; because He speaks to us, who teaches us; but He that teaches us not, even if He speaks, He speaks not to us. Who now teaches us, but the unchangeable truth? For even when we are admonished through a changeable creature, we are but led to the unchangeable truth; where we learn truly, while we stand and hear Him, and rejoice greatly because of the Bridegroom's voice, restor-ing us to Him, from whom we are. It is therefore the beginning, because if it did not abide, there should not, when we went astray, be anywhere to return. But when we return from error, it is through knowing that we return; and that we may know, He teaches us, because He is the beginning, and speaks to us.

9. *How the word of God speaks unto the heart*

In this beginning, O God, have You made heaven and earth, in Your word, in Your Son, in Your power, in Your wisdom, in Your truth; wondrously speaking, and wondrously making. Who shall comprehend? Who declare it? What is that which gleams through me, and strikes my heart without hurting it; and I shudder and kindle? I shudder, inasmuch as I am unlike it; I kindle, inasmuch as I am like it. It is wisdom, wisdom's self which gleams through me; severing my cloudiness which yet again mantles over me, fainting from it, through the darkness which for my punishment gathers upon me. For my strength is brought down in need, so that I cannot support my blessings, till You, Lord, who have been gracious to all mine iniquities, shall heal all my infirmities. For You shall also redeem my life from corruption, and crown me with loving kindness and tender mercies, and shall satisfy my desire with good things, because my youth shall be renewed like an eagle's. For in hope we are saved, wherefore we through patience wait for Your promises. Let him that is able, hear You inwardly discoursing out of Your oracle: I will boldly cry out, How wonderful are Your works, O Lord, in wisdom have You made them all; and this wisdom is the beginning, and in that beginning did You make heaven and earth.

10. *God's will knows no beginning*

Lo, are they not full of their old leaven, who say to us, What was God doing before He made heaven and earth? For if (say they) He were unemployed and worked not, why does He not also henceforth, and for ever, as He did heretofore? For did any new motion arise in God, and a new will to make a creature, which He had never before made, how then would that be a true eternity, where there arises a will, which was not? For the will of God is not a creature, but before the creature; seeing nothing could be created, unless the will of the creator had preceded. The will of God then belongs to His very substance. And if anything have arisen in God's substance, which before was not, that substance cannot be truly called eternal. But if the will of God from eternity has been that the creature should be, why was not the creature also from eternity?

11. *God's eternity not to be measured by the parts of time*

Those who speak thus, do not yet understand You, O wisdom of God, light of minds, do not yet understand how the things be made, which through You and in You are made: yet they strive to comprehend things eternal, whilst their heart flutters between the motions of things past and to come, and is still unstable. Who shall hold it and fix it, that it be settled awhile, and awhile catch the glory of that ever-fixed eternity, and compare it with the times which are never fixed, and see that it cannot be compared? And that a long time cannot become long, but out of many motions passing by, which cannot be prolonged altogether; but that in the eternal nothing passes, but the whole is present; whereas no time is all at once present? And that all time past is driven on by time to come, and all to come follows upon the past; and all past and to come, is created, and flows out of that which is ever present? Who shall hold the heart of man, that it may stand still, and see how eternity ever still-standing, neither past nor to come, utters the times past and to come? Can my hand do this, or the hand of my mouth by speech bring about a thing so great?

12. *What God did before the creation of the world*

See, I answer him that asks, What did God before He made heaven and earth? I answer not as one is said to have answered in jest (eluding the pressure of the question), He was preparing hell (says he) for those who pry into mysteries. Better a seer than a sneer. So I answer not; for rather had I answer, I know not, what I know not, than so as to raise a laugh at him who asks deep questions and gain praise for one who gives false answers. But I say that You, our God, are the creator of every creature: and if by the name 'heaven and earth' every creature be understood, I boldly say, that before God made heaven and earth, He did not make anything. For if He made, what did He make but a creature? And I wish I knew whatsoever I desire to know to my profit, as certainly as I know, that no creature was made, before there was made any creature.

13. *That before those times which God created, there was no time*

But if any light-winged brain rove over the images of times which are past, and wonder that You the God almighty and all-creating and all-supporting, maker of heaven and earth, did for innumerable ages forbear from so great a work, before You would make it; let him awake and consider, that he wonders at false conceits. For whence could innumerable ages pass by, which You made not, You the author and creator of all ages? Or what times should there be, which were not made by You? Or how should they pass by, if they never were? Seeing then You are the creator of all times, if any time was before You made heaven and earth, why say they that You did forego working? For that very time did You make, nor could times pass by, before You made those times. But if before heaven and earth there was no time, why is it demanded, what You then did? For there was no 'then', when there was no time.

Nor do You by time, precede time: else should You not precede all times. But You precede all things past, by the sublimity of an ever-present eternity; and surpass all future because they are future, and when they come, they shall be past; but You are the same, and Your years fail not. Your years neither come nor go; whereas ours both come and go, that they all may come. Your years stand together, because they do stand; nor are departing thrust out by coming years, for they pass not away; but ours shall all be, when they shall no more be. Your years are one day; and Your day is not daily, but today, seeing Your today gives not place unto tomorrow, for neither does it replace yesterday. Your today, is eternity; therefore did You beget the co-eternal, to whom You said, This day have I begotten You. You have made all things; and before all times You are: neither in any time was time not.

14. *Of the nature and three differences of time*

At no time then had You not made anything, because time itself You made. And no times are co-eternal with You, because You remain always; whereas if they remained always, they would not be times. For what is time? Who can readily and briefly explain this? Who can even in thought comprehend it, so as to utter a word about it? But what in speaking do we mention more familiarly and knowingly, than time? We understand, when we speak of it; and we understand also, when we hear it spoken of by another. What then is time? If no one asks me, I know: if I wish to explain it to one that asks, I know not: yet I say boldly that I know, that if nothing passed away, time past were not; and if nothing were coming, a time to come were not; and if nothing were, time present were not. Those two times then, past and future, how are they, seeing the past is no longer, and the future is not yet? But the present, should it always be present, and never pass into time past, verily it should not be time, but eternity. If time present (if it is to be time) only comes into existence because it passes into time past, how can we say this also is, whose cause of being is, that it shall not be; so that, I suppose, we can only truly say that time is, because it is tending not to be?

15. *No time can be said to be long*

And yet we say, 'a long time' and 'a short time'; still, only of time past or to come. A long time past (for example) we call an hundred years since; and a long time to come, an hundred years hence. But a short time past, we call (say) ten days since; and a short time to come, ten days hence. But in what sense is that long or short, which is not? For the past is not now; and the future is not yet. Let us not then say, 'it is long'; but of the past, 'it has been long'; and of the future, 'it will be long'. O my Lord, my light, shall not here also Your truth mock at man? For that past time which was long, was it long when it was now past, or when it was yet present? For then might it be long, when there was, what could be long; but when past, it was no more; wherefore it could not be long, since it was not at all. Let us not then say, 'time past has been long': for we shall not find, what has been long, seeing that since it was past, it is no more, but let us say, 'that present time was long'; because, when it was present, it was long. For it had not yet passed away, so as not to be; and therefore there was something which could be long; but after it was past, that ceased also to be long, which ceased to be.

Let us see then, you soul of man, whether present time can be long: for to You it is given to feel and to measure length of time. What will you answer me? Are a hundred years, when present, a long time? See first, whether a hundred years can be present. For if the first of these years be now current, it is present, but the other ninety and nine are to come, and therefore are not yet, but if the second year be current, one is now past, another present, the rest to come. And so if we assume any middle year of this hundred to be present, all before it are past; all after it, are to come; wherefore a hundred years cannot be present. But see at least whether that one which is now current, itself is present; for if the current month be its first, the rest are to come; if the second, the first is already past, and the rest are not yet. Therefore, neither is the year now current present; and if not present as a whole, then is not the year present. For twelve months are a year; of which any one month, the current month, is present; the rest are past, or to come. Although neither is that current month present, but one day only, the rest being to come, if it be the first; past, if the last; if any of the middle, then between past and to come.

See how the present time, which alone we found could be called long, is abridged to the length scarce of one day. But let us examine that also; because neither is one day present as a whole. For it is made up of four and twenty hours of night and day: of which, the first has the rest to come; the last has them past; and any of the middle has those before it past, those behind it to come. And that one hour itself passes away in flying particles. Whatsoever of it has flown away, is past; whatsoever remains, is to come. If an instant of time be conceived, which cannot be divided into the smallest particles of moments, that alone is it, which may be called present. Which yet flies with such speed from future to past, as not to be lengthened out with the least stay. For if it be, it is divided into past and future. The present has no space. Where then is the time, which we may call long? Is it to come? Of it we do not say, 'it is long'; because it is not yet, so as to be long; but we say, 'it will be long'. When therefore will it be? For if even when it is yet to come, it shall not be long (because what can be long, as yet is not), and so it shall then be long, when from future which as yet is not, it shall begin now to be, and have become present, that so there should exist what may be long; then does time present cry out in the words above, that it cannot be long.

16. *Of our measuring of times*

And yet, Lord, we perceive intervals of times, and compare them, and say some are shorter, and others longer. We measure also, how much longer or shorter this time is than that; and we answer, 'This is double, or treble; and that but once, or only just so much as that.' But we measure times as they are passing, by perceiving them; but past, which now are not, or the future, which are not yet, who can measure? Unless a man shall presume to say, that can be measured, which is not. When then time is passing, it may be perceived and measured; but when it is past, it cannot, because it is not.

17. *Where time past, and to come, now are*

I ask, Father, I affirm not: O my God, rule and guide me. Who will tell me that there are not three times (as we learned when boys, and taught boys): past, present, and future; but present only, because those two are not? Or are they also; and when from future it becomes present, does it come out of some secret place; and so, when retiring, from present it becomes past? For where did they, who foretold things to come, see them, if as yet they be not? For that which is not, cannot be seen. And they who relate things past, could not relate them, if in mind they did not discern them, and if they were not, they could no way be discerned. Things then past and to come, are.

18. *How times past, and to come, are present now*

Permit me, Lord, to seek further, O my hope. Let not my purpose be confounded. For if times past and future exist, I wish to know where they exist. Which yet if I cannot, yet I do know, wherever they be, they are not there as future or past, but as present. For if there also they be future, they are not yet there; if there also they be past, they are no longer there. Wherever they are, then, and whatever they are, they are there only as present. Although when past facts are related, there are drawn out of the memory, not the things themselves which are past, but words conceived by the images of the things, which through the senses they have left in passing, as traces in the mind. Thus my childhood, which now is not, is in time past, which now is not: but now when I recall its image, and tell of it, I behold it in the present, because it is still in my memory. Whether there be a like cause of foretelling things to come also; that of things which as yet are not, the images may be perceived before, already existing, I confess, O my God, I know not. This indeed I know, that we generally think before on our future actions, and that that forethinking is present, but the action whereof we forethink is not yet, because it is to come. Which, when we have set upon, and have begun to do what we were forethinking, then shall that action be; because then it is no longer future, but present.

Which way soever then this secret fore-perceiving of things to come be, that only can be seen, which is. But what now is, is not future, but present. When then things to come are said to be seen, it is not themselves which as yet are not (that is, which are to be), but their causes perchance or signs are seen, which already are. Therefore they are not future but present to those who now see that, from which the future, being foreconceived in the mind, is foretold. Which fore-conceptions again now are; and those who foretell those things, do behold the conceptions present before them. Let now the numerous variety of things furnish me some example. I behold the day-break, I foreshow, that the sun is about to rise. What I behold, is present; what I foresignify, to come; not the sun, which already is; but the sun-rising, which is not yet. And yet did I not in my mind imagine the sun-rising itself (as now while I speak of it), I could not foretell it. But neither is that day-break which I discern in the sky, the sun-rising, although it goes before it; nor that imagination of my mind; which two are seen now present, that the other which is to be may be foretold. Future things then are not yet: and if they be not yet, they are not: and if they are not, they cannot be seen; yet foretold they may be from things present, which are already, and are seen.

19. *He asks God, how future things are known*

You then, ruler of Your creation, by what way do You teach souls things to come? For You did teach Your prophets. By what way do You, to whom nothing is to come, teach things to come; or rather of the future, do teach things present? For that which is not, neither can it be taught. Too far is this way out of my ken: it is too mighty for me, I cannot attain unto it; but from You I can, when You shall vouchsafe it, O sweet light of my hidden eyes.

20. *These three differences of times, how they are to be called*

What now is clear and plain is, that neither things to come nor past are. Nor is it properly said, There be three times: past, present, and to come; yet perchance it might be properly said, There be three times; a present of things past, a present of things present, and a present of things future. For these three do exist in some sort, in the soul, but otherwhere do I not see them; present of things past, memory; present of things present, sight; present of things future, expectation. If thus we be permitted to speak, I see three times, and I confess there are three. Let it be said too, There be three times, past, present, and to come: in our incorrect way. See, I object not, nor gainsay, nor find fault, if what is so said be but understood, that neither what is to be, now is, nor what is past. For but few things are there, which we speak properly, most things improperly; still the things intended are understood.

21. *How time may be measured*

Very well. I said just now, we measure times as they pass, so as to be able to say, this time is twice so much as that one; or, this is just so much as that; and so of any other parts of time which be measurable. Wherefore, as I said, we measure times as they pass. And if any should ask me, How know you? I might answer, I know, because we measure, and we cannot measure things that are not; and things past and to come, are not. But time present how do we measure, seeing it has no space? It is measured while passing, but when it shall have passed, it is not measured; for there will be nothing to be measured. But whence, by what way, and whither passes it while it is being measured? Whence, but from the future? Which way, but through the present? Whither, but into the past? From that therefore, which is not yet, through that which has no space, into that which now is not. Yet what do we measure, if not time in some space? For we do not say, single, and double, and triple, and equal, or any other like way that we speak of time, except of spaces of times. In what space then do we measure time passing? In the future, whence it passes? But what is not yet, we measure not. Or in the present, by which it passes? But no space, we cannot measure: or in the past, to which it passes? But neither do we measure that, which now is not.

22. *He begs God to resolve a difficulty*

My soul is on fire to know this most intricate enigma. Shut it not up, O Lord my God, good Father; through Christ I beseech You, do not shut up these familiar, yet hidden things, from my desire, that it be hindered from penetrating them; but let them dawn through Your enlightening mercy, O Lord. Whom shall I enquire of concerning these things? And to whom shall I more fruitfully confess my ignorance, than to You, to whom these my studies, so vehemently kindled toward Your scriptures, are not troublesome? Give what I love; for I do love, and this have You given me. Give, Father, who truly know to give good gifts unto Your children. Give, because I have taken upon me to know, and trouble is before me until You do open it. By Christ I beseech You, in His name, holy of holies, let no man disturb me. For I believed, and therefore do I speak. This is my hope, for this do I live, that I may contemplate the delights of the Lord. Behold, You have made my days old, and they pass away, and how, I know not. And we talk of time, and time, and times, and times, How long is it since he said this? How long since he did this? and, How long since I saw that? and, This syllable has twice the time of that single short syllable. These words we speak, and these we hear, and are understood and understand. Most manifest and ordinary they are, and the self-same things again are but too deeply hidden, and the discovery of them were new.

23. *He clears this question, what time is*

I heard once from a learned man, that the motions of the sun, moon, and stars, constituted time, and I assented not. For why should not the motions of all bodies rather be times? Or, if the lights of heaven should cease, and a potter's wheel run round, should there be no time by which we might measure those whirlings, and say, that either it moved with equal pauses, or if it turned sometimes slower, other times quicker, that some rounds were longer, others shorter? Or, while we were saying this, should we not also be speaking in time? Or, are there in our words some syllables short, others long, for any reason other than that those are sounded in a shorter time, these in a longer? God, grant to men to see in a small thing evidence common to things great and small. The stars and lights of heaven are by way of signs, for seasons, for years, and for days. Indeed they are; yet neither should I say, that the going round of that wooden wheel was a day, nor yet he, that there was therefore no time.

I desire to know the force and nature of time, by which we measure the motions of bodies, and say (for example) this motion is twice as long as that. For I ask, seeing 'day' denotes not the stay only of the sun upon the earth (according to which day is one thing, night another), but also its whole circuit from east to east again; according to which we say, 'there passed so many days', the night being included when we say, 'so many days', and the nights not reckoned apart – seeing then a day is completed by the motion of the sun and by his circuit from east to east again, I ask, does the motion alone make the day, or the stay in which that motion is completed, or both? For if the first be the day, then should we have a day, although the sun should finish that course in so small a space of time, as one hour comes to. If the second, then should not that make a day, if between one sun-rise and another there were but so short a stay, as one hour comes to; but the sun must go four and twenty times about, to complete one day. If both, then neither could that be called a day; if the sun should run his whole round in the space of one hour; nor that if, while the sun stood still, so much time should overpass, as the sun usually makes his whole course in, from morning to morning. I will not there-fore now ask, what that is which is called day; but what time is, whereby we, measuring the circuit of the sun, should say that it was finished in half the time it was wont, if so be it was finished in so small a space as twelve hours; and comparing both times, should call this a single time, that a double time; even supposing the sun to run his round from east to east, sometimes in that single, sometimes in that double time. Let no man then tell me, that the motions of the heavenly bodies constitute times, because, when at the prayer of one, the sun had stood still, till he could achieve his victorious battle, the sun stood still, but time went on. For in its own allotted space of time was that battle waged and ended. I perceive time then to be a certain extension. But do I perceive it, or seem to perceive it? You, Light and Truth, will show me.

24. *It is time, by which we measure the movement of bodies*

Do You bid me assent, if any define time to be 'motion of a body'? You do not bid me. For that no body is moved, but in time, I hear; this You say; but that the motion of a body *is* time, I hear not; You say it not. For when a body is moved, I by time measure, how long it moves, from the time it began to move until it left off? And if I did not see whence it began, and it continue to move so that I see not when it ends, I cannot measure, save perchance from the time I began, until I cease to see. And if I look long, I can only pronounce it to be a long time, but not how long; because when we say 'how long', we do it by comparison; as, 'this is as long as that', or 'twice so long as that', or the like. But when we can mark the distances of the places, whence and whither goes the body moved, or his parts, if it moved as in a lathe, then can we say precisely, in how much time the motion of that body or his part, from this place unto that, was finished. Seeing therefore the motion of a body is one thing, that by which we measure how long it is, another, who sees not, which of the two is rather to be called time? For if a body both sometimes moves, and sometimes stands still, then we measure, not his motion only, but his standing still too by time; and we say, 'it stood still, as much as it moved'; or 'it stood still twice or thrice so long as it moved'; or any other space which our measuring has either ascertained, or guessed; more or less, as the saying goes. Time then is not the motion of a body.

25. *He prays again*

And I confess to You, O Lord, that I still know not what time is, and again I confess unto You, O Lord, that I know that I speak this in time, and that having long spoken of time, that 'long' itself is long only by the lapse of time. How then know I this, seeing I know not what time is? Or is it perchance that I know not how to express what I know? Woe is me, that do not even know, what I know not. Behold, O my God, before You I lie not; but as I speak, so is my heart. You shall light my candle; You, O Lord my God, will enlighten my darkness.

26. *Measuring the feet and syllables of a verse*

Does not my soul most truly confess unto You, that I do measure times? Do I then measure, O my God, and know not what I measure? I measure the motion of a body in time; and do I not measure the time itself? Or could I indeed measure the motion of a body how long it were, and in how long space it could come from this place to that, without measuring the time in which it is moved? This same time then, how do I measure? Do we by a shorter time measure a longer, as by the space of a cubit, the space of a rood? For so indeed we seem by the space of a short syllable, to measure the space of a long syllable, and to say that this is double the other. Thus measure we the spaces of stanzas, by the spaces of the verses, and the spaces of the verses, by the spaces of the feet, and the spaces of the feet, by the spaces of the syllables, and the spaces of long, by the space of short syllables; not measuring by pages (for then we measure spaces, not times); but when we utter the words and they pass by, and we say, It is a long stanza, because composed of so many verses; long verses, because consisting of so many feet; long feet, because prolonged by so many syllables; a long syllable because double to a short one. But neither do we this way obtain any certain measure of time;

because it may be, that a shorter verse, pronounced more fully, may take up more time than a longer, pronounced hurriedly. And so for a verse, a foot, a syllable. Whence it seemed to me, that time is nothing else than protraction; but of what, I know not; and it is a surprise, if it be not of the mind itself. For what, I beseech You, O my God, do I measure, when I say, either indefinitely, This is a longer time than that, or definitely, This is double that? That I measure time, I know; and yet I measure not time to come, for it is not yet; nor present, because it is not protracted by any space; nor past, because it now is not. What then do I measure? Times passing, not past? As I said originally.

27. He begins to resolve the earlier question, how we measure time

Courage, my mind, and press on mightily. God is our helper, He made us, and not we ourselves. Press on where truth begins to dawn. Suppose, now, the voice of a body begins to sound, and does sound, and sounds on. Ah, it ceases; now there is silence; that voice is past, and is no more a voice. Before it sounded, it was to come, and could not be measured, because as yet it was not; and now it cannot, because it is no longer. Then therefore while it sounded, it might, because there then was what might be measured. But yet even then it was not at a stay; for it was passing on, and passing away. Could it rather be measured by that? For while passing, it was being extended into some space of time, in which it could be measured, since the present has no space. If that was possible, then imagine another voice has begun to sound, and still sounds in one continued tenor without any interruption; let us measure it while it sounds; seeing when it has left sounding, it will then be past, and nothing left to be measured; let us measure it distinctly, and tell how much it is. But it sounds still, nor can it be measured but from the instant it began, unto the end when it finished. For the actual interval is what we measure, from some beginning unto some end. Wherefore, a voice that is not yet ended, cannot be measured, so that it may be said how long or short it is; nor can it be called equal to another, or double to a single, or the like. But when ended, it no longer is, so how may it then be measured? And yet we measure times; but yet neither those which are not yet, nor those which no longer are, nor those which are not lengthened out by some pause, nor those which have no bounds. We measure neither times to come, nor past, nor present, nor while they are passing; and yet we do measure times.

'*Deus creator omnium*': this verse of eight syllables alternates between short and long syllables. The four short then, the first, third, fifth, and seventh, are but single, in respect of the four long, the second, fourth, sixth, and eighth. Every one of these to every one of those, has a double time: I pronounce them, report on them, and find it so, as one's plain sense perceives. By plain sense then, I measure a long syllable by a short, and I sensibly find it to have twice so much; but when one sounds after the other, if the former be short, the latter long, how shall I detain the short one, and how, measuring, shall I apply it to the long, that I may find this to have twice so much; seeing the long does not begin to sound, unless the short leaves sounding? And that very long one do I measure while it is present, seeing I measure it not till it be ended? Now its ending is its passing away. What then is it I measure? Where is the short syllable by which I measure? Where the long which I measure? Both have sounded, have flown, passed away, are no more; and yet I measure, and confidently answer (so far as is presumed on a practiced sense) that as to space of time this syllable is but single, that double. And yet I could not do this, unless they were already past and ended. It is not then themselves, which now are not, that I measure, but something in my memory, which there remains fixed.

It is in You, my mind, that I measure times. Interrupt me not, that is, do not interrupt yourself with the tumults of your impressions. In You I measure times; the impression, which things as they pass by cause in You, remains even when they are gone; this it is which, still present, I measure, not the things which pass by to make this impression. This I measure, when I measure times. Either then this is time, or I do not measure times. What when we measure silence, and say that this silence has held as long time as did that voice? Do we not stretch out our thought to the measure of a voice, as if it sounded, that so we may be able to report of the intervals of silence in a given space of time? For though both voice and tongue be still, yet in thought we go over poems, and verses, and any other discourse, or dimensions of motions, and report as to the spaces of times, how much this is in respect of that, no otherwise than if vocally we did pronounce them. If a man would utter a lengthened sound, and had settled in thought how long it should be, he has in silence already gone through a space of time, and committing it to memory, begins to utter that speech, which sounds on, until it be brought unto the end proposed. Indeed, it has sounded, and will sound; for so much of it as is finished, has sounded already, and the rest will sound. And thus passes it on, until the present intent conveys over the future into the past; the past increasing by the diminution of the future, until by consumption of the future, all is past.

28. *We measure times in our mind*

But how is that future diminished or consumed, which as yet is not? Or how that past increased, which is now no longer, save that in the mind which enacts this, there be three things done? For it expects, it considers, it remembers; so that which it expects, through that which it considers, passes into that which it remembers. Who therefore denies, that things to come do not yet exist? And yet, there is in the mind an expectation of things to come. And who denies that past things no longer exist? And yet is there still in the mind a memory of things past. And who denies that the present time is without space, because it passes away in a moment? And yet our consideration continues, through which that which shall be proceeds to become absent. It is not then future time, that is long, for as yet it is not: but a long future is 'a long expectation of the future', nor is it time past, which now is not, that is long; but a long past is 'a long memory of the past'.

I am about to repeat a psalm that I know. Before I begin, my expectation is extended over the whole; but when I have begun, how much soever of it I shall separate off into the past, is extended along my memory; thus the life of this action of mine is divided between my memory as to what I have repeated, and expectation as to what I am about to repeat; but 'consideration' is present with me, that through it what was future, may be conveyed over, so as to become past. Which the more it is done again and again, so much the more the expectation being shortened, is the memory enlarged: till the whole expectation be at length exhausted, when that whole action being ended, shall have passed into memory. And this which takes place in the whole psalm, the same takes

place in each several portion of it, and each several syllable; the
same holds in that longer action, whereof this psalm may be part;
the same holds in the whole life of man, whereof all the actions of
man are parts; the same holds through the whole age of the sons of
men, whereof all the lives of men are parts.

29. *How the mind lengthens out itself*

But because Your loving-kindness is better than all lives, behold,
my life is but a distraction, and Your right hand upheld me, in
my Lord the Son of man, the mediator betwixt You, the One,
and us many, in many things and through many things, that
through Him I may lay hold, in whom I have been laid hold
of, and may be re-collected from my old occupations, to follow
this one, forgetting the past, not drawn aside but drawn on,
and not to things which shall be and shall pass away, but to
those things which are before. And so, not as one drawn aside,
but as one drawn on, I pursue the prize of my heavenly calling,
where I may hear the voice of Your praise, and contemplate
Your delights, which are neither to come nor to pass away. But
now are my years spent in mourning. And You, O Lord, are my
comfort, my Father everlasting, but I am in pieces, falling into
times whose order I know not; and my thoughts, even the
inmost bowels of my soul, are rent and mangled with varied
tumults, until I run together in You, purified and molten by the
fire of Your love.

30. *He goes on in the same discourse*

Now will I stand, and become firm in You, in my mould, Your
truth; nor will I endure the questions of men, who in their
culpable disease thirst for more than they can contain, and say,
What did God before He made heaven and earth? Or, How
came it into His mind to make anything, having never before
made anything? Give them, O Lord, well to bethink themselves
what they say, and to find, that 'never' makes no sense when
'time' is not. This then that He is said 'never to have made';
what else is it than to say, There was no time when he made it?
Let them see therefore, that time cannot be without created
being, and cease to speak that vanity. Let them even stretch out
towards those things which are before; and understand You

before all times, the eternal creator of all times, and that no times be co-eternal with You, nor any creature, even if there be any creature before all times.

31. *How God is known, and how the creature*

O Lord my God, what a depth is that recess of Your mysteries, and how far from it have the consequences of my transgressions cast me! Heal mine eyes, that I may share the joy of Your light. Certainly, if there be mind gifted with such vast knowledge and foreknowledge, as to know all things past and to come, as I know one well-known psalm, truly that mind is passing wonderful, and amazing to the point of horror; in that nothing past, nothing to come in after-ages, is any more hidden from Him, than for me, when I sung that psalm, was hidden from me – what, and how much, had passed away since the beginning; and what, and how much, there remained unto the end. But far be it that You the creator of the universe, the creator of souls and bodies, far be it that You should in such wise know all things past and to come. Far, far more wonderfully, and far more mysteriously, do You know them. It is not like someone singing something he knows, or hearing some well-known song, whose feelings are altered, and his senses distracted, through expectation of the words to come, and the remembering of those that are past. Not so does anything happen unto You, unchangeably eternal, that is, the eternal creator of minds. Like then as You in the beginning knew the heaven and the earth, without any variety of Your knowledge, so made You in the beginning heaven and earth, without any distraction of Your action. Whoso understands, let him confess unto You; and whoso understands not, let him confess unto You. Oh how high are You, and yet the humble in heart are Your dwelling-place; for You raise up those that are bowed down, and they fall not, whose elevation You are.

Book 12

1. *The difficulty of finding out the truth*

My heart, O Lord, touched with the words of Your holy scripture, is much busied, amid this poverty of my life. And therefore most times is the poverty of human understanding copious in words, because enquiring has more to say than discovering, and demanding is longer than obtaining, and our hand that knocks, has more work to do than our hand that receives. We hold the promise, who shall make it null? If God be for us, who can be against us? Ask, and ye shall have; seek, and ye shall find; knock, and it shall be opened unto you. For every one that asks, receives; and he that seeks, finds; and to him that knocks, shall it be opened. These be Your own promises: and who need fear to be deceived, when the truth promises?

2. *That the heaven we see is but earth, in comparison with the heaven of heavens, which we see not*

The lowliness of my tongue confesses unto Your Highness, that You made heaven and earth — this heaven which I see, and this earth that I tread upon, from which comes this earth that I bear about me; You made it. But where is that heaven of heavens, O Lord, which we hear of in the words of the psalm? The heaven of heavens are the Lord's; but the earth has He given to the children of men? Where is that heaven which we see not, to which all this which we see is earth? For this corporeal whole, not being wholly everywhere, has in such wise received its portion of beauty in these lower parts, whereof the lowest is this our earth; but to that heaven of heavens, even the heaven of our earth is but earth: yea both these great bodies may not absurdly be called earth, in comparison with that unknown heaven, which belongs to the Lord, not to the sons of men.

3. *Of the darkness upon the face of the deep*

And now this earth was invisible and without form, and there was I know not what depth of abyss, upon which there was no light, because it had no shape. Therefore did You command it to be written, that darkness was upon the face of the deep; what else than the absence of light? For had there been light, where should it have been but by being over all, rising and giving light? Where then light was not, what was the presence of darkness, but the absence of light? Darkness therefore was upon it, because light was not upon it; as where sound is not, there is silence. And what is it to have silence there, but to have no sound there? Have not You, O Lord, taught his soul, which confesses unto You? Have not You taught me, Lord, that before You formed and diversified this formless matter, there was nothing, neither color, nor figure, nor body, nor spirit? And yet not altogether nothing; for there was a certain formlessness, without any beauty.

4. *Of the chaos, and what Moses called it*

How then should it be called, that it might be in some measure conveyed to those of duller mind, but by some familiar word? And what, among all parts of the world, can be found nearer to an absolute formlessness, than earth and deep? For, occupying the lowest stage, they are less beautiful than the other higher parts are, transparent all and shining. Why then may I not conceive the formlessness of matter (which You had created without beauty, whereof to make this beautiful world) to be suitably intimated unto men, by the name of earth invisible and without form?

5. *That this chaos is hard to conceive*

So that when thought seeks what the sense may conceive under this, and says to itself, It is no intellectual form, as life, or justice; because it is the matter of bodies; nor object of sense, because being invisible, and without form, there was in it no object of sight or sense — while man's thought thus says to itself, it may endeavor either to know it, by being ignorant of it; or to be ignorant, by knowing it.

6. *Saint Augustine's own thoughts about chaos*

As for me, Lord, if I would, by my tongue and my pen, confess unto
You the whole, whatever You have taught me of that matter – the
name whereof hearing before, and not understanding, because
they who told me of it understood it not, so I conceived of it as
having innumerable forms and diverse, and therefore did not
conceive it at all; my mind revolved foul and horrible 'forms', out
of all order, but yet 'forms'; and I called this lacking in form –
not that it wanted all form, but because it had such as my mind,
presented with it, would turn from, as unwonted and jarring,
and human frailness would be troubled at. And still that which I
conceived, was without form, not as being deprived of all form,
but in comparison of more beautiful forms; and true reason did
persuade me, that I must utterly strip it of all remnants of form
whatsoever, if I would conceive matter absolutely without form;
and I could not; for sooner could I imagine that not to be at all,
which should be deprived of all form, than conceive a thing
betwixt form and nothing, neither formed, nor nothing, a formless almost nothing. So my mind gave over to question thereupon
with my spirit, it being filled with the images of formed bodies,
and changing and varying them, as it willed; and I bent myself
to the bodies themselves, and looked more deeply into their
changeableness, by which they cease to be what they have been,
and begin to be what they were not; and this same shifting from
form to form, I suspected to be through a certain formless state,
not through a mere nothing; yet this I longed to know, not
to suspect only. If then my voice and pen would confess unto
You the whole, whatsoever knots You did open for me in this
question, what reader would hold out to take in the whole? Nor
shall my heart for all this cease to give You honor, and a song of
praise, for those things which it is not able to express. For the
changeableness of changeable things, is itself capable of all those
forms, into which these changeable things are changed. And this
changeableness, what is it? Is it soul? Is it body? Is it that which
constitutes soul or body? If one could say, 'a nothing something',
an 'is, is not', I would say, this were it: and yet in some way it had
an existence even then, as being capable of receiving these visible
and compound figures.

7. *Heaven is greater than earth*

But whence had it this degree of being, but from You, from Whom are all things, so far forth as they are? But so much the further from You, the more unlike You; for it is not a matter of place. You therefore, Lord, who are not one thing in one place, and something else in another, but the self-same, and the self-same, and the self-same, holy, holy, holy, Lord God Almighty, did in the beginning, which is of You, in Your wisdom, which was born of Your own substance, create something, and that out of nothing. For You created heaven and earth; not out of Yourself, for so should they have been equal to Your only begotten Son, and thereby to You also; whereas no way were it right that anything should be equal to You, which was not of You. And anything else besides You was there not, whereof You might create them, O God, one trinity, and threefold unity; and therefore out of nothing did You create heaven and earth; a great thing, and a small thing; for You are almighty and good, to make all things good, even the great heaven and the petty earth. You were, and nothing was there besides, out of which You created heaven and earth; things of two sorts; one near You, the other near to nothing; one to which You alone should be superior; the other, to which nothing should be inferior.

8. *Chaos was created out of nothing;*
and out of that, all things

That heaven of heavens was for Yourself, O Lord; but the earth which You gave to the sons of men, to be seen and touched, was not such as we now see and touch. It was invisible, without form, and there was a deep, upon which there was no light; or, darkness was above the deep, that is, more than in the deep. Because this deep of waters, visible now, has even in its depths, a light proper for its nature: perceivable in whatever degree unto the fishes, and creeping things in the bottom of it. But that whole deep was almost nothing, because hitherto it was altogether without form; yet there was already that which could be formed. For You, Lord, made the world of a matter without form, which You made out of nothing, into almost nothing, thereof to make those great things, which we sons of men wonder at. For very wonderful is this corporeal heaven; of which firmament between water and water, the second day, after the creation of light, You said, Let it be made, and it was made. Which firmament You called heaven: the heaven, that is, to this earth and sea, which You made the third day, by giving a visible figure to the formless matter, which You made before all days. For already had You made one heaven, before all days; but that was the heaven of this heaven, because in the beginning You had made heaven and earth. But this same earth which You made was formless matter, because it was invisible and without form, and darkness was upon the deep, that of this invisible earth, without form, of which formlessness, of which almost nothing, You might make all these things of which this changeable world consists and does not consist; whose very changeableness appears therein, that times can be observed and numbered in it. For times are made by the alterations of things, while the figures, the matter whereof is the invisible earth mentioned earlier, are varied and turned.

9. *What that heaven of heavens is*

And therefore the Spirit, the teacher of Your servant, when it recounts You to have in the beginning created heaven and earth, speaks nothing of times, nothing of days. For verily that heaven of heavens which You created in the beginning, is some intellectual creature which, although no ways co-eternal unto You, the Trinity, yet partakes of Your eternity, and does through the sweetness of that most happy contemplation of Yourself, strongly restrain its own changeableness; and without any fall since its first creation, sticking close unto You, is placed beyond all the rolling vicissitude of times. Yea, neither is this very formlessness of the earth, invisible and without form, numbered among the days. For where no figure nor order is, there does nothing come, or go; and where this is not, there plainly are no days, nor any change of intervals of time.

10. *His desire to understand the scriptures*

O let the light, the truth, the light of my heart, not mine own darkness, speak unto me. I lapsed into those things, and became darkened; but even thence, even thence I loved You. I went astray, and remembered You. I heard Your voice behind me, calling to me to return, and scarcely heard it, through the tumultuousness of the enemies of peace. And now, behold, I return in distress, thirsting for Your spring. Let no man forbid me! Of this will I drink, and so live. Let me not be mine own life; relying on myself I lived ill, death was I to myself; and I revive in You. Do You speak unto me, do You discourse unto me. I have believed Your books, and their words be most full of mystery.

11. *What he learnt of God*

Already You have told me with a strong voice, O Lord, in my inner ear, that You are eternal, who alone have immortality; since You can not be changed as to figure or motion, nor is Your will altered by times: seeing no will which varies is immortal. This is in Your sight clear to me. Let it be made clearer and clearer to me, I beseech You; and in the manifestation thereof, let me with sobriety abide under Your wings. You have told me also with a strong voice, O Lord, in my inner ear, that You have made all natures and substances, which are not what You are, and yet are; and that alone is not from You, which is not, and the motion of the will from You who are, unto that which is in a less degree, is because such motion is transgression and sin; and that no man's sin does either hurt You, or disturb the order of Your government, first or last. This is in Your sight clear unto me. Let it be made clearer and clearer to me, I beseech You: and in the manifestation thereof, let me with sobriety abide under Your wings.

You have told me also with a strong voice, in my inner ear, that neither is that creature co-eternal with You, whose sole happiness You are, and which with a most persevering purity, drawing its nourishment from You, does in no place and at no time put forth its natural mutability; and, You being ever present with it, unto whom with its whole affection it keeps itself, having neither future to expect, nor conveying into the past what it remembers, neither altered by any change, nor drawn into any times. O blessed creature, if such there be, for holding fast to Your blessedness; blessed in You, its eternal inhabitant and its enlightener! Nor do I find by what name I may rather call the heaven of heavens which is the Lord's, than Your house, which contemplates Your delights without any defection of going forth to another; one pure mind, most harmoniously one, by that settled estate of peace of holy spirits, the citizens of Your city in heavenly places; far above those heavenly places that we see.

By this may the soul, whose pilgrimage is made long and far away, by this may she understand, if she now thirsts for You, if her tears be now become her bread, while they daily say unto her, Where is Your God? If she now seeks of You one thing, and desires it, that she may dwell in Your house all the days of her life (and what is her life, but You? And what Your days, but Your eternity, as Your years which fail not, because You are ever the same?); by this then may the soul that is able, understand how far You are, above all times, eternal; seeing Your house which at no time went into a far country, although it be not co-eternal with You, yet by continually and unfailingly holding fast to You, suffers no changeableness of times. This is in Your sight clear unto me, and let it be clearer and clearer unto me, I beseech You, and in the manifestation thereof, let me with sobriety abide under Your wings.

There is, behold, I know not what formlessness in those changes of these last and lowest creatures; and who shall tell me (unless such a one as through the emptiness of his own heart, wonders and tosses himself up and down amid his own fancies?), who but such a one would tell me, that if all figure be so wasted and consumed away, that there should only remain that formlessness, through which the thing was changed and turned from one figure to another, that that could exhibit the vicissitudes of times? For plainly it could not, because, without the variety of motions, there are no times: and no variety, where there is no figure.

12. *Of two creatures not within the compass of time*

These things considered, as much as You give, O my God, as much as You stir me up to knock, and as much as You open to me when I do knock, two things I find that You have made, not within the compass of time, neither of which is co-eternal with You. One, which is so formed, that without any ceasing of contemplation, without any interval of change − since though changeable, it has not been changed − it may thoroughly enjoy Your eternity and unchangeableness; the other which was so formless, that it had nothing which could be changed from one form into another, whether of motion, or of repose, so as to become subject unto time. But this You did not leave thus formless, because before all days, You in the beginning did create heaven and earth; the two things that I spoke of. And the earth was invisible and without form, and darkness was upon the deep. In which words is the formlessness conveyed unto us (that such capacities may hereby be drawn on by degrees, as are not able to conceive an utter privation of all form, without yet coming to nothing), out of which another heaven might be created, together with a visible and well-formed earth: and the waters diversly ordered, and whatsoever further is in the formation of the world, recorded to have been, in some days, created; being of such nature, that the successive changes of times may take place in them, as being subject to appointed alterations of motions and of forms.

13. *The nature of the heaven of heavens described*

This then is what I conceive, O my God, when I hear Your scripture saying, In the beginning God made heaven and earth: and the earth was invisible and without form, and darkness was upon the deep, and not mentioning what day You created them; this is what I conceive, that because of the heaven of heavens – that intellectual heaven, whose intelligences know all at once, not in part, not darkly, not through a glass, but as a whole, in manifestation, face to face; not this thing now, and that thing anon; but (as I said) know all at once, without any succession of times – and because of the earth invisible and without form, without any succession of times, which succession presents 'this thing now, that thing anon'; because where is no form, there is no distinction of things: it is, then, on account of these two, a primitive formed, and a primitive formless: the one, heaven, but the heaven of heaven, the other earth, but the earth invisible and without form; because of these two do I conceive, did Your scripture say without mention of days, In the beginning God created heaven and earth. For forthwith it subjoined what earth it spoke of; and also, in that the firmament is recorded to be created the second day, and called heaven, it conveys to us of which heaven He before spoke, without mention of days.

14. *The depth of holy scripture*

Wondrous depth of Your words! whose surface, behold! is before us, inviting to little ones; yet are they a wondrous depth. O my God, a wondrous depth! It is awful to look therein; an awfulness

of honor, and a trembling of love. The enemies thereof I hate
vehemently; O that You would slay them with Your two-edged
sword, that they might no longer be enemies unto it: for so do I
love to have them slain unto themselves, that they may live unto
You. But behold others, not faultfinders, but extollers of the book
of Genesis; 'The spirit of God,' say they, 'who by His servant
Moses wrote these things, would not have those words thus
understood; He would not have it understood as you say, but
otherwise, as we say.' Unto whom, with You as judge, O God of
us all, do I thus answer.

15. *The difference between the creator and the creatures;
some discourse on the heaven of heavens*

'Will you affirm that to be false, which truth tells me loudly in my
inner ear, concerning the eternity of the creator, that His substance is no ways changed by time, nor His will separate from His
substance? Wherefore He wills not one thing now, another anon,
but once, and at once, and always, He wills all things that He wills;
not again and again, and not now this, now that; nor wills
afterwards, what before He willed not, nor wills not, what before
He willed; because such a will is changeable, and no changeable
thing is eternal: but our God is eternal. Again, the things He tells
me in my inner ear, the expectation of things to come, becomes
sight, when they are come, and this same sight becomes memory,
when they be past. Now all thought which thus varies is mutable;
and what is mutable is not eternal: but our God is eternal.' These
things I collect, and put together, and find that my God, the
eternal God, has not upon any new will made any creature, nor
does His knowledge admit of anything transitory.

'What will ye say then, O ye gainsayers? Are these things false?'
'No,' they say; 'What then? Is it false, that every nature already
formed, or matter capable of form, can only be from Him who
is supremely good, because He supremely is?' 'No, we do not
deny this either,' say they. 'What then? Do you deny this, that
there is some sublime creature, with so chaste a love holding fast
unto the true and truly eternal God, that although not co-eternal
with Him, yet is it not detached from Him, nor dissolved into
the variety and vicissitude of times, but it reposes in the most true
contemplation of Him only?' Because You, O God, unto him

that loves You so much as You command, do show Yourself, and suffice him; and therefore does he not decline from You, nor toward himself. This is the house of God, not of earthly mould, nor of celestial bulk corporeal but spiritual, and partaker of Your eternity, because without defect for ever. For You have made it fast for ever and ever, You have given it a law which it shall not pass. Yet is it not co-eternal with You, O God, because not without beginning; for it was made.

For even if we find no time before it – for wisdom was created before all things; not that wisdom which is altogether equal and co-eternal unto You, our God, His Father, and by whom all things were created, and in whom, as the beginning, You created heaven and earth; but that wisdom which is created, that is, the intellectual nature, which by contemplating the light, is light. For this, though created, is also called wisdom. But what difference there is betwixt the light which enlightens, and that which is enlightened, so much is there betwixt the wisdom that creates, and that which is created; as betwixt the righteousness which justifies, and the righteousness which is made by justification. For we also are called Your righteousness; for so says a certain servant of Yours, That we might be made the righteousness of God in Him. Therefore since a certain created wisdom was created before all things, the rational and intellectual mind of that chaste city of Yours, our mother which is above, and is free and eternal in the heavens (in what heavens, if not in those that praise You, the heaven of heavens? Because this is also the heaven of heavens for the Lord) – even if we find no time before it (because what has been created before all things, precedes also the creation of time), yet is the eternity of the creator Himself before it, from whom, being created, it took the beginning, not indeed of time (for time itself was not yet), but of its creation.

Hence it is from You, our God, in such a way as to be altogether other than You, and not the self-same: because though we find time neither before it, nor even in it (it being fit ever to behold Your face, nor is ever drawn away from it, wherefore it is not varied by any change), yet is there in it a liability to change, whence it would wax dark, and chill, but that by a strong affection holding fast to You, like perpetual noon, it shines and glows from You. O house, full of light and charm! I have loved your beauty, and the place of the habitation of the glory of my Lord, your builder and possessor. Let my wandering sigh after You, and I say to Him that made You, let Him take possession of me also in You, seeing He has made me likewise. I have gone astray like a lost sheep: yet upon the shoulders of my shepherd, who built you, hope I to be brought back to You.

'What say you to me, O ye gainsayers that I was speaking unto, who yet believe Moses to have been the holy servant of God, and his books the oracles of the Holy Ghost? Is not this house of God, not co-eternal indeed with God, yet after its measure, eternal in the heavens, when you seek for changes of times in vain, because you will not find them? For that, whose good it is ever to hold fast to God, surpasses all extension, and all revolving periods of time.' 'It is,' say they. 'What then of all that which my heart loudly uttered unto my God, when inwardly it heard the voice of His praise, what part thereof do you affirm to be false? Is it that the matter was without form, in which because there was no form, there was no order? But where no order was, there could be no vicissitude of times: and yet this almost nothing,' inasmuch as it was not altogether nothing, was from Him certainly, from whom is whatsoever is, in what degree soever it is.' 'This also,' say they, 'do we not deny.'

16. *Against those who deny divine truth, and of his own delight in it*

In Your presence, O my God, do I wish now to parley a little with those who allow all these things to be true, which Your truth whispers unto my soul. As for those who deny these things, let them bark and deafen themselves as much as they please; I will essay to persuade them to be quiet, and to open in them a way for Your word. But if they refuse, and repel me, I beseech, O my God, do not You be silent to me. Speak You truly in my heart; for You alone so speak: and I send them away to blow upon the dust, and raise it up into their own eyes: let me enter my chamber, and sing there a song of loves unto You; groaning with groanings unutterable, in my wanderings, and remembering Jerusalem, my heart stretching up towards it, Jerusalem my country, Jerusalem my mother, and You who rule over her, the enlightener, father, guardian, husband, the pure and strong delight, and solid joy, and all good things unspeakable, yea all at once, because the one sovereign and true good. Nor will I be turned away, until You gather all that I am, from this dispersed and disordered estate, into the peace of that our most dear mother, where the first-fruits of my spirit are already (whence I am ascertained of these things), and You conform and confirm it for ever, O my God, my mercy. But those who do not affirm all these truths to be false, who honor Your holy scripture, set forth by holy Moses, placing it, as we, on the summit of authority to be followed, and do yet contradict me in some thing, I answer thus: You must be judge, O our God, between my confessions and these men's contradictions.

17. *What the names 'heaven' and 'earth' signify*

For they say, 'Though these things be true, yet did not Moses have in view those two things, when, by revelation of the Spirit, he said, In the beginning God created heaven and earth. He did not under the name of heaven, signify that spiritual or intellectual creature which always beholds the face of God; nor under the name of earth, that formless matter.' 'What then?' 'What we say,' they reply, 'is what that man of God meant, what he declared by those words.' 'And what is that?' 'By the name of heaven and earth,' say they, 'would he first signify, universally and briefly, all this visible world; so as afterwards by the enumeration of the several days, to arrange in detail, and, as it were, piece by piece, all those things which it pleased the Holy Ghost thus to enounce. For such were that rude and carnal people to which he spoke, that he thought them fit to be entrusted with the knowledge of such works of God only as were visible.' They agree, however, that the words 'earth invisible and without form', and 'that darksome deep' (out of which it is subsequently shown, that all these visible things which we all know, were made and arranged during those 'days') may, not incongruously, be understood of this formless first matter.

What now if another should say, that this same formlessness and confusedness of matter, was for this reason first conveyed under the name of heaven and earth, because out of it was created and perfected this visible world with all those natures which most manifestly appear in it, which is ofttimes called by the name of heaven and earth? What again if another say, that invisible

and visible nature is not indeed inappropriately called heaven and
earth; and so, that the universal creation, which God made in His
wisdom, that is, in the beginning, was comprehended under those
two words? Notwithstanding, since all things be made not of the
substance of God, but out of nothing (because they are not the same
that God is, and there is a mutable nature in them all, whether they
abide, as does the eternal house of God, or be changed, as the soul
and body of man are); therefore the common matter of all things
visible and invisible (as yet unformed though capable of form), out
of which was to be created both heaven and earth (i.e. the invisible
and visible creature when formed), was identified by the same
names given to the earth invisible and without form and the
darkness upon the deep, but with this distinction, that by the earth
invisible and without form is understood corporeal matter, ante-
cedent to its being qualified by any form; and by the darkness upon
the deep, spiritual matter, before it underwent any restraint of its
unlimited fluidness, or received any light from wisdom?

It yet remains for a man to say, if he will, that the already
perfected and formed natures, visible and invisible, are not signified under the name of heaven and earth, when we read, In the
beginning God made heaven and earth, but that the yet unformed
commencement of things, the stuff apt to receive form and making,
was called by these names, because therein were confusedly contained, not as yet distinguished by their qualities and forms, all
those things which being now digested into order, are called
heaven and earth, the one being the spiritual, the other the
corporeal, creation.

18. *Different expounders may understand the same text different ways*

All which things being heard and well considered, I will not argue
about words: there is no profit in that, beyond putting off the
hearers. But the law is good to build on, if a man use it lawfully:
for that the end of it is charity, out of a pure heart and good
conscience, and faith unfeigned. Well did our Master know this,
upon which two commandments He hung all the Law and the
Prophets. And how does it hinder me, O my God, You light of
my eyes in secret, if I zealously confess these things, since different
things may be understood under these words which yet are all

true – how, I say, does it hinder me, if I understand what the writer meant differently from how somebody else understands it? All we who read are doing our best to trace out and to understand his meaning whom we read; and seeing we believe him to speak truly, we dare not imagine him to have said anything, which we either know or think to be false. While every man endeavors then to understand in the holy scriptures, the same as the writer understood, what hurt is it, if a man understand what You, the light of all true-speaking minds, do show him to be true, although he whom he reads, understood not this, seeing he also understood a truth, though not this truth?

19. *Of some particular apparent truths*

For true it is, O Lord, that You made heaven and earth; and it is true too, that the beginning is Your wisdom, in which You created all: and true again, that this visible world has for its greater part the heaven and the earth, which briefly comprise all made and created natures. And true too, that whatsoever is mutable, gives us to understand a certain want of form, whereby it receives a form, or is changed or turned. It is true, that which so holds fast to the unchangeable form, that though it is subject to change, it never does change, is not subject to any time. It is true, that that formlessness which is almost nothing, cannot be subject to the alteration of times. It is true, that that whereof a thing is made, may by a certain mode of speech, be called by the name of the thing made of it; whence that formlessness, whereof heaven and earth were made, might be called heaven and earth. It is true, that of things having form, there is not any nearer to having no form, than the earth and the deep. It is true, that not only every created and formed thing, but whatsoever is capable of being created and formed, You made, from whom are all things. It is true, that whatsoever is formed out of that which had no form, was unformed before it was formed.

20. *He interprets Genesis i.1 differently*

Out of all these truths, of which they doubt not whose inward eye You have enabled to see such things, and who unshakenly believe Your servant Moses to have spoken in the spirit of truth – of all these, then, he takes one, who says, In the beginning God

made the heaven and the earth; that is, In His word co-eternal
with Himself, God made the intelligible and the sensible, or the
spiritual and the corporeal creature. He takes another, who says,
In the beginning God made heaven and earth; that is, In His
word co-eternal with Himself, did God make the universal bulk
of this corporeal world, together with all those apparent and
known creatures, which it contains. And he another, who says,
In the beginning God made heaven and earth; that is, In His
word co-eternal with Himself, did God make the formless matter
of creatures spiritual and corporeal. He another, that says, In
the beginning God created heaven and earth; that is, In His
word co-eternal with Himself, did God create the formless matter
of the creature corporeal, wherein heaven and earth lay as yet
confused, which, being now distinguished and formed, we at this
day see in the bulk of this world. He another, who says, In the
beginning God made heaven and earth; that is, In the very
beginning of creating and working, did God make that formless
matter, confusedly containing in itself both heaven and earth; out
of which, being formed, do they now stand out, and are apparent,
with all that is in them.

21. These words, 'the earth was void etc.' variously understood

And as regards understanding the words following, out of all those
truths, he chooses one to himself, who says, But the earth was
invisible, and without form, and darkness was upon the deep; that
is, That corporeal thing that God made, was as yet a formless matter
of corporeal things, without order, without light. Another, he
who says, The earth was invisible and without form, and darkness
was upon the deep; that is, This all, which is called heaven and
earth, was still a formless and darksome matter, of which the
corporeal heaven and the corporeal earth were to be made, with
all things in them which are known to our corporeal senses.
Another, he who says, The earth was invisible and without form,
and darkness was upon the deep; that is, This all, which is called
heaven and earth, was still a formless and a darksome matter; out
of which was to be made, both that intelligible heaven, elsewhere
called the heaven of heavens, and the earth, that is, the whole
corporeal nature, under which name is comprised this corporeal

heaven also; in a word, out of which every visible and invisible creature was to be created. Another, he who says, The earth was invisible and without form, and darkness was upon the deep. The scripture did not call that formlessness by the name of heaven and earth; but that formlessness, says he, already was, which he called the earth invisible without form, and darkness upon the deep; of which he had before said, that God had made heaven and earth, namely, the spiritual and corporeal creature. Another, he who says, The earth was invisible and without form, and darkness was upon the deep; that is, There already was a certain formless matter, of which the scripture said before, that God made heaven and earth; namely, the whole corporeal bulk of the world, divided into two great parts, upper and lower, with all the common and known creatures in them.

22. *That the waters are also included under the names of heaven and earth*

For should any attempt to dispute against these two last opinions, thus: If you will not allow that this formlessness of matter seems to be called by the name of heaven and earth, therefore there was something which God had not made, out of which to make heaven and earth; for neither has scripture told us, that God made this matter, unless we understand it to be signified by the name of heaven and earth, or of earth alone, when it is said, In the beginning God made the heaven and earth; so that in what follows, 'and the earth was invisible and without form' (although it pleased Him so to call the formless matter), we are to understand no other matter, but that which God made, whereof is written above, God made heaven and earth. Those who maintain either of these two last opinions will, upon hearing this, return for answer, We do not deny this formless matter to be indeed created by God, that God from whom, certainly, come all good things; for as we affirm that to be a greater good, which is created and formed, so we confess that to be a lesser good which is made capable of creation and form, yet still good. However, we say scripture has not set down, that God made this formlessness, as also it has not set down many other things; as the Cherubim, and Seraphim, and the things the apostle explicitly mentions: thrones, dominions, principalities, powers. And that God made

these, is quite clear. Or if in that which is said, He made heaven
and earth, all things be comprehended, what shall we say of the
waters, upon which the Spirit of God moved? For if they be
comprised in this word earth, how then can formless matter be
meant in that name of earth, when we see the waters so beautiful?
Or if it be so taken, why then is it written, that out of the same
formlessness, the firmament was made, and called heaven; when
that the waters were made, is not written? For the waters remain
not formless and invisible, seeing we behold them flowing in
so comely a manner. But if they then received that beauty,
when God said, Let the waters under the firmament be gathered
together, that so the gathering together be itself the forming of
them, what will be said as to those waters above the firmament?
Seeing neither if formless would they have been worthy of so
honorable a seat, nor is it written, by what word they were
formed. If then Genesis is silent as to God's making of anything,
which yet that God did make neither sound faith nor well-
grounded understanding doubts, nor again will any sober teaching
dare to affirm these waters to be co-eternal with God, on the
ground that we find them to be mentioned in the book of
Genesis, but when they were created, we do not find; why (seeing
truth teaches us) should we not understand that formless matter
(which this scripture calls the earth invisible and without form,
and darksome deep) to have been created of God out of nothing,
and therefore not to be co-eternal to Him; although this history
has omitted to show when it was created?

23. In interpreting holy scripture, truth is
to be sought in a charitable fashion

These things then being heard and perceived, to the best of my
weak capacity (which I confess unto You, O Lord, that know it),
two sorts of disagreement I see may arise, when a thing is in words
related by true reporters: one, concerning the truth of the things,
the other, concerning the meaning of the person reporting. It
is one thing to ask, about the making of what is created, what
the truth is; a quite different question to ask, what Moses, that
excellent minister of Your faith, wanted his reader and hearer to
understand by those words. In the first category, let them reject all
those who claim to know things that are false; and in the second,

let them reject all who claim that Moses said things that are false. But let me be united in You, O Lord, and delight myself in You, with those, the ones that feed on Your truth, in the largeness of charity, and let us approach together unto the words of Your book, and seek in them for Your meaning, through the meaning of Your servant, by whose pen You have dispensed them.

24. *Scripture is true, even if we do not understand its full scope or depth*

But which of us shall, among those so many truths, which occur to enquirers in those words, as they are differently understood, so discover that one meaning, as to affirm, This Moses thought, and, This would he have understood in that history, with the same confidence as he would, This is true, whether Moses thought this or that? For behold, O my God, I Your servant, who have in this book vowed a sacrifice of confession unto You, and pray, that by Your mercy I may pay my vows unto You, can I, with the same confidence wherewith I affirm, that in Your incommutable world You created all things visible and invisible, affirm also, that Moses meant no other than this, when he wrote, In the beginning God made heaven and earth? No. Because I see not in his mind, that he thought of this when he wrote these things, as I do see it in Your truth to be certain. For he might have been thinking of the commencement of creating, when he said In the beginning; and by heaven and earth, in this place he might intend no formed and perfected nature, whether spiritual or corporeal, but both of them inchoate and as yet formless. For I perceive, that whichsoever of the two had been said, it might have been truly said; but which of the two he thought of in these words, I do not so perceive. Although, whether it were either of these, or any sense beside (that I have not here mentioned), which this great man saw in his mind, when he uttered these words, I doubt not but that he saw it truly, and expressed it aptly.

25. *We are not to break charity over a different exposition of scripture*

Let no man try and make trouble for me then, by saying, Moses thought not as you say, but as I say: for if he should ask me, How know you that Moses thought that which you infer out of his

words? I ought to take it in good part, and would answer perchance as I have above, or something more at large, if he were
unyielding. But when he says, Moses meant not what you say,
but what I say, yet denies not that what each of us say, may
both be true, O my God, life of the poor, in whose bosom is no
contradiction, pour down a softening dew into my heart, that I
may patiently bear with such as say this to me, not because they
have a divine spirit, and have seen in the heart of Your servant
what they speak, but because they be proud; not knowing Moses'
opinion, but loving their own, not because it is truth, but because
it is theirs. Otherwise they would equally love another true
opinion, as I love what they say, when they say true: not because
it is theirs, but because it is true; and on that very ground not
theirs because it is true. But if the reason they love it, is because it
is true, then is it both theirs and mine; as being in common to all
lovers of truth. But when they contend that Moses did not mean
what I say, but what they say, this I will not have, do not love:
for even if it were so, yet that their rashness belongs not to
knowledge, but to overboldness, and not insight but vanity was
its parent. And therefore, O Lord, are Your judgments terrible;
seeing Your truth is neither mine, nor his, nor another's, but
belonging to us all, whom You call publicly to partake of it;
warning us terribly, not to account it private to ourselves, lest we
be deprived of it. For whosoever challenges that as proper to
himself, which You propound to all to enjoy, and would have
that his own which belongs to all, is driven from what is in
common to his own — that is, from truth, to a lie. For he that
speaks a lie, speaks it of his own.

Hearken, O God, You best judge; truth itself, hearken to what
I shall say to this gainsayer; hearken, for before You do I speak,
and before my brethren, who employ Your law lawfully, to the
end of charity: hearken and behold, if it please You, what I shall
say to him. For this brotherly and peaceful word do I return unto
him: If we both see what you say to be true, and both see what I
say to be true, where, I pray You, do we see it? Neither I in you,
nor you in me; but both in the unchangeable truth itself, which is
above our souls. Seeing then we strive not about the very light of
the Lord God, why strive we about the thoughts of our neighbour, which we cannot so see as the unchangeable truth is seen:

for that, if Moses himself had appeared to us and said, This I meant; neither so should we see it, but should believe it. Let us not then be puffed up for one against another, above that which is written: Let us love the Lord our God with all our heart, with all our soul, and with all our mind: and our neighbour as ourself. With a view to which two precepts of charity, unless we believe that Moses meant, whatsoever in those books he did mean, we shall make God a liar, imagining otherwise of our fellow servant's mind, than he has taught us. Behold now, how foolish it is, in such abundance of most true meanings as may be extracted out of those words, rashly to affirm, which of them Moses principally meant; and with pernicious contentions to offend charity itself, for whose sake he spoke everything, whose words we go about to expound.

26. *What style is fit to write the scriptures in*

And yet I, O my God, You height of my humility, and rest of my labour, who hear my confessions, and forgive my sins: seeing You command me to love my neighbour as myself, I cannot believe that You gave a lesser gift unto Moses Your faithful servant, than I would wish or desire You to have given me, had I been born in the time he was, and had You set me in that office, that by the service of my heart and tongue those books might be dispensed, which for so long after were to profit all nations, and through the whole world from such an eminence of authority, were to surmount all sayings of false and proud teachings. I should have desired verily, had I then been Moses (for we all come from the same lump, and what is man, saving that You are mindful of him?) I would then, had I been then what he was, and been ordered by You to write the book of Genesis, have desired such a power of expression and such a style to be given me, that both they who cannot yet understand how God created, might not reject the sayings as beyond their capacity; and they who had attained thereto, might find what true opinion soever they had by thought arrived at, not passed over in those few words of that Your servant: and should another man by the light of truth have discovered another, neither should that fail of being discoverable in those same words.

27. *Drawing from the fountain*

For as a fountain within a narrow compass, is more plentiful, and supplies a tide for more streams over larger spaces, than any one of those streams which, after a wide interval, is derived from the same fountain; so the relation of that dispenser of Yours, which was to benefit many who were to discourse thereon, does out of a modest measure of language, overflow into streams of clearest truth, whence every man may draw out for himself such truth as he can upon these subjects; one, one truth; another, another, by larger circumlocutions of discourse. For some, when they read or hear these words, conceive that God is like a man, or some mass endued with unbounded power, which by some new and sudden resolution, exterior to itself, did as it were at a certain distance, create heaven and earth, two great bodies above and below, wherein all things were to be contained. And when they hear, God said, Let it be made, and it was made; they conceive of words begun and ended, sounding in time, and passing away; after whose departure, that came into being, which was commanded so to do; and whatever of the like sort men's acquaintance with the material world would suggest. In whom, being yet little ones and carnal, while their weakness is by this humble kind of speech, carried on, as in a mother's bosom, their faith is wholesomely built up, whereby they hold assured, that God made all natures, which in admirable variety their eye beholds around. Which words, if any despising, as too simple, with a proud weakness, shall stretch himself beyond the guardian nest; he will, alas, fall miserably. Have pity, O Lord God, lest they who go by the way trample on the unfledged bird. Send Your angel to replace it into the nest, that it may live, till it can fly.

28. *How diversely this scripture is understood*

But others, unto whom these words are no longer a nest, but deep shady fruit-bowers, see the fruits concealed therein, fly joyously around, and with cheerful notes seek out, and pluck them. For reading or hearing these words, they see that all times past and to come, are surpassed by Your eternal and stable abiding; and yet that there is no creature formed in time, not of Your making. And because Your will is the same that You are, You made all things, not by any change of will, nor by a will which before was not, not out of Yourself, in Your own likeness, which is the form of all things; but out of nothing, a formless unlikeness, which should be formed by Your likeness (recurring to You who are one, according to their appointed capacity, so far as is given to each thing in his kind); and all might be made very good, whether they abide around You, or being in gradation removed in time and place, made or undergo the beautiful variations of the universe. These things they see, and rejoice, in the little degree they here may, in the light of Your truth.

Another bends his mind on that which is said, In the beginning God made heaven and earth; and beholds therein wisdom, the beginning because it too speaks unto us. Another likewise bends his mind on the same words, and by beginning understands the commencement of things created: In the beginning He made, as if it were said, He at first made. And among them that understand In the beginning to mean, In Your wisdom You created heaven and earth, one believes the matter out of which the heaven and earth were to be created, to be there called heaven and earth; another, natures already formed and distinguished; another, one nature possessing form, and that spiritual, under the name heaven, another formless, a corporeal matter, under the name earth. They again who by the names heaven and earth, understand matter as yet formless, out of which heaven and earth were to be formed, do not understand it in one way; one understands, that matter out of which both the intelligible and the sensible creature were to be perfected; another, that only, out of which this sensible corporeal mass was to be made, containing in its vast bosom these visible and ordinary natures. Neither do they, who believe the creatures already ordered and arranged, to be in this place called heaven and earth, understand the same; but the one understands, both the invisible and visible, the other, the visible only, in which we behold this lightsome heaven, and darksome earth, with the things in them contained.

29. *How many ways a thing may be said to be first*

But he that no otherwise understands In the beginning He made, than if it were said, At first He made, can only truly understand heaven and earth of the matter of heaven and earth, that is, of the universal intelligible and corporeal creation. For if he would understand thereby the universe, as already formed, it may be rightly demanded of him, If God made this first, what made He afterwards? and after the universe, he will find nothing; whereupon must he against his will hear another question; How did God make this first, if nothing after? But when he says, God made matter first formless, then formed, there is no absurdity, if he be but qualified to discern, what precedes by eternity, what by time, what by choice, and what by its origin. By eternity, as God is before all things; by time, as the flower before the fruit; by choice, as the fruit before the flower; by origin, as the sound before the tune. Of these four, the first and last mentioned, are with extreme difficulty understood; the two middle, easily. For a rare and too lofty a vision is it, to behold Your eternity, O Lord, unchangeably making things changeable; and being thereby prior to them. And who, again, is of so sharpsighted understanding, as to be able without great pains to discern, how the reason the sound is before the tune is because a tune is a formed sound; and a thing not formed, may exist; whereas that which exists not, cannot be formed. Thus is the matter before the thing made; not because it makes it, seeing it is itself the thing made; nor is it before by interval of time, for we do not first in time utter formless sounds without singing, and subsequently adapt or fashion them into the form of a chant, as wood or silver, whereof a chest or vessel is fashioned. For such materials do by time also precede the forms of the things made of them, but in singing it is not so; for when it is sung, its sound is heard; for there is not first a formless sound, which is afterwards formed into a chant. For each sound, so soon as made, passes away, nor can you find aught to recall and by art to compose. So then the chant is concentrated in its sound, and this its sound is its matter. And this indeed is formed, that it may be a tune; and therefore (as I said) the matter of the sound is before the form of the tune; not before, through any power it has to make it a tune; for a sound is no way the workmaster of the tune; but is something corporeal, subjected to the soul which sings, whereof to make a tune. Nor is it first in time; for it is given forth together with the tune; nor first in choice, for a sound is not better than a tune, a tune being not only a sound, but a beautiful sound. But it is first in origin, because a tune receives not form to become a sound, but a sound receives a form to become a tune. By this example, let him that is able understand how the matter of things was first made, and called heaven and earth, because heaven and earth were made out of it. Yet was it not made first in time; because the forms of things give rise to time; but that was without form, but now is, in time, an object of sense together with its form. And yet nothing can be related of that matter, but as though prior in time, whereas in value it is last (because things formed are superior to things without form) and is preceded by the eternity of the creator: that so out of nothing there might be whereof somewhat might be created.

30. *The scriptures are to be searched, with respect for the writer*

In this diversity of the true opinions, let truth herself produce concord. And may our God have mercy upon us, that we may lawfully use the law, the end of the commandment, pure charity. By this if man demands of me, Which of these was the meaning of Your servant Moses? this were not the language of my *Confessions*, should I not confess unto You, I know not; and yet I know that those senses are true, those carnal ones excepted, of which I have spoken what seemed necessary. And even those hopeful little ones who so think, have this benefit, that the words of Your book affright them not, delivering high things lowlily, and with few words a copious meaning. And all we who, I confess, see and express the truth delivered in those words, let us love one another, and jointly love You our God, the fountain of truth, if we are athirst for it, and not for vanities; yea, let us so honor this Your servant, the dispenser of this scripture, full of Your spirit, as to believe that, when by Your revelation he wrote these things, he intended that, which among them chiefly excels both for light of truth, and fruitfulness of profit.

31. *Truth is so to be received, whoever speaks it*

So when one says, Moses meant as I do; and another, Nay, but as I do, I suppose that I speak more reverently, Why not rather as both, if both be true? And if there be a third, or a fourth, yea if any other sees any other truth in those words, why may not he be believed to have seen all these, through whom the One God has tempered the holy scriptures to the senses of many, who should see therein things true but different? For my part, certainly (and fearlessly I speak it from my heart), were I to write anything with claims to supreme authority, I should prefer so to write, that any truth to be found on those matters, might be conveyed in my words, rather than set down my own meaning so clearly as to exclude the rest, which if they were false, could not offend me. I will not therefore, O my God, be so rash, as not to believe, that You vouchsafed as much to that great man. He without doubt, when he wrote those words, perceived and thought on what truth soever we have been able to find, yea and whatsoever we have not been able, nor yet are, but which may be found in them.

32. *He prays to obtain right meaning*

Lastly, O Lord, who are God and not flesh and blood, if man did see less, could anything be concealed from Your good spirit (who shall lead me into the land of uprightness), which You Yourself by those words were about to reveal to readers in times to come, though he through whom they were spoken, perhaps among many true meanings, thought on one in particular? Which if so it be, let that which he had in mind be of all the highest. But to us, O Lord, do You either reveal that same, or any other true one which pleases You; that so, whether You discover the same to us, as to that Your servant, or some other by occasion of those words, yet You may feed us, not error deceive us. Behold, O Lord my God, how much we have written upon a few words, how much I beseech You! What strength of ours, yea what ages would suffice for all Your books in this manner? Permit me then in these more briefly to confess unto You, and to choose some one true, certain, and good sense that You shall inspire me, even though many should occur, where many may occur; with this faith in my confession, that if I should say that which Your minister intended, that is right and best; for this should I endeavor, which if I should not attain, yet I should speak that, which Your truth willed by his words to tell me, which revealed also unto him, what it willed.

Book 13

1. *He calls upon God*

I call upon You, O my God, my mercy, who created me, and forgot not me, who did forget You. I call You into my soul which, by the longing You breathe into her, You are preparing to receive You. Forsake me not now calling upon You, since You were there ahead of me before I called, and urged me with much variety of repeated calls, that I would hear You from afar, and be converted, and call upon You, that called after me; for You, Lord, blotted out all my evil deservings, so as not to give retribution to the work of my hands, wherewith I fell from You; and You have been ahead of all my well deservings, so as to repay me with the work of Your hands wherewith You made me; because before I was, You were; nor was I anything, to which You might grant to be; and yet behold, I am, out of Your goodness, which goes before all this which You have made me, and whereof You have made me. For neither had You need of me, nor am I any such good, as to be helpful unto You, my Lord and God; not in serving You, as though You would tire in working; or lest Your power might be less, if lacking my service: nor cultivating Your service, as a land that must remain uncultivated, unless I cultivated You: but serving and worshipping You, that I might receive a well-being from You, from whom it comes, that I have a being capable of well-being.

2. *Of the creatures' dependency on their creator*

From the fullness of Your goodness, does Your creature subsist, that so a good, which was no benefit to You, nor (though coming from You) could be equal to You, might yet not be lacking, since it could be made of You. For what did heaven and earth, which You made in the beginning, deserve of You? Let those spiritual and corporeal natures which You made in Your wisdom, say wherein they deserved of You, to depend thereon (even in that their several inchoate and formless state, whether spiritual or corporeal, ready to fall away into an immoderate liberty and far-distant unlikeliness unto You – the spiritual, even without form, superior to the corporeal, though formed, and the corporeal though without form, better than were it altogether nothing), and so to depend upon Your word, as formless, unless by the same word they were brought back to Your unity, endued with form and from You, the one sovereign good, were made all very good. How did they deserve of You, even to be without form, since they had not been even this, but from You?

How did corporeal matter deserve of You, to be even invisible and without form? seeing it were not even this, but that You made it, and therefore because it was not, could not deserve of You to be made. Or how could the inchoate spiritual creature deserve of You, even to ebb and flow darksomely like the deep – unlike You, unless it had been by the same word turned to that, by whom it was created, and by Him so enlightened, become light; though not equally, yet conformably to that form which is equal unto You? For as in a body, to be is not one with being beautiful, else could it not be deformed; so likewise to a created spirit to live is not one with living wisely; else should it be wise unchangeably. But good it is for it always to hold fast to You; lest what light it has obtained by turning to You, it lose by turning from You, and relapse into life resembling the darksome deep. For we ourselves also, who as to the soul are a spiritual creature, turned away from You our light, were in that life sometimes darkness; and still labour amidst the relics of our darkness, until in Your only One we become Your righteousness, like the mountains of God. For we have been Your judgments, which are like the great deep.

3. All things are by the grace of God

That which You said in the beginning of the creation, Let there be light, and there was light; I do, not unsuitably, understand of the spiritual creature: because there was already a sort of life, which You might illuminate. But as it had no claim on You for a life, which could be enlightened, so neither now that it was, had it any, to be enlightened. For neither could its formless estate be pleasing unto You, unless it became light, and that not by existing simply, but by beholding the illuminating light, and holding fast to it; and so, that it lived, and lived happily, it owes to nothing but Your grace, being turned by a better change unto that which cannot be changed into worse or better; which You alone are, because You alone simply are; unto You it being not one thing to live, another to live blessedly, seeing You are Your own blessedness.

4. *God does not need the creatures; they do need Him*

What then could be wanting unto Your good, which You Yourself are, although these things had either never been, or remained without form; which you made, not out of any want, but out of the fullness of Your goodness, restraining them and converting them to form, not as though Your joy were fulfilled by them? For to You, being perfect, is their imperfection displeasing, and that is why they were perfected by You, and please You; not because You were imperfect, and were also to be perfected by their perfecting. For Your good spirit indeed was borne over the waters, not borne up by them, as if he rested upon them. For those, on whom Your good spirit is said to rest, he causes to rest in himself. But Your incorruptible and unchangeable will, in itself all-sufficient for itself, was borne upon that life which You had created; to which, living is not one with happy living, seeing it lives also, ebbing and flowing in its own darkness: for which it remains to be converted unto Him, by whom it was made, and to live more and more by the fountain of life, and in His light to see light, and to be perfected, and enlightened, and beautified.

5. *The Holy Trinity*

Lo, now the Trinity appears unto me in a glass darkly, which is You my God, because You, O Father, in Him who is the beginning of our wisdom, which is Your wisdom, born of Yourself, equal unto You and co-eternal, that is, in Your Son, created heaven and earth. Much now have we said of the heaven of heavens, and of the earth invisible and without form, and of the darksome deep, in reference to the wandering instability of its spiritual deformity, had it not been converted unto Him, from whom it had its then degree of life, and by His enlightening become a beauteous life, and the heaven of that heaven, which was afterwards set between water and water. And under the name

of God, I now held the Father, who made these things, and under
the name of beginning, the Son, in whom He made these things;
and believing, as I did, my God as the Trinity, I searched further
in His holy words, and lo, Your Spirit moved upon the waters.
Behold the Trinity, my God, Father, and Son, and Holy Ghost,
creator of all creation.

6. *Of the Spirit moving upon the waters*

But what was the cause, O true-speaking light? Unto You lift I up
my heart, let it not teach me vanities, dispel its darkness; and tell
me, I beseech You, by our mother charity, tell me the reason, I
beseech You, why after the mention of heaven, and of the earth
invisible and without form, and darkness upon the deep, Your
scripture should then at length mention Your Spirit? Was it
because it was meet that the knowledge of Him should be conveyed, as being 'borne above'; and this could not be said, unless
that were first mentioned, over which Your Spirit may be understood to have been borne. For neither was He borne above the
Father, nor the Son, nor could He rightly be said to be borne
above, if He were borne over nothing. First then was that to be
spoken of, over which He might be borne; and then He, whom it
was meet not otherwise to be spoken of than as being borne. But
wherefore was it not meet that the knowledge of Him should be
conveyed otherwise, than as being borne above?

7. *Of the working of the Holy Ghost*

Hence let him that is able, follow with his understanding Your
apostle, where he thus speaks: Because Your love is shed abroad in
our hearts by the Holy Ghost which is given unto us: and where
concerning spiritual gifts, he teaches and shows unto us a more
excellent way of charity; and where he bows his knee unto You for
us, that we may know the supereminent knowledge of the love of
Christ. And therefore from the beginning, was He borne supereminent above the waters. To whom shall I speak this? How speak
of the weight of evil desires, downwards to the steep abyss; and
how charity raises up again by Your Spirit which was borne above
the waters? To whom shall I speak it? How speak it? For it is not in
space that we are merged and emerge. What can be more, and yet
what less like? They be affections, they be loves; the uncleanness of

our spirit flowing away downwards with the love of cares, and the holiness of Your raising us upward by love of carefree repose; that we may lift our hearts unto You, where Your Spirit is borne above the waters; and come to that supereminent repose, when our soul shall have passed through the waters which yield no support.

8. *How God helps weak souls*

Angels fell away, man's soul fell away; they pointed to the abyss in that dark depth, ready for the whole spiritual creation, had not You said from the beginning, Let there be light, and there was light, and every obedient intelligence of Your heavenly city held fast to You, and rested in Your Spirit, which is borne unchangeably over every thing changeable. Otherwise, even the heaven of heavens had been in itself a darksome deep; but now it is light in the Lord. For even in that miserable restlessness of the spirits, who fell away and discovered their own darkness, when bared of the clothing of Your light, do You sufficiently reveal how noble You made the rational creation; to which nothing less than You (and so not even herself) suffices to yield a happy rest. For You, O our God, shall lighten our darkness: from You rises our garment of light; and then shall our darkness be as the noon day. Give Yourself unto me, O my God, restore Yourself unto me: behold I love, and if it be too little, I would love more strongly. I cannot measure so as to know, how much love is yet lacking to me, ere my life may run into Your embracements, nor turn away, until it be hidden in the hidden place of Your presence. This only I know, that woe is me except in You: not only without but within myself also; and all abundance, which is not my God, is emptiness to me.

9. *Why the Spirit moved only upon the waters*

But was not either the Father, or the Son, borne above the waters? If this means, in space, like a body, then neither was the Holy Spirit; but if the unchangeable supereminence of divinity above all things changeable, then were both Father and Son and Holy Ghost borne upon the waters. Why then is this said of Your Spirit only, why is it said only of Him? As if there had been a place where He was, who is not in a place, of whom only it is written, that He is Your gift? In Your gift we rest; there we enjoy You. Our rest is our place. Love lifts us up thither, and Your good Spirit lifts up our lowliness from the gates of death. In Your good pleasure is our peace. The body by its own weight strives towards its own place. Weight makes not downward only, but to his own place. Fire tends upward, a stone downward. They are urged by their own weight, they seek their own places. Oil poured below water, is raised above the water; water poured upon oil, sinks below the oil. They are urged by their own weights to seek their own places. When out of their order, they are restless; restored to order, they are at rest. My weight, is my love; thereby am I borne, whithersoever I am borne. We are inflamed, by Your gift we are kindled; and are carried upwards; we glow inwardly, and go forwards. We ascend Your ways that be in our heart, and sing a song of degrees; we glow inwardly with Your fire, with Your good fire, and we go, because we go upwards to the peace of Jerusalem: for gladdened was I in those who said unto me, We will go up to the house of the Lord. There has Your good pleasure placed us, that we may desire nothing else, but to abide there for ever.

10. *All is of God's gift*

Blessed creature, which being itself other than You, has known no other condition, than that, so soon as it was made, it was, without any interval, raised up by Your gift, which is borne above every thing changeable, in that calling whereby You said, Let there be light, and there was light. Whereas in us this took place at different times, in that we were darkness, and are made light: but of that is said, what it would have been, had it not been enlightened. And this is so spoken, as if it had been unsettled and darksome before; that so the cause whereby it was made otherwise might appear, namely, that being turned to the light unfailing it became light. Whoso can, let him understand this; let him ask of You. Why should he trouble me, as if I could enlighten any man that comes into this world?

11. *Of some impressions or resemblances of the Holy Trinity, that be in man*

Who comprehends the almighty Trinity? And who speaks not of it, if indeed it be it? Rare is the soul, which speaks of it, and knows what it speaks of. They contend and strive, yet without peace, no man sees that vision. I could wish that men would consider three things, that are in themselves. These three be indeed far other than the Trinity: I do but tell, where they may practice themselves, and there prove and feel how far they be. Now the three I spoke of are: to be, to know, and to will. For I am, and know, and will: I am knowing and willing: and I know myself to be, and to will: and I will to be, and to know. In these three then, let him discern that can, how inseparable a life there is, yea one life, mind, and one essence, yea lastly how inseparable a distinction there is, and yet a distinction. Surely a man has it before him; let him look into himself, and see, and tell me. But when he discovers and can say anything of these, let him not therefore think that he has found that unchangeable which is above these, which is unchangeably, and knows unchangeably, and wills unchangeably; whether because of these three, there is a trinity there too, or whether all three be in each, so that the three belong to each; or whether both ways at once, wondrously, simply and yet manifoldly, an infinite limit to itself within itself; whereby it is, and is known unto itself and suffices to itself, unchangeably the self-same, by the abundant greatness of its unity – who will easily decide? Who will in any way express it? Who will, in any way, pronounce rashly thereon?

12. *The water in baptism takes effect through the Holy Spirit*

Proceed in your confession; say to the Lord your God, O my faith, Holy, Holy, Holy, O Lord my God, in Your name have we been baptized, Father, Son, and Holy Ghost; in Your name do we baptize, Father, Son, and Holy Ghost, because among us also, in His Christ did God make heaven and earth, namely, the spiritual and carnal people of His Church. Yea and our earth, before it received the form of doctrine, was invisible and without form; and we were covered with the darkness of ignorance. For You chastened man for iniquity, and Your judgments were like the great deep unto him. But because Your Spirit was borne above the waters, Your mercy forsook not our misery, and You said, Let there be light, Repent ye, for the kingdom of heaven is at hand. Repent ye, let there be light. And because our soul was troubled within us, we remembered You, O Lord, from the land of Jordan, and that mountain equal unto You, but little for our sakes: and our darkness displeased us, we turned unto You, and there was light. And, behold, we were once darkness, but are now light in the Lord.

13. *His devout longing for God*

But as yet by faith and not by sight, for by hope we are saved; but hope that is seen, is not hope. As yet does deep call unto deep, but now in the voice of Your water-spouts. As yet, he that says, I could not speak unto you as unto spiritual, but as unto carnal, even he as yet does not think himself to have apprehended, and forgets those things which are behind, and reaches forth to those which are before, and groans being burdened, and his soul thirsts after the living God, as the hart after the water-brooks, and says, When shall I come? desiring to put on his habitation which is from heaven; and calls upon this lower deep, saying, Be not conformed to this world, but be transformed by the renewing of your mind. And, Be not children in under-standing, but be ye children in malice, that in understanding ye may be perfect; and, O foolish Galatians, who has bewitched you? But now no longer in his own voice; but in Yours who sent Your Spirit from above; through Him who ascended up on high, and set open the flood-gates of His gifts, that the force of His streams might make glad your city. After her does this friend of the bridegroom sigh, having now the first-fruits of the Spirit laid up with him, yet still groaning within himself, waiting for the adoption, to wit, the redemption of his body; for her he sighs, a member of the bride; for him he is jealous, as being a friend of the bridegroom; for her he is jealous, not for himself; because in the voice of Your water-spouts, not in his own voice, does he call to that other depth, over whom being jealous he fears, lest as the serpent beguiled Eve through his subtilty, so their minds should be corrupted from the purity that is in our bridegroom Your only Son. O what a light of beauty will that be, when we shall see Him as He is, and those tears be passed away, which have been my meat day and night, whilst they daily say unto me, Where is now Your God?

14. *Our misery is comforted by faith and hope*

Behold, I too say, My God, where are You? See, where You are! In You I breathe a little, when I pour out my soul by myself in the voice of joy and praise, the sound of him that keeps holy-day. Yet still it is sad, because it relapses, and becomes a deep, or rather perceives itself still to be a deep. Unto it speaks my faith which You have kindled to enlighten my feet in the night, Why are you sad, O my soul, and why do you trouble me? Hope in the Lord; His word is a lantern unto your feet: hope and endure, until the night, the mother of the wicked, until the wrath of the Lord, be overpast, whereof we also were once children, who were at one time darkness, relics whereof we bear about us in our body, dead because of sin; until the day break, and the shadows fly away. Hope you in the Lord; in the morning I shall stand in Your presence, and contemplate You: I shall for ever confess unto You. In the morning I shall stand in Your presence, and shall see the health of my countenance, my God, who also shall quicken our mortal bodies, by the Spirit that dwells in us, because He has in mercy been borne over our inner darksome and floating deep: from whom we have in this pilgrimage received an earnest, that we should now be light: whilst we are saved by hope, and are the children of light, and the children of the day, not the children of the night, nor of the darkness, which yet sometime we were. Betwixt whom and us, in this uncertainty of human knowledge, You alone divide; You, who prove our hearts, and call the light, day, and the darkness, night. For who discerns us, but You? And what have we, that we have not received of You? Out of the same lump vessels are made unto honor, whereof others also are made unto dishonor.

15. *By 'firmament' is meant scripture*

Or who, except You, our God, made for us that firmament of authority over us in Your divine scripture? As it is said, For heaven shall be folded up like a scroll; and now is it stretched over us like a skin. For Your divine scripture is of more eminent authority, since those mortals by whom You dispense it unto us, underwent mortality. And You know, Lord, You know, how You with skins did clothe men, when they by sin became mortal. Whence You have like a skin stretched out the firmament of Your book, that is, Your harmonizing words, which by the ministry of mortal men You spread over us. For by their very death was that solid firmament of authority, in Your discourses, set forth by them, more eminently extended over all that be under it; which whilst they lived here, was not so eminently extended. You had not as yet spread abroad the heaven like a skin; You had not as yet enlarged in all directions the glory of their deaths.

Let us look, O Lord, upon the heavens, the work of Your fingers; clear from our eyes that cloud, with which You have covered them. There is Your testimony, which gives wisdom unto the little ones: perfect, O my God, Your praise out of the mouth of babes and sucklings. For we know no other books, which so destroy pride, which so destroy the enemy and the defender, who resists Your reconciliation by defending his own sins. I know not, Lord, I know not any other such pure words, which so persuade me to confess, and make my neck pliant to Your yoke, and invite me to serve You for nothing. Let me understand them, good Father: grant this to me, who am placed under them: because for those placed under them, have You established them.

Other waters there be above this firmament, I believe immortal, and separated from earthly corruption. Let them praise Your name, let them praise You, the supercelestial people, Your angels; who have no need to gaze up at this firmament, or by reading to know of Your word. For they always behold Your face, and there read without any timed syllables, what wills Your eternal will; they read, they choose, they love. They are ever reading; and that never passes away which they read; for by choosing, and by loving, they read the very unchangeableness of Your counsel. Their book is never closed, nor their scroll folded up; seeing You Yourself are this to them, and are eternally; because You have ordained them above this firmament, which You have firmly settled over the infirmity of the lower people, where they might gaze up and learn Your mercy, announcing in time You who made times. For Your mercy, O Lord, is in the heavens, and Your truth reaches unto the clouds. The clouds pass away, but the heaven abides. The preachers of Your word pass out of this life into another; but Your scripture is spread abroad over the people, even unto the end of the world. Even heaven and earth shall pass away, but Your words shall not pass away. Because the scroll shall be rolled together: and the grass over which it was spread, shall with the goodliness of it pass away; but Your word remains for ever, which now appears unto us under the dark image of the clouds, and through the glass of the heavens, not as it is: because to us also, though the well-beloved of Your Son, it has not yet been made clear what we shall be. He looked through the lattice of our flesh, and spoke us tenderly, and kindled us, and we are hot on His scent. But when He shall appear, then shall we be like Him, for we shall see Him as He is. As He is, Lord, will our sight be.

16. *God is unchangeable*

For altogether, how You are, You alone know; who are unchangeably, and know unchangeably, and will unchangeably. Your essence knows, and wills unchangeably; and Your knowledge is, and wills unchangeably; and Your will is, and knows unchangeably. Nor seems it right in Your eyes, that as the unchangeable light knows itself, so should it be known by the thing enlightened, and changeable. Therefore is my soul like a land where no water is, because as it cannot of itself enlighten itself, so can it not of itself satisfy itself. For so is the fountain of life with You, just as in Your light we shall see light.

17. *What is meant by dry land, and by the sea*

Who gathered the embittered together into one society? For they have all one end, a temporal and earthly felicity, for attaining whereof they do all things, though they waver up and down with an innumerable variety of cares. Who, Lord, but You, said, Let the waters be gathered together into one place, and let the dry land appear, which thirsts after You? For the sea also is Yours, and You have made it, and Your hands prepared the dry land. Nor is the bitterness of men's wills, but the gathering together of the waters, called sea; for You restrain the wicked desires of men's souls, and set them their bounds, how far they may be allowed to pass, that their waves may break one against another: and thus You make it a sea, by the order of Your dominion over all things.

But the souls that thirst after You, and that appear before You (being by other bounds divided from the society of the sea), You water by a sweet spring, that the earth may bring forth her fruit, and You, Lord God, so commanding, our soul may bud forth works of mercy according to their kind, loving our neighbour in the relief of his bodily necessities, having seed in itself according to its likeness, when from feeling of our infirmity, we sympathize, so as to relieve the needy; helping them, as we would be helped if we were in like need; not only in things easy, as in herb yielding seed, but also in the protection of our assistance, with our best strength, like the tree yielding fruit: that is, well-doing in rescuing him that suffers wrong, from the hand of the powerful, and giving him the shelter of protection, by the mighty strength of just judgment.

18. *He continues his allegory, on the works of the creation*

So, Lord, so, I beseech You, let there spring up, as You make it do, as You give cheerfulness and ability, let truth spring out of the earth, and righteousness look down from heaven, and let there be lights in the firmament. Let us break our bread to the hungry, and bring the houseless poor to our house. Let us clothe the naked, and despise not those of our own flesh. Which fruits having sprung out of the earth, see it is good: and let our temporary light break forth; and ourselves, from this lower fruitfulness of action, arriving at the delightfulness of contemplation, obtaining the word of life above, appear like lights in the world, holding fast to the firmament of Your scripture. For there You instruct us, to divide between things intellectual and things of sense, as betwixt the day and the night; or between souls given either to things intellectual or things of sense, so that now not only You in the secret of Your judgment, as before the firmament was made, divide between the light and the darkness, but Your spiritual children also set and ranked in the same firmament (now that Your grace is laid open throughout the world), may give light upon the earth, and divide betwixt the day and the night, and be for signs of times, that old things are passed away, and, behold, all things are become new; and that our salvation is nearer than when we believed: and that the night is far spent, and the day is at hand: and that You will crown Your year with blessing, sending the labourers of Your goodness into Your harvest, in sowing whereof others have laboured, and sending also into another field, whose harvest shall be in the end. Thus grant You the prayers of him that asks, and bless the years of the just; but You are the same, and in Your years which fail not, You prepare a garner for our passing years. For You by an eternal counsel do in their proper seasons bestow heavenly blessings upon the earth. For here is given by the Spirit the word of wisdom, as it were the greater light; (for those who delight in the light of perspicuous truth), as it were at the beginning of the day; there, is given the word of knowledge by the same Spirit, as it were the lesser light; here, faith; there, the gift of healing; here, the working of miracles; there, prophecy; here, discerning of spirits; there, divers kinds of tongues. And all these as it were stars. For all these work the one and self-same spirit, dividing to every man his own as He will; and causing stars to appear manifestly, to profit withal. But the word of knowledge, wherein are contained all sacraments, which are varied in their seasons as it were the moon, and those other notices of gifts, which are reckoned up in order, as it were stars, inasmuch as they come short of that brightness of wisdom, which gladdens the forementioned day, are only for the rule of the night. For they are necessary to such as that Your most prudent servant could not speak unto as unto spiritual, but as unto carnal; even he who speaks wisdom among those that are perfect. But the natural man, as it were a babe in Christ and fed on milk, until he be strengthened for solid meat and his eye be enabled to behold the sun, let him not dwell in a night forsaken of all light, but be content with the light of the moon and the stars. So do You speak to us, our all-wise God, in Your book, Your firmament; that we may discern all things, in an admirable contemplation; though as yet in signs and in times, and in days and in years.

19. *Our hearts are to be cleaned, that they may be capable of virtue; the allegory of the creation continued*

But first, wash you, be clean; put away evil from your souls, and from before mine eyes, that the dry land may appear. Learn to do good, act as judge for the fatherless, plead for the widow, that the earth may bring forth the green herb for meat, and the tree bearing fruit; and come, let us reason together, says the Lord, that there may be lights in the firmament of the heaven, and they may shine upon the earth. That rich man asked of the good Master, what he should do to attain eternal life. Let the good Master, whom he thought a man and nothing more (but He is good because He is God), tell him, if he would enter into life, he must keep the commandments: let him put away from him the bitterness of malice and wickedness;

not kill, not commit adultery, not steal, not bear false witness; that the dry land may appear, and bring forth the honoring of father and mother, and the love of our neighbour. All these (says he) have I kept. Whence then so many thorns, if the earth be fruitful? Go, root up the spreading thickets of covetousness; sell that you have, and be filled with fruit, by giving to the poor, and you shall have treasure in heaven; and follow the Lord if you will be perfect, associated with those among whom He speaks wisdom, who knows what to distribute to the day, and to the night, that you also may know it, and for You there may be lights in the firmament of heaven; which will not be, unless your heart be there: nor will that be, unless your treasure be there; as you have heard of the good Master. But that barren earth was grieved; and the thorns choked the word.

But you, chosen generation, you weak things of the world, who have forsaken all, that you may follow the Lord; go after Him, and confound the mighty; go after Him, you beautiful feet, and shine in the firmament, that the heavens may declare His glory, dividing between the light of the perfect, though not as the angels, and the darkness of the little ones, though not despised. Shine over the earth; and let the day, lightened by the sun, utter unto day, speech of wisdom; and night, shining with the moon, show unto night, the word of knowledge. The moon and stars shine for the night; yet does not the night obscure them, seeing they give it light in its degree. For behold God saying, as it were, Let there be lights in the firmament of heaven; there came suddenly a sound from heaven, as it had been the rushing of a mighty wind, and there appeared cloven tongues like as of fire, and it sat upon each of them. And there were made lights in the firmament of heaven, having the word of life. Run to and fro everywhere, you holy fires, you beauteous fires; for you are the light of the world, nor are you put under a bushel; He whom you hold fast unto, is exalted, and has exalted you. Run to and fro, and be known unto all nations.

20. *An allegory upon the creation of spiritual things*

Let the sea also conceive and bring forth your works; and let the waters bring forth the moving creature that has life. For you, separating the precious from the vile, are made the mouth of God, by whom He says, Let the waters bring forth, not the living creature which the earth brings forth, but the moving creature having life, and the fowls that fly above the earth. For Your sacraments, O God, by the ministry of Your holy ones, have moved amid the waves of temptations of the world, to hallow the gentiles in Your name, in Your baptism. And amid these things, many great wonders were wrought, as it were great whales: and the voices of Your messengers flying above the earth, in the open firmament of Your book (that being set over them, as their authority under which they were to fly, whithersoever they went). For there is no speech nor language, where their voice is not heard: seeing their sound is gone through all the earth, and their words to the end of the world, because You, Lord, multiplied them by blessing.

Speak I untruly, or do I mingle and confound, and not distinguish between the lucid knowledge of these things in the firmament of heaven, and the material works in the wavy sea, and under the firmament of heaven? For of those things whereof the knowledge is substantial and defined, without any increase by generation, as it were lights of wisdom and knowledge, yet even of them, the material operations are many and divers; and one thing growing out of another, they are multiplied by Your blessing, O God, who have refreshed the fastidiousness of mortal senses; that so one thing in the understanding of our mind may, by the motions of the body, be many ways set out, and expressed. These sacraments have the waters brought forth; but in Your word. The necessities of the people estranged from the eternity of Your truth, have brought them forth, but in Your gospel; because the waters themselves cast them forth, the diseased bitterness whereof was the cause, why they were sent forth in Your word.

All things are fair if You make them; but behold, You Yourself, that made all, are unutterably fairer; from whom had not Adam fallen, the brackishness of the sea had never flowed out of him, that is, the human race so profoundly curious, and tempestuously swelling, and restlessly tumbling up and down; and then had there been no need of Your dispensers, in many waters, fashioning mysterious doings and sayings in a physical and perceptible manner. For that is how those creeping and flying creatures now strike me; people imbued with these, and consecrated by physical sacraments, should get no further, unless their soul has a spiritual life, and after the word of admission, is looking towards perfection.

21. *An allegory upon the creation of birds and fishes; meaning by them such as have received the Lord's supper, who are more perfect Christians than the merely baptized*

And hereby, in Your word, not the deepness of the sea, but the earth separated from the bitterness of the waters, brings forth, not the moving creature that has life, but the living soul. For now has it no more need of baptism, as the heathen have, and as itself had, when it was covered with the waters (for no other entrance is there into the kingdom of heaven, since You have appointed that this should be the entrance); nor does it seek after the wonders of miracles to work belief; for it is not such, that unless it sees signs and wonders, it will not believe, now that the faithful earth is separated from the waters that were bitter with infidelity; and tongues are for a sign, not to them that believe, but to them that believe not. Neither then does that earth which You have founded upon the waters, need that flying kind, which at Your word the waters brought forth. Send Your word into it by Your messengers: for we speak of their working, yet it is You that work in them that they may work out a living soul in it. The earth brings it forth, because the earth is the cause that they work this in the soul; as the sea was the cause that they wrought upon the moving creatures that have life, and the fowls that fly under the firmament of heaven, of whom the earth has no need; although it feeds upon that fish which was taken out of the deep, upon that table which You have prepared in the presence of them that believe. For the reason he was taken out of the deep, was that he might feed the dry land; and the fowl, though bred in the sea, is yet multiplied upon the earth. For of the first preachings of the evangelists, man's infidelity was the cause; yet are the faithful also exhorted and blessed by them manifoldly, from day to day. But the living soul takes its beginning from the earth: for it profits only those already among the faithful, to contain themselves from the love of this world, that so their soul, which was dead while it lived in death-bringing pleasures, may live unto You, Lord, for You are the life-giving delight of the pure heart.

Therefore let Your ministers now work upon the earth – not as upon the waters of infidelity, by preaching and speaking by miracles, and sacraments, and mystic words; wherein ignorance, the mother of admiration, might be intent upon them, out of a reverence towards those secret signs – such is the entrance unto the faith for the sons of Adam forgetful of You, while they hide themselves from Your face, and become a darksome deep – but let Your ministers work now as on the dry land, separated from the whirlpools of the great deep: and let them be a pattern unto the faithful, by living before them, and stirring them up to imitation. For thus do men hear, so as not to hear only, but to do also. Seek the Lord, and your soul shall live, that the earth may bring forth the living soul. Be not conformed to the world. Keep yourselves from it: the soul lives by avoiding what it dies by seeking. Keep yourselves from the wild savagery of pride, the sluggish voluptuousness of luxury, and the false name of knowledge: that so the wild beasts may be tamed, the cattle broken to the yoke, the serpents, harmless. For these be the motions of our mind under an allegory; that is to say, the haughtiness of pride, the delight of lust, and the poison of curiosity, are the motions of a dead soul; for the soul dies not so as to lose all motion; it dies by forsaking the fountain of life, and so is taken up by this transitory world, and is conformed unto it.

But Your word, O God, is the fountain of life eternal; and passes not away: wherefore this departure of the soul is restrained by Your word, when it is said unto us, Be not conformed unto this world; that so the earth may in the fountain of life bring forth a living soul; that is, a soul made continent in Your word, by Your evangelists, by following the followers of Your Christ. For this is after his kind, because a man is wont to imitate his friend. Be you (says he) as I am, for I also am as you are. Thus in this living soul shall there be good beasts, in meekness of action (for You have commanded, Go on with your business in meekness, so shall you be beloved by all men); and good cattle, which neither if they eat, shall they over-abound, nor, if they eat not, have any lack; and good serpents, not dangerous, to do hurt, but wise to take heed; and only making so much search into this temporal nature, as may suffice that eternity be clearly seen, being understood by the things that are made. For these creatures are obedient unto reason, when, restrained from their lethal prevailing upon us, they live and are good.

22. Of regeneration by the Spirit; an allegory
upon the creation of man

For behold, O Lord, our God, our creator, when our affections have been restrained from the love of the world, by which we died through evil-living; and begun to be a living soul, through good living; and Your word which You spoke by Your apostle, is made good in us, Be not conformed to this world: there follows that also, which You presently subjoined, saying, But be you transformed by the renewing of your mind; not now after your kind, as though following your neighbour who went before you, nor as living after the example of some better man (for You said not, Let man be made after his kind, but, Let us make man after our own image and similitude), that we might prove what Your will is. For to this purpose spoke that dispenser of Yours (who begat children by the gospel), that the children he had might not be for ever babes, whom he must be fain to feed with milk, and cherish as a nurse; Be ye transformed (says he) by the renewing of your mind, that you may prove what is that good and acceptable and perfect will of God. Wherefore You say not, Let man be made, but Let us make man. Nor said You, 'according to his kind'; but, 'after our image and likeness'. For man being renewed in his mind, and beholding and understanding Your truth, needs not man as his director, so as to follow after his kind; but by Your direction proves what is that good, that acceptable and perfect will of Yours: yes, You teach him, now made capable, to discern the trinity of the unity, and the unity of the trinity. Wherefore to what is expressed in the plural, Let us make man, is yet subjoined in the singular, And God made man: and to that expressed in the plural, 'after our likeness', is subjoined in the singular, 'after the image of God'. Thus is man renewed in the knowledge of God, after the image of Him that created him: and being made spiritual, he judges all things (all things which are to be judged), yet is himself judged of no man.

23. What things a Christian may judge of; an allegory
upon man's dominion over things created

But that he judges all things, this answers to his having dominion over the fish of the sea, and over the fowls of the air, and over all cattle and wild beasts, and over all the earth, and over every creeping thing that creeps upon the earth. For this he does by the understanding of his mind, whereby he perceives the things of the Spirit of God; whereas otherwise, man being placed in honor, had no understanding, and is compared unto the brute beasts, and is become like unto them. In Your church therefore, O our God, according to Your grace which You have bestowed upon it (for we are Your workmanship created unto good works), not those only who are spiritually set over, but they also who spiritually are subject to those that are set over them – for in this way did You make man male and female, in Your grace spiritual, where there is neither male nor female, depending on the sex of body, because neither Jew nor Greek, neither bond nor free. Spiritual persons (whether such as are set over, or such as obey) do judge spiritually; not of that spiritual knowledge which shines in the firmament (for they ought not to judge as to so supreme authority), nor may they judge of Your book itself, even though something there shines not clearly; for we submit our understanding unto it, and hold for certain, that even what is closed to our sight, is yet rightly and truly spoken. For so man, though now spiritual and renewed in the knowledge of God after His image that created him, ought to be a doer of the law, not a judge. Neither does he judge of that distinction of spiritual and carnal men, who are known unto Your eyes, O our God, and have not as yet discovered themselves unto us by works, that by their fruits we might know them: but You, Lord, do even now know them, and have divided and called them in secret, before the firmament was made. Nor does he, though spiritual, judge the unquiet people of this world; for what has he to do, to judge them that are outside, knowing not which of them shall hereafter come into the sweetness of Your grace; and which continue in the perpetual bitterness of ungodliness?

Man therefore, whom You have made after Your own image, received not dominion over the lights of heaven, nor over that hidden heaven itself, nor over the day and the night, which You called before the foundation of the heaven, nor over the gathering together of the waters, which is the sea; but he received dominion over the fishes of the sea, and the fowls of the air, and over all cattle, and over all the earth, and over all creeping things which creep upon the earth. For he judges and approves what he finds right, and he disallows what he finds amiss, whether in the celebration of those sacraments by which such are initiated, as Your mercy searches out in many waters: or in that, in which that fish is set forth, which taken out of the deep, the devout earth feeds upon: or in the expressions and signs of words, subject to the authority of Your book — such signs as proceed out of the mouth, and sound forth, flying as it were under the firmament, by interpreting, expounding, discoursing, disputing, consecrating, or praying unto You, so that the people may answer, Amen. The vocal pronouncing of all which words, is occasioned by the deep of this world, and the blindness of the flesh, which cannot see thoughts, so there is need to speak aloud into the ears; so that, although flying fowls be multiplied upon the earth, yet they derive their beginning from the waters. The spiritual man judges also by approving what is right, and reproving what he finds amiss, in the works and lives of the faithful — their alms as it were the earth bringing forth fruit; he judges of the living soul, by the taming of the affections in chastity, in fasting, in holy meditations; and of those things, which are perceived by the senses of the body. Upon all these is he now said to judge, wherein he has also power of correction.

24. *An allegory upon 'increase and multiply'*

But what is this, and what kind of mystery? Behold, You bless mankind, O Lord, that they may increase and multiply, and replenish the earth; do You not thereby give us a hint to understand something? Why did You not as well bless the light, which You called day; nor the firmament of heaven, nor the lights, nor the stars, nor the earth, nor the sea? I might say that You who created, O God, created us after Your image; I might say, that it had been Your good pleasure to bestow this blessing peculiarly upon man, had You not in like manner blessed the fishes and the whales, that they should increase and multiply, and replenish the waters of the sea, and that the fowls should be multiplied upon the earth. I might say likewise, that this blessing pertained properly unto such creatures as are bred of their own kind, had I found it given to the fruit-trees, and plants, and beasts of the earth. But now neither unto the herbs, nor the trees, nor the beasts, nor serpents is it said, Increase and multiply; notwithstanding all these as well as the fishes, fowls, or men, do by generation increase and continue their kind.

What then shall I say, O truth my light? That it was idly said, because without meaning? Not so, O Father of piety, far be it from a minister of Your word to say so. And if I understand not what You mean by that phrase, let my betters, that is, those of more understanding than myself, make better use of it, according as You, my God, have given to each man to understand. But let my confession also be pleasing in Your eyes, wherein I confess unto You, that I believe, O Lord, that You spoke not so in vain; nor will I suppress, what this lesson suggests to me. For it is true, nor do I see what should hinder me from thus understanding the figurative sayings of Your Bible. For I know one thing to be in many ways signified by the body, which is understood in one way by the mind; and another thing to be understood in many ways by the mind, which is signified in one way by the body. Behold, the single love of God and our neighbour, by what manifold sacraments and innumerable languages, and in each several language, in how innumerable modes of speaking, it is corporeally expressed. Thus do the offspring of the waters increase and multiply. Observe again, whosoever reads this; behold, what scripture delivers and the voice utters, in one only way, In the beginning God created heaven and earth; is it not understood in many ways, not through any deceit of error, but by different kinds of true understandings? Thus do man's offspring increase and multiply.

If therefore we conceive of the natures of the things themselves, not allegorically, but properly, then does the phrase 'increase and multiply' agree unto all things that come of seed. But if we treat of the words as figuratively spoken (which I rather suppose to be the purpose of the scripture, which does not, surely, superfluously ascribe this benediction to the offspring of aquatic animals and man only); then do we find 'multitude' to belong to creatures spiritual as well as corporeal, as in heaven and earth, and to righteous and unrighteous, as in light and darkness; and to holy authors who have been the ministers of the Law unto us, as in the firmament which is settled betwixt the waters and the waters; and to the society of people yet in the bitterness of infidelity, as in the sea; and to the zeal of holy souls, as in the dry land; and to works of mercy belonging to this present life, as in the herbs bearing seed, and in trees bearing fruit; and to spiritual gifts set forth for edification, as in the lights of heaven; and to affections formed unto temperance, as in the living soul. In all these instances we meet with multitudes, abundance, and increase; but what shall in such wise increase and multiply that one thing may be expressed many ways, and one expression understood many ways, we find not, except in signs corporeally expressed, and in things mentally conceived. By signs corporeally expressed we understand the generations of the waters, necessarily occasioned by the depth of the flesh; by things mentally conceived, human generations, on account of the fruitfulness of reason. And for this end do we believe You, Lord, to have said to these kinds, Increase and multiply. For in this blessing, I conceive You to have granted us a power and a faculty, both to express several ways what we understand but one; and to understand several ways, what we read to be obscurely delivered but in one. Thus are the waters of the sea replenished, which are not moved but by several significations: thus with human increase is the earth also replenished, whose dryness appears in its longing, and reason rules over it.

25. *He compares the fruits of the earth to the duties of piety*

I would also say, O Lord my God, what the following scripture minds me of; Yea, I will say, and not fear. For I will say the truth, Yourself inspiring me with what You willed me to deliver out of those words. But by no other inspiration than Yours, do I believe myself to speak truth, seeing You are the truth, and every man a liar. He therefore that speaks a lie, speaks of what is his; that therefore I may speak truth, I will speak of what is Yours. Behold, You have given unto us for food every herb bearing seed which is upon all the earth; and every tree, in which is the fruit of a seed which can be sown. And not to us alone, but also to all the fowls of the air, and to the beasts of the earth, and to all creeping things; but unto the fishes and to the great whales, have You not given them. Now we said that by these fruits of the earth were signified, and figured in an allegory, the works of mercy which are provided for the necessities of this life out of the fruitful earth. Such an earth was the devout Onesiphorus, unto whose house You gave mercy, because he often refreshed Your Paul, and was not ashamed of Paul's chain. Thus did also the brethren, and such fruit did they bear, who out of Macedonia supplied what was lacking to him. But how grieved he for some trees, which did not afford him the fruit due unto him, where he says, At my first answer no man stood by me, but all men forsook me. I pray God that it may not be laid to their charge. For these fruits are due to such as minister the spiritual doctrine unto us out of their understanding of the divine mysteries; and they are due to them, as men; yea and due to them also, as the living soul, which gives itself as an example, in all continency; and due unto them also, as flying creatures, for their blessings which are multiplied upon the earth, because their sound went out into all lands.

26. *The pleasure and profit to us from a*
good turn done to our neighbour

But they are fed by these fruits, that are delighted with them; nor are they delighted with them, whose god is their belly. Nor indeed in those that show this character, is it the things they do which are the fruit, but the mind with which they do them. He therefore that served God, and not his own belly, I plainly see why he rejoiced; I see it, and I rejoice with him. For he had received from the Philippians, what they had sent by Epaphroditus unto him: and yet I perceive why he rejoiced. For whereat he rejoiced, upon that he fed; for, speaking in truth, I rejoiced (says he) greatly in the Lord, that now at the last your care of me has flourished again, wherein you were once careful, but it became wearisome unto you. These Philippians then had now dried up, with a long weariness, and withered as it were as to bearing this fruit of a good work; and he rejoices for them, that they flourished again, not for himself, that they supplied his wants. Therefore he adds, Not that I speak in respect of want, for I have learned in whatsoever state I am, therewith to be content. I know both how to be abased, and I know also how to abound; in all things, and in general, I am instructed both to be full, and to be hungry; both to abound, and to suffer need. I can do all things through Him who strengthens me.

Whereat then rejoice you, O great Paul? Whereat rejoice you? Whereon feed you, O man renewed in the recognition of God, after the image of Him that created you, you living soul, of so much continency, you tongue in your flight, speaking mysteries? (for to such creatures is this food due) What is it that feeds You? Joy. I will hear what follows: Notwithstanding (he says) you have well done, that you did communicate with my affliction. At this he rejoices,

on this he feeds; because they had well done, not because his strait
was eased; and he says unto You, You have enlarged me when
I was in distress, for that he knew to abound, and to suffer want,
in You who strengthen him. For you Philippians also know (says
he), that in the beginning of the gospel, when I departed from
Macedonia, no church communicated with me as concerning giving and receiving, but you only. For even to Thessalonica you sent
once and again unto my necessity. Unto these good works, he now
rejoices that they are returned; and is gladdened that they flourished
again, as when a fruitful field resumes its green.

Was it for his own necessities, because he said, You sent unto
my necessity? Rejoices he for that? Verily not for that. And how
do we know this? Because himself says immediately, Not because
I desire a gift, but I desire fruit. I have learned of You, my God,
to distinguish betwixt a gift and fruit. A gift is the thing itself
given by him who imparts these necessaries unto us; as money,
meat, drink, clothing, shelter, help: but the fruit is the good and
right will of the giver. For the good Master does not say, He
that receives a prophet, but added, In the name of a prophet: nor
does He only say, He that receives a righteous man, but added, In
the name of a righteous man. So verily shall the one receive the
reward of a prophet, the other, the reward of a righteous man:
nor says He only, He that shall give to drink a cup of cold water
to one of my little ones; but added, In the name of a disciple: and
so concludes, Verily I say unto you, he shall not lose his reward.
The gift is, to receive a prophet, to receive a righteous man, to
give a cup of cold water to a disciple: but the fruit, to do this in
the name of a prophet, in the name of a righteous man, in the
name of a disciple. With fruit was Elijah fed by the widow that
knew she fed a man of God, and therefore fed him: but by the
raven was he fed with a gift. Nor was the inner man of Elijah so
fed, but the outer only; which might also for want of that food
have perished.

27. *An allegory upon the fishes and the whales*

I will then speak what is true in Your sight, O Lord, that when
carnal men and infidels (for the gaining and initiating whom, the
initiatory sacraments and the mighty workings of miracles are
necessary, which we suppose to be signified by the name of fishes

and whales) undertake the bodily refreshment of your children, or otherwise succour them with something useful for this present life, should they be ignorant, why this is to be done, and to what end; neither do they feed these, nor are these fed by them; because neither do the one do it out of an holy and right intent, nor do the other rejoice at their gifts, whose fruit they as yet behold not. For the mind is fed upon that which makes it glad. And therefore do not the fishes and whales feed upon such meats, as the earth brings not forth until after it was separated and divided from the bitterness of the waves of the sea.

28. *Very good, why added last of all?*

And You, O God, saw every thing that You had made, and, behold, it was very good. Yea we also see the same, and behold, all things are very good. Of the several kinds of Your works, when You had said, Let them be made, and they were made, You saw each that it was good. Seven times have I counted it to be written, that You saw that that which You made was good: and this is the eighth, that You saw every thing that You had made, and, behold, it was not only good, but also very good, as being now all together. For severally, they were only good; but all together, both good and very good. All beautiful bodies express the same, by reason that a body consisting of members all beautiful, is far more beautiful than the same members by themselves are, by whose well-ordered blending the whole is perfected; notwithstanding that the members severally be also beautiful.

29. *God's works are good for ever*

And I looked narrowly to find, whether seven or eight times You saw that Your works were good, when they pleased You; but in Your seeing I found no times, whereby I might understand that You saw so often, what You made. And I said, Lord, is not this Your scripture true, since You are true, and being truth, have set it forth? Why then do You say unto me, that in Your seeing there be no times; whereas this Your scripture tells me, that what You made each day, You saw that it was good: and when I counted them, I found how often. Unto this You answer me, for You are my God, and with a strong voice tell Your servant in his inner ear, breaking through my deafness and crying, O man, that which

My scripture says, I say: and yet does that speak in time; but time has no relation to My word; because My word exists in equal eternity with Myself. So the things which you see through My spirit, I see; just as what you speak by My spirit, I speak. And so when you see those things in time, I see them not in time; as when you speak them in time, I speak them not in time.

30. *Against those who dislike God's works*

And I heard, O Lord my God, and drank up a drop of sweetness out of Your truth, and understood, that certain men there be who mislike Your works; and say, that many of them You made, compelled by necessity; such as the fabric of the heavens, and harmony of the stars; and that You made them not of what was Yours, but that they were otherwhere and from other sources created, for You to bring together and compact and combine, when out of Your conquered enemies You raised up the walls of the universe; that they, bound down by the structure, might not again be able to rebel against You. For other things, they say You neither made them, nor even compacted them, such as all flesh and all very minute creatures, and whatsoever has its root in the earth; but that a mind at enmity with You, and another nature not created by You, and contrary unto You, did, in these lower stages of the world, beget and frame these things. Frenzied are they who say thus, because they see not Your works by Your spirit, nor recognize You in them.

31. *The godly allow that which is pleasing to God*

But they who by Your spirit see these things, You see in them. Therefore when they see that these things are good, You see that they are good; and whatsoever things for Your sake please, You please in them, and what things through Your spirit please us, they please You in us. For what man knows the things of a man, save the spirit of a man, which is in him? Even so the things of God no one knows, but the spirit of God. Now we (says he) have received, not the spirit of this world, but the spirit which is of God, that we might know the things that are freely given to us of God. And I am admonished, Truly the things of God no one knows, but the spirit of God: how then do we also know, what things are given us of God? Answer is made me. Because the things which we know by His spirit, even these no one knows, but the spirit of God. For as it is rightly said unto those that were to speak by the spirit of God, It is not you that speak: so is it rightly said to them that know through the spirit of God, It is not you that know. And no less then is it rightly said to those that see through the spirit of God, It is not you that see; so whatsoever through the spirit of God they see to be good, it is not they, but God that sees that it is good. It is one thing then for a man to think that to be ill which is good, as the forenamed do; another, that that which is good, a man should see that it is good (as Your creatures be pleasing unto many, because they be good, whom yet You please not in them, when they prefer to enjoy them, to You); and another, that when a man sees a thing that it is good, God should in him see that it is good, so, namely, that He should be loved in that which He made, who cannot be loved, but by the Holy Ghost which He has given. Because the love of God is shed abroad in our hearts by the Holy Ghost, which is given unto us: by whom we see that whatsoever in any degree is, is good. For it is from Him, who Himself is not in degree, but who is, what He is.

32. *He briefly sums up the works of God*

Thanks be to You, O Lord. We behold the heaven and earth, whether the corporeal part, superior and inferior, or the spiritual and corporeal creature; and in the adorning of these parts, whereof the general mass of the world, or rather the universal creation, does consist, we see light made, and divided from the darkness. We see the firmament of heaven, whether that primary body of the world, between the spiritual upper waters and the inferior corporeal waters, or (since this also is called heaven) this space of air through which wander the fowls of heaven, betwixt those waters which are in vapors borne above them, and in clear nights distill down in dew; and those heavier waters which flow along the earth. We behold a face of waters gathered together in the fields of the sea; and the dry land both denuded, and formed so as to be visible and harmonized, the mother of plants and trees. We behold the lights shining from above, the sun to suffice for the day, the moon and the stars to cheer the night; and that by all these, times should be marked and signified. We behold on all sides a moist element, replenished with fishes, beasts, and birds;

because the grossness of the air, which bears up the flights of birds, thickens itself by the exhalation of the waters. We behold the face of the earth decked out with earthly creatures, and man, created after Your image and likeness, even through that Your very image and likeness (that is the power of reason and understanding), set over all irrational creatures. And as in his soul there is one power which has dominion by directing, another made subject, that it might obey; so was there for the man, corporeally also, made a woman, who in mind, in her reasonable understanding, should have an equal nature, but in the sex of her body, should be subject to the sex of her husband, to the extent that the appetite of doing is driven to derive the skill of right-doing from the reason of the mind. These things we behold, and they are severally good, and all together very good.

33. *How every creature ought to praise the creator*

Your works praise You, that we may love You; and we love You, that Your works may praise You. They from time have their beginning and ending, rising and setting, growth and decay, form and privation. They have then their succession of morning and evening, part secretly, part apparently; for they were made of nothing, by You, not of You; not of any matter not Yours, or that was before, but of matter con-created (that is, at the same time created by You), because to its state without form, You without any interval of time did give form. For seeing the matter of heaven and earth is one thing, and the form another, You made the matter of merely nothing, but the form of the world out of the matter without form: yet both together, so that the form should follow the matter, without any interval of delay.

34. *The order and various fruit of a Christian life*

We have also examined what You willed to be shadowed forth, whether by the creation, or the relation of things in such an order. And we have seen, that things singly are good, and together very good, in Your word, in Your only-begotten, both heaven and earth, the head and the body of the church, in Your predestination before all times, without morning and evening. But when You began to execute in time the things predestinated, to the end You might reveal hidden things, and rectify our disorders; for our sins hung over us, and we had sunk into the dark deep; and Your good spirit was borne over us, to help us in due season; and You did justify the impious, and distinguish them from the wicked; and You placed the firmament of authority of Your book between those placed above, who were to be docile unto You, and those under, who were to be subject to them: and You gathered together the society of unbelievers into one conspiracy, that the zeal of the faithful might appear, and they might bring forth works of mercy, even distributing to the poor their earthly riches, to obtain heavenly. And after this did You kindle certain lights in the firmament, Your holy ones, having the word of life; and shining with an eminent authority set on high through spiritual gifts; after that again, for the initiation of the unbelieving gentiles, did You out of corporeal matter produce the sacraments, and visible miracles, and forms of words according to the firmament of Your book, by which the faithful should be blessed and multiplied. Next did You form the living soul of the faithful, through affections well ordered by the vigor of continency: and after that, the mind subjected to You alone and needing to imitate no human authority, have You renewed after Your image and likeness; and did subject its rational actions to the excellency of the understanding, as the woman to the man; and to all offices of Your ministry, necessary for the perfecting of the faithful in this life, You willed, that for their temporal uses, good things, fruitful to themselves in time to come, be given by the same faithful. All these we see, and they are very good, because You who have given unto us Your spirit, by which we might see them and in them love You, see them in us.

35. He prays for peace

O Lord God, give peace unto us (for You have given us all things): the peace of rest, the peace of the sabbath, which has no evening. For all this most beautiful array of things very good, when they shall have finished their courses, is to pass away, for in them there was morning and evening.

36. Why the seventh day has no evening

But the seventh day has no evening, nor has it setting, because You have sanctified it to an everlasting continuance; that that which You did after Your works which were very good, resting the seventh day (although You made them without effort), that may the voice of Your book announce beforehand unto us, that we also after our works (which are very good, precisely because You have given them us), shall rest in You also in the sabbath of eternal life.

37. *When God shall rest in us*

For then shall You rest in us, as now You work in us; and so shall that be Your rest through us, as these are Your works through us. But You, Lord, ever work, and are ever at rest. Nor do You see in time, nor are moved in time, nor rest in time; and yet You make things which are seen in time, yea the times themselves, and the rest which results from time.

38. *God beholds created things one way, and man another*

We therefore see these things which You made, because they are: but they are, because You see them. And we see without, that they are, and within, that they are good, but You saw them there, when made, where You saw them, yet to be made. And we were at a later time moved to do well, after our hearts had conceived of Your spirit; but in the former time we were moved to do evil, forsaking You; but You, the One, the good God, did never cease doing good. And we also have some good works, of Your gift, but not eternal; after them we trust to rest in Your great hallowing. But You, being the good which needs no good, are ever at rest, because Your rest is You Yourself. And what man can teach man to understand this? Or what angel, an angel? Or what angel, a man? Let it be asked of You, sought in You, knocked for at You; so, so shall it be received, so shall it be found, so shall it be opened.

Amen.

Gratias Tibi Domine